Wars and Peace Treaties
1816–1991

Erik Goldstein

London and New York

First published 1992
by Routledge
11 New Fetter Lane, London EC4P 4EE

Simultaneously published in the USA and Canada
by Routledge
a division of Routledge, Chapman and Hall, Inc.
29 West 35th Street, New York, NY 10001

Typeset in 10/12pt Times by Leaper & Gard Ltd, Bristol, England
Printed in England by Clays Ltd, St Ives plc

British Library Cataloguing in Publication Data
Goldstein, Erik
  Wars and peace treaties.
  I. Title
  355.02

Library of Congress Cataloging in Publication Data
Goldstein, Erik.
  Wars and peace treaties / Erik Goldstein.
      p.   cm.
  Includes index.
  1. Military history, Modern – 19th century. 2. Military history,
  Modern – 20th century. I. Title.
  D361.G65   1991
  904'.7 – dc20   91-18744

ISBN 0–415–07822–9

For my parents,
Jack and Ranka Goldstein

Contents

List of maps   xii
Chronological list of wars   xiii
Preface   xvii
List of abbreviations   xix

1 Post-Napoleonic Revolutionary Wars   1
Neapolitan War 1821   1
Franco-Spanish War 1823   3
Belgo-Dutch War 1830–3   4

2 Wars of German Unification   6
First Schleswig-Holstein War 1848–50   6
Second Schleswig-Holstein War 1863–4   8
Seven Weeks' War (Austro-Prussian War) 1866   10
Franco-Prussian War 1870–1   12

3 Wars of Italian Unification   14
Austro-Piedmontese War 1848–9   14
Austrian War with France and Piedmont 1859   17
Italo-Austrian War 1866   18

4 Decline of the Ottoman Empire   20
Greek War of Independence 1821–32   20
Russo-Ottoman War 1828–9   22
First Ottoman-Egyptian War 1831–3   24
Second Ottoman-Egyptian War 1839–40   25
Montenegrin-Ottoman War 1852–3   26
Crimean War 1853–6   27
Montenegrin-Ottoman War 1858   29
Montenegrin-Ottoman War 1861–2   30
Montenegrin-Serbian-Ottoman War 1876   30
Russo-Ottoman War 1877–8   32
Serbo-Bulgarian War 1885   34
Graeco-Ottoman War 1897   35
Italo-Ottoman War (Tripolitanian War) 1911–12   36

Balkan Wars 1912–13	38
First Balkan War 1912–13	38
Second Balkan War 1913	40

5 World Wars and Related Conflicts — 42
First World War 1914–18 — 42
Western Front — 44
Eastern Front — 45
Balkan Front — 46
Ottoman Front — 46
Colonial and Non-European Front — 46
War at Sea — 47
Polish-Soviet War 1920 — 50
Graeco-Turkish War 1920–2 — 51
Second World War 1939–45 — 53
Polish War 1939 — 53
War in the West 1939–45 — 56
Winter War (Russo-Finnish War) 1939–40 — 57
Balkan War 1940–5 — 59
German-Soviet War 1941–5 — 61
Sino-Japanese War 1931–45 — 62
Changkufeng Incident (Khasan Incident) 1938 — 65
Nomonhan Incident (Khalin Gol) 1939 — 66
Pacific War 1941–5 — 67

6 Central Asian Wars — 72
Russo-Persian War 1826–8 — 72
Persia-Herat War 1837–8 — 74
First Anglo-Afghan War 1839–42 — 75
Anglo-Persian War 1856–7 — 76
Second Anglo-Afghan War 1878–80 — 78
Third Anglo-Afghan War 1919 — 79
Soviet-Afghan War 1979–89 — 80

7 South Asian Wars — 82
First Sikh War 1845–6 — 82
Second Sikh War 1848–9 — 84
Kashmir Dispute (First Indo-Pakistani War) 1947–9 — 85
Sino-Indian War 1962 — 86
Second Indo-Pakistani War 1965 — 88
Third Indo-Pakistani War (Bangladesh War of Independence) 1971 — 89

8 Anglo-Burmese Wars — 92
First Anglo-Burmese War 1824–6 — 92
Second Anglo-Burmese War 1852 — 94
Third Anglo-Burmese War 1885 — 95

9   East Asian Wars   97
First Opium War 1839–42   97
Second Opium War 1856–60   99
First Franco-Indochinese War 1858–62   100
Second Franco-Indochinese War 1881–3   102
Sino-French War 1883–5   103
Sino-Japanese War 1894–5   104
Boxer Rebellion 1900   106
Russo-Japanese War 1904–5   107
Franco-Vietminh War 1946–54   109
Korean War 1950–3   111
Malaysian-Indonesian Confrontation 1963–6   112
Vietnam War 1964–73   114
Sino-Soviet Dispute 1969   116
Vietnam-Kampuchea War 1978–9   118
Sino-Vietnamese War 1979   119

10   Middle Eastern Wars   122
First Arab-Israeli War 1948–9   122
Suez War (Second Arab-Israeli War) 1956   125
Six Day War (Third Arab-Israeli War) 1967   127
October War (Fourth Arab-Israeli War) 1973   128
Lebanon Conflict 1976–   130
North Yemen-South Yemen Dispute 1979   132
First Gulf War (Iran-Iraq War) 1980–8   133
Second Gulf War (Kuwait Crisis) 1990–1   135

11   West African Colonial Wars   139
Ashanti Wars 1824–1900   139
    First Ashanti War 1824–31   139
    Second Ashanti War 1873–4   141
    Third Ashanti War 1895–6   143
    Fourth Ashanti War 1900   143
Barra War 1831   144
First Dahomey War 1890   145
Second Dahomey War 1892–4   146
Benin War 1897   148
Sokoto War 1903   149

12   Southern African Colonial Wars   151
Zulu War 1879   151
Transvaal Revolt (First Boer War) 1880–1   154
Second Boer War 1899–1902   155

13   Struggle for the Horn of Africa   158
Anglo-Ethiopian War 1867–8   158
Egyptian-Ethiopian War 1875–6   159

First Italo-Ethiopian War 1887–9   160
Second Italo-Ethiopian War 1895–6   162
Sudanese War 1896–9   163
Third Italo-Ethiopian War (Abyssinian Crisis) 1935–6   164

14 Somalian Wars   167
Ethiopia-Somalia Dispute 1964   167
Kenya-Somalia Dispute (Shifta War) 1963–7   169
Ogaden War (Ethiopia-Somalia War) 1977–8   170

15 Maghreb Wars   172
Bizerta Crisis (Franco-Tunisian Dispute) 1961   172
War of the Sands (Morocco-Algeria Dispute) 1963   173
Saharan War 1975–   174

16 Post-Independence African Wars   177
South Africa-Angola War 1975–91   177
Chad-Libya War 1978–87   180
Tanzania-Uganda Dispute 1978–9   182
Christmas War (Burkina Faso-Mali War) 1985   183

17 South American Wars   185
Argentine-Brazilian War 1825–8   185
Peru-Gran Colombia War 1828–9   187
War of the Peruvian-Bolivian Confederation 1836–40   188
Peruvian-Bolivian War 1841–2   190
First Ecuador-Colombia War 1862   191
Second Ecuador-Colombia War 1862–4   192
Peruvian-Spanish War 1864–6   193
War of the Triple Alliance (López War) 1864–70   194
War of the Pacific 1879–84   196
War of Acre 1902   198
Chaco War 1932–5   199
First Ecuador-Peru War (Zarumilla-Marañón War) 1941   200
Second Ecuador-Peru War 1981   201
Falklands War 1982   202

18 North and Central American Wars   205
Mexican-American War 1846–8   205
Mexican-French War 1861–7   207
Spanish-American War 1898   208
Honduran-Nicaraguan War 1907   210
El Salvador-Honduras War (Football War) 1969   211

Appendices   213
A First World War: Entry of countries into hostilities and
      declarations of war   213

B Second World War: Entry of countries into hostilities
    and declarations of war   215
C Post-Second World War Peace Treaties   220
D United Nations Peacekeeping Operations   221
E Major Arms Control Agreements   224

Further reading   227
Index   239

Maps

 1 Europe in 1815 (inset: the Lowlands)   2
 2 Unification of Germany   7
 3 Italian unification   15
 4 Decline of the Ottoman Empire   21
 5 Balkan Peninsula to 1913   39
 6 Europe in 1914   43
 7 First World War: postwar settlements   48
 8 Second World War: Europe in 1939   54
 9 Second World War: Asia   63
10 Central Asia   72
11 South Asia   83
12 Anglo-Burmese Wars   93
13 Modern Middle East   123
14 Colonial West Africa   140
15 Colonial Southern Africa   152
16 Somalia   168
17 Modern Africa   178
18 South America   186
19 North and Central America   206

Chronological list of wars

1821	Neapolitan War
1821–32	Greek War of Independence
1823	Franco-Spanish War
1824–6	First Anglo-Burmese War
1824–31	First Ashanti War
1825–8	Argentine-Brazilian War
1826–8	Russo-Persian War
1828–9	Peru-Gran Colombia War
1828–9	Russo-Ottoman War
1830–3	Belgo-Dutch War
1831	Barra War
1831–3	First Ottoman-Egyptian War
1836–40	War of the Peruvian-Bolivian Confederation
1837–8	Persia-Herat War
1839–40	Second Ottoman-Egyptian War
1839–42	First Anglo-Afghan War
1839–42	First Opium War
1841–2	Peruvian-Bolivian War
1845–6	First Sikh War
1846–8	Mexican-American War
1848–9	Austro-Piedmontese War
1848–50	First Schleswig-Holstein War
1848–9	Second Sikh War
1852	Second Anglo-Burmese War
1852–3	Montenegrin-Ottoman War
1853–6	Crimean War
1856–7	Anglo-Persian War
1856–60	Second Opium War
1858	Montenegrin-Ottoman War
1858–62	First Franco-Indochinese War
1859	Austrian War with France and Piedmont
1861–2	Montenegrin-Ottoman War
1861–7	Mexican-French War

1862	First Ecuador-Colombia War
1862–4	Second Ecuador-Colombia War
1863–4	Second Schleswig-Holstein War
1864–6	Peruvian-Spanish War
1864–70	War of the Triple Alliance (López War)
1866	Seven Weeks' War (Austro-Prussian War)
1866	Italo-Austrian War
1867–8	Anglo-Ethiopian War
1870–1	Franco-Prussian War
1873–4	Second Ashanti War
1875–6	Egyptian-Ethiopian War
1876	Montenegrin-Serbian-Ottoman War
1877–8	Russo-Ottoman War
1878–80	Second Anglo-Afghan War
1879	Zulu War
1879–84	War of the Pacific
1880–1	Transvaal Revolt (First Boer War)
1882–3	Second Franco-Indochinese War
1883–5	Sino-French War
1885	Serbo-Bulgarian War
1885	Third Anglo-Burmese War
1887–9	First Italo-Ethiopian War
1890	First Dahomey War
1892–4	Second Dahomey War
1894–5	Sino-Japanese War
1895–6	Second Italo-Ethiopian War
1895–6	Third Ashanti War
1896–9	Sudanese War
1897	Benin War
1897	Graeco-Ottoman War
1898	Spanish-American War
1899–1902	Second Boer War
1900	Boxer Rebellion
1900	Fourth Ashanti War
1902	War of Acre
1903	Sokoto War
1904–5	Russo-Japanese War
1907	Honduran-Nicaraguan War
1911–12	Italo-Ottoman War (Tripolitanian War)
1912–13	First Balkan War
1913	Second Balkan War
1914–18	First World War
1919	Third Anglo-Afghan War
1920	Polish-Soviet War
1920–2	Graeco-Turkish War

1931–45	Sino-Japanese War
1932–5	Chaco War
1935–6	Third Italo-Ethiopian War (Abyssinian Crisis)
1939–40	Winter War (Russo-Finnish War)
1939–45	Second World War
1941	First Ecuador-Peru War (Zarumilla-Marañón War)
1946–54	Franco-Vietminh War
1947–9	Kashmir Dispute (First Indo-Pakistani War)
1948–9	First Arab-Israeli War
1950–3	Korean War
1956	Suez War (Second Arab-Israeli War)
1961	Bizerta Crisis (Franco-Tunisian Dispute)
1962	Sino-Indian War
1963	War of the Sands (Morocco-Algeria Dispute)
1963–6	Malaysian-Indonesian Confrontation
1963–7	Kenya-Somalia Dispute (Shifta War)
1964	Ethiopia-Somalia Dispute
1964–73	Vietnam War
1965	Second Indo-Pakistani War
1967	Six Day War (Third Arab-Israeli War)
1969	El Salvador-Honduras War (Football War)
1969	Sino-Soviet Dispute
1971	Third Indo-Pakistani War (Bangladesh War of Independence)
1973	October War (Fourth Arab-Israeli War)
1975–	Saharan War
1975–91	South Africa-Angola War
1976–	Lebanon Conflict
1977–8	Ogaden War (Ethiopia-Somalia War)
1977–87	Chad-Libya War
1978–9	Tanzania-Uganda Dispute
1978–9	Vietnam-Kampuchea War
1979	North Yemen-South Yemen Dispute
1979	Sino-Vietnamese War
1979–89	Soviet-Afghan War
1980–8	First Gulf War (Iran-Iraq War)
1981	Second Ecuador-Peru War
1982	Falklands War
1985	Christmas War (Burkina Faso-Mali War)
1990–1	Second Gulf War (Kuwait Crisis)

Preface

The idea for this book had its origins in an earlier work written by Arthur Ponsonby, MP, *Wars & Peace Treaties, 1815 to 1914,* published in 1918 by George Allen & Unwin Ltd. It came out as the First World War was ending and the Paris Peace Conference was about to convene to determine the peace treaties. It was meant then as a handy, quick guide to the more significant wars of the previous hundred years, and how they were settled. For its time it was a remarkably balanced work, not showing much sign of a sense of European or British superiority. Each entry considered who were the belligerents, what was the background cause of the war, what provided the occasion for the outbreak of hostilities, how the course of the war developed and, finally, what was the political result achieved. It was thought useful in this book to take the straightforward approach initiated by Ponsonby and to cover the period from the fall of Napoleon to the present day.

This work does not claim to be comprehensive, for it is almost impossible to find any agreed definition or list of wars which could serve as the guidelines to make it so. Ponsonby covered 40 wars for the century he wrote on; this work has picked 74 conflicts for the period dealt with by Ponsonby and overall covers 124 wars. The general criterion for choosing the conflicts described has been that they should be wars between states recognized as having the ingredients of sovereignty and as participating in the international system. Civil wars have been omitted, for to include them would have swelled the book to an unmanageable size. Some wars, however, occur in tandem with civil wars, for instance the Lebanon Crisis and the South Africa-Angola War, and these have been included for their international dimension. The colonial wars of the last century present a particular problem, especially in Africa. Here several wars are included as approximating to the general guidelines, although there are others that fall into a grey area. Minor border skirmishes are omitted, but major border fighting is included where it has an important international dimension, for example the Sino-Soviet Dispute of 1969.

I am greatly indebted to several individuals for their advice and comments on various sections of this work and I would like to express my very great thanks to my colleagues Arnold Hughes, David Armstrong, Stuart Croft and Martin Kolinsky at the University of Birmingham, and to John Maurer at the United States Naval War College, as well as to George J. Marcopoulos of Tufts University. The responsibility for whatever deficiencies may exist rests with the author.

EG

Abbreviations

ADF	Arab Deterrent Force
ALA	Arab Liberation Army
ANC	African National Congress
ASEAN	Association of South East Asian Nations
CGDK	Coalition Government of Democratic Kampuchea
CMEA	Council for Mutual Economic Assistance (Comecon)
CSCE	Conference on Security and Cooperation in Europe
ECOWAS	Economic Community of West African States
FNLA	National Front for the Liberation of Angola
FROLINAT	National Liberation Front (Chad)
GUNT	Government d'union nationale de transition (Chad)
ICJ	International Court of Justice
MNF	Multinational Force (Lebanon)
MPLA	People's Movement for the Liberation of Angola
NDF	National Democratic Front (North Yemen)
NFD	Northern Frontier District (of Kenya)
OAS	Organization of American States
OAU	Organization of African Unity
OPEC	Organization of Petroleum Exporting Countries
PDPA	People's Democratic Party of Afghanistan
PDRY	People's Democratic Republic of Yemen
PLO	Palestine Liberation Organization
POLISARIO	Popular Front for the Liberation of Saguia el Hamra and Rio de Oro
SADR	Saharawi Arab Democratic Republic
SAIRI	Supreme Assembly of the Islamic Revolution in Iraq
SLA	South Lebanon Army
SWAPO	South West Africa People's Organization
TEZ	Total Exclusion Zone
UN	United Nations
UNAVEM	United Nations Angola Verification Mission
UNEF	United Nations Emergency Force
UNIFIL	United Nations Interim Force in Lebanon

UNIIMOG	United Nations Iran-Iraq Military Observer Group
UNIKOM	United Nations Iraq-Kuwait Observation Mission
UNIPOM	United Nations India-Pakistan Observation Mission
UNITA	National Union for the Total Independence of Angola
UNLF	Uganda National Liberation Front
UNMOGIP	United Nations Military Observation Group in India and Pakistan
UNSCOP	United Nations Special Committee on Palestine
UNTAG	United Nations Transition Assistance Group (Namibia)
UNTSO	United Nations Truce Supervision Organization (Middle East)
WSLF	Western Somalia Liberation Front
YAR	Yemen Arab Republic

1 Post-Napoleonic Revolutionary Wars

Neapolitan War 1821

Belligerents: **Naples**
                     Austria

Cause

The revolution in the Kingdom of Naples (officially the Kingdom of the Two Sicilies) was sparked by the Spanish Revolution of 1820. The revolutionaries forced a constitution, modelled on the 1812 Spanish constitution, on an unwilling king, Ferdinand I. Metternich, the Austrian foreign minister, saw the revolution as a threat to his country's influence in Italy and pushed for Great Power intervention to restore the old order. This was discussed by the Great Powers at the Congress of Troppau (Oct. 1820). The result was the Troppau Doctrine, supported by the conservative powers (Austria, Prussia and Russia), which called for international intervention to prevent what they considered to be illegal institutions from being established in a European state.

Occasion

At the subsequent Congress of Laibach (Jan. 1821) the powers requested the presence of King Ferdinand, who was allowed to attend by his government after promising his support for the constitution. He reneged on this promise as soon as he had escaped from Naples, however, and immediately requested Austrian assistance to regain his throne and traditional rights. Ferdinand assured the Congress that the Neapolitan army would offer little resistance, observing: 'You may dress it in blue or green or in red, but whichever you do it will run.'

Course of War

An Austrian army entered the Kingdom of Naples in support of Ferdinand I. At the Battle of Rieti (7 March 1821) a Neapolitan army of 100,000

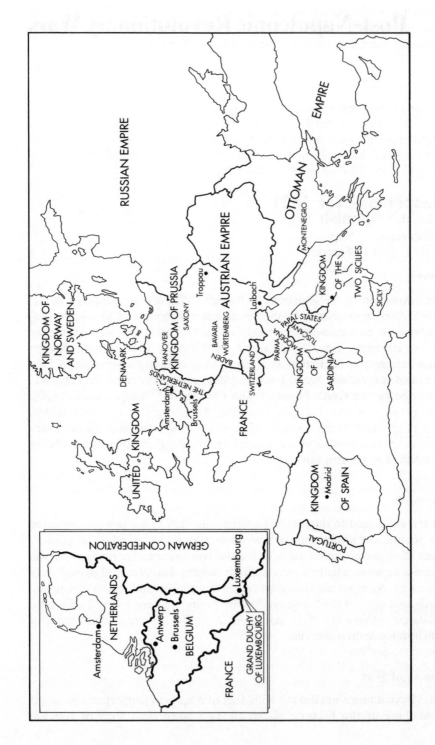

1 Europe in 1815 (inset: the Lowlands)

under General Pepe was defeated by an Austrian army numbering 80,000. The revolutionary forces collapsed with little resistance. The Austrians occupied Naples and restored Ferdinand I (23 March).

Political result

Ferdinand was restored as King of Naples, where he reigned until his death in 1825, taking a harsh revenge on his opponents. The British Prime Minister, Gladstone, would later say of Naples that it was 'the negation of God erected into a form of government'. Pepe subsequently became a general in the 1848–9 war between Piedmont and Austria.

Franco-Spanish War 1823

Belligerents: **France**
             Spain

Cause

In 1815, after the Napoleonic Wars, King Ferdinand VII was restored to the Spanish throne, but his incompetent, authoritarian and brutal rule led to a military revolt in 1820 which forced him to reimpose the suppressed constitution of 1812. Ferdinand became a virtual prisoner until in 1822 he appealed successfully for help to the Holy Alliance, a grouping of conservative powers committed to 'legitimist' principles.

Occasion

The Spanish problem was debated at the Congress of Verona (Oct. 1822), where the Holy Alliance powers of France, Prussia and Austria demanded that the Spanish government restore Ferdinand to his full powers. A French intervention was authorized to restore Ferdinand, although Britain strongly objected to this, fearing traditional French ambitions to dominate the Iberian peninsula. France indeed hoped the campaign would restore some of its military prestige, while impressing the conservative powers with post-Napoleonic France's commitment to political stability in Europe.

Course of War

The French army, 'the Hundred Thousand Sons of St Louis', led by the Duc d'Angoulême, a nephew of the French king, Louis XVIII, crossed into Spain (7 April 1823). There was little significant resistance to a French army whose aim was to restore the traditional powers of the Spanish king. The Constitutionalists fled Madrid, taking the king with them, and the capital fell to the French (24 May). The only significant battle of the campaign took place at Cadiz, where the Constitutionalist government had taken refuge (31 Aug.). The one-month siege of Cadiz ended after Ferdinand promised leniency to the Constitutionalists. He later broke this promise and took a terrible toll in reprisals on the Constitutionalists. The Duc d'Angoulême, distressed by Ferdinand's actions, returned to France (Nov.), although some 45,000 French soldiers remained in Spain until 1828.

Political result

This war began a long period of political instability, lasting at least until 1874 and arguably until the Spanish Civil War (1936–9), as the struggle between liberals and conservatives continued.

Belgo-Dutch War 1830–3

Belligerents: **Belgium**
                     Netherlands

Cause

At the Congress of Vienna (1814–15) a large Kingdom of the Netherlands was created, in part to act as a barrier against French ambitions. It consisted of the modern Netherlands and Belgium, under William I of Orange, who was also made Grand Duke of Luxembourg. The government of the new kingdom was dominated by Protestant Dutchmen, much to the growing irritation of predominantly Roman Catholic Belgium, the southern part of which was also French-speaking.

Occasion

The 1830 revolution in Paris sent shock waves throughout Europe and helped to precipitate a revolution in Brussels. The rising began when, during a performance of Auber's opera *La Muette de Portici,* the duet 'Amour sacre de la patrie' so overcame the audience that they flooded into the street and raised the flag of revolt (25 Aug. 1830).

Course of War

A Dutch army of 14,000 marched south into Belgium to restore royal authority and occupied the upper part of Brussels. When the Dutch attempted to occupy the lower town they met great popular opposition; after three days of fighting the Dutch army withdrew. This retreat caused support for the rebellion to spread throughout Belgium, and a provisional government was formed at Brussels which proclaimed Belgium independent (4 Oct.). Antwerp, however, remained under Dutch control. When a

Belgian army approached the city the Dutch forces withdrew into the citadel, from where they bombarded the city for two days, an action which only increased anti-Dutch feeling (27 Oct.).

A Great Power conference at London met to discuss the crisis, as the Lowlands were considered a vital part of the European security system. The powers ordered an armistice (4 Nov.) and recognized Belgian independence with Leopold of Saxe-Coburg as king. King William, however, refused to give up and invaded Belgium with an army of 50,000 (2 Aug. 1831), whereas the Belgian army mustered at this time no more than 25,000. In the 'Ten Days Campaign' the Belgians were overwhelmed, Louvain was occupied (11 Aug.) and Brussels was threatened. It was only when France intervened with an army of 60,000 in support of the Belgians that William was forced to withdraw.

The London Conference now proposed peace terms which, while acceptable to the Belgians, were rejected by the Dutch king. To apply pressure on the Dutch an Anglo-French fleet blockaded the Dutch coast (5 Nov. 1832) and the French army re-entered Belgium and laid siege to Antwerp. The Dutch garrison at Antwerp finally surrendered (23 Dec. 1832), effectively bringing the war to a close. An armistice was agreed (21 May 1833), leaving the Dutch with two forts controlling the Scheldt. It was not, however, until 1839 that the Dutch king signed a final settlement.

Political result

By the Treaty of London (19 April 1939), the Netherlands recognized Belgium's independence. Belgium was declared neutral, with Britain, Austria, France, Prussia and Russia signing the treaty as guarantors. It was over Germany's violation of Belgian neutrality in 1914 that Britain entered the First World War.

Remarks

The Grand Duchy of Luxembourg had also revolted and attempted to join Belgium, although the city of Luxembourg was controlled by the Prussians, who garrisoned it as a fortress of the German Confederation under the terms of the 1815 Vienna settlement. Under the Treaty of London Luxembourg was divided in two, the larger, French-speaking western part going to Belgium (it is now the Belgian province of Luxembourg), while the smaller, eastern portion was retained by William as its grand duke. In 1867, on the dissolution of the German Confederation after the Seven Weeks' War, the Prussian garrison was withdrawn, the fortifications were dismantled and Luxembourg was declared neutral. In 1890, on the death of the Dutch King William III without a male heir, Luxembourg passed to a distant cousin, while the Netherlands (where Salic Law did not apply) was inherited by his daughter Wilhelmina.

2 Wars of German Unification

In the wake of the Napoleonic Wars the Congress of Vienna in 1815 created the German Confederation, comprising 39 states of varying sizes and importance. The two most important members were Austria and Prussia, and their struggle for the mastery of Germany would eventually destroy the Confederation and see the establishment of a united Germany ruled from the Prussian capital of Berlin. In 1821 a confederal army was created, but was never very effective because of inter-state tension.

First Schleswig-Holstein War 1848–50

Belligerents: Denmark
Prussia, German Confederation

Cause

The Schleswig-Holstein question was one of the most complex diplomatic problems of the nineteenth century; it revolved around growing German nationalism and was eventually used by Prussia as part of its bid for mastery in Germany. The duchies of Schleswig and Holstein possessed a curious status. They were ruled by the king of Denmark but were administratively separate from Denmark and from each other; although indivisible from each other, Holstein alone was a member of the German Confederation. Both duchies were predominantly German-speaking, but Danish prevailed in northern Schleswig along the Danish border.

Occasion

In 1848, with the accession of the childless King Frederick VII to the Danish throne and the likely extinction of the direct line of the dynasty, a succession crisis arose. While Denmark allowed inheritance in the female line, the duchies adhered to the traditional German Salic Law, which permitted only male succession. Succession through the female line would result in splitting the duchies from Denmark, an event the Danes were

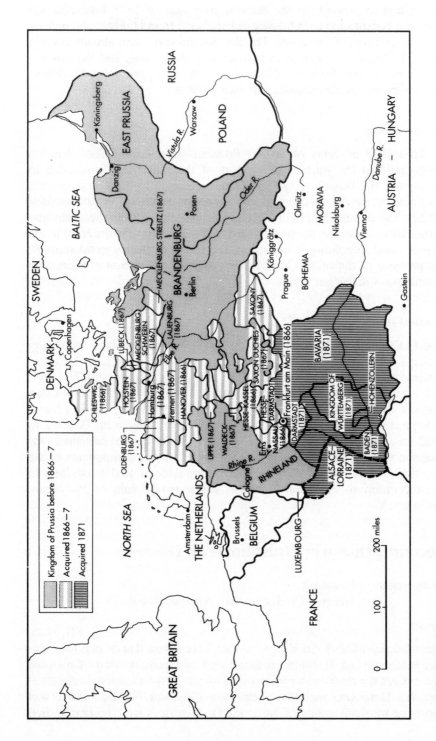

2 Unification of Germany

Kingdom of Prussia before 1866–7

Acquired 1866–7

Acquired 1871

GREAT BRITAIN

NORTH SEA

THE NETHERLANDS
Amsterdam

BELGIUM
Brussels

LUXEMBOURG

FRANCE

0   100   200 miles

SWEDEN

DENMARK
Copenhagen

BALTIC SEA

SCHLESWIG (1866)

HOLSTEIN (1867)

LÜBECK (1867)

MECKLENBURG SCHWERIN (1867)

MECKLENBURG STRELITZ (1867)

Hamburg

Bremen (1867)

HANOVER (1866)

Elbe R.

LAUENBURG (1867)

BRANDENBURG

Berlin

SAXONY (1867)

OLDENBURG (1867)

LIPPE (1867)

WALDECK (1867)

HESSE-KASSEL (1866)

SAXON DUCHIES (1867)

HESSE (1867)

NASSAU (1866)

Frankfurt am Main (1866)

DARMSTADT (1871)

Ems

Rhine R.

Cologne

RHINELAND

ALSACE-LORRAINE (1871)

HOHENZOLLERN

KINGDOM OF WÜRTTEMBERG (1871)

BAVARIA (1871)

BADEN (1871)

Danzig

EAST PRUSSIA

Köningsberg

Vistula R.

Warsaw

POLAND

Posen

Oder R.

Königgrätz

Prague

BOHEMIA

Olmütz

MORAVIA

Nikolsburg

Vienna

Danube R.

Gastein

AUSTRIA – HUNGARY

RUSSIA

determined to prevent. In the revolutionary year of 1848 Frederick VII granted a constitution to Schleswig, separating it from Holstein and making it an integral part of Denmark. The duchies, however, had already risen in revolt. In Prussia revolutionary activity was also strong, and the government saw in the Schleswig-Holstein revolt an opportunity to deflect popular interest while enhancing its own prestige.

Course of War

In April 1848 an army of 30,000 Prussian and German Confederation troops entered the duchies in support of the rebels and succeeded in driving out the Danish army. The Danes appealed to the Great Powers, who had previously guaranteed the union of Schleswig with Denmark (1820). The powers, looking for an opportunity to maintain the status quo in the Baltic, moved to support Denmark. Prussia withdrew its army in the face of Swedish military intervention, the threat of British naval support, the pressure of the other Great Powers and the distraction of increasing revolutionary activity at home.

Political result

The Convention of Malmö (26 Aug. 1848) brought about a temporary settlement by which Prussia agreed to most Danish demands. An international conference in London failed to reach a final settlement, however, and hostilities were renewed on 3 April 1849. Strong Anglo-Russian pressure on Prussia finally forced a peace. The Treaty of Berlin (2 July 1850) restored the rights and control of the Danish king in the duchies. In 1852 Frederick VII established a unitary state, with a central parliament for common matters and autonomy on local issues for the components of the kingdom. The London Protocol of 1852 gave international recognition to the succession to the Danish crown, which would pass to the future Christian IX.

Second Schleswig-Holstein War 1863–4

Belligerents: Denmark
German Confederation, Austria, Prussia

Cause

After the crisis of 1848–50, King Frederick VII continued his efforts to ensure that Schleswig and Holstein remained part of Denmark. Part of his plan was to treat the duchies as two separate issues. He granted a new constitution for Denmark, including Schleswig (28 Sept. 1863), which was approved by parliament (13 Nov. 1863). Two days later Frederick died and was succeeded by his cousin, Christian IX, in accordance with the terms of the London Protocol of 1852. Christian IX signed the new constitution, thereby provoking protests in Schleswig-Holstein that the 1852 constitutional arrangements were being violated.

Occasion

The German Confederation acted in support of the German population and forces from Hanover and Saxony entered the duchies on behalf of the Confederation (24 Dec. 1863). Both Austria and Prussia refused to support this action, fearing a wider European war. However, the Prussian chancellor, Bismarck, was intent on annexation of the duchies, awaiting only an appropriate moment. Prussia, together with Austria, proposed to the German Diet (28 Dec. 1863) that the Confederation should occupy Schleswig until the 1852 settlement was restored. This suggestion was rejected and Prussia and Austria opted to intervene as independent powers. They agreed in advance that the future of the duchies would only be decided by their common consent. On 1 February 1864 the Austro-Prussian force crossed the Eider river, for centuries the southern frontier of the Danish domains.

Course of War

The campaign was fought in two phases. The first (1 Feb.–25 April 1864) ended with a truce, the German forces having taken effective control of the duchies. The chief military action was the siege of Dybbøl (Düppel), which cost the Danes 1,800 dead but also inflicted heavy casualties on the Prussians. The Prussians pressed home their advantage by invading Denmark itself. The truce, brought about at British insistence, failed to lead to a settlement and hostilities resumed (25 June). The result was a clear defeat for the Danes, who agreed to a new truce (1 Aug.).

Political result

By the Treaty of Vienna (30 Oct. 1864), the Danish king renounced all his rights in the duchies to Prussia and Austria. Residents were allowed six years to decide whether they wished to opt for Danish nationality and to leave the duchies. The Gastein Convention (14 Aug. 1865) between Austria and Prussia specified that Austria would administer Holstein, while Prussia would administer Schleswig together with a naval base in Holstein.

Remarks

The problem of the future of Schleswig-Holstein led to the Seven Weeks' War of 1866 between Austria and Prussia. After that the duchies were annexed to Prussia, but continued to be a source of Danish-German tension. After the First World War a plebiscite led to the return of predominantly Danish northern Schleswig to Denmark (5 May 1920). In 1940 Hitler again annexed this area, which in turn reverted to Denmark in 1945, since when the matter has ceased to be a source of conflict.

Seven Weeks' War (Austro-Prussian War) 1866

Belligerents: **Prussia, Italy**
Austria, Hanover, Saxony, Württemberg, Baden, Hesse-Cassel, Hesse-Darmstadt, Nassau, Frankfurt

Cause

The underlying cause of the war was the rivalry between Austria and Prussia for predominance in Germany. Bismarck hoped to use the Schleswig-Holstein question to enhance Prussia's position by creating an incident which could be used to break Austria's traditional dominance of the German states.

Occasion

Austria and Prussia, in the aftermath of the Second Schleswig-Holstein War, concluded the Gastein Convention (14 Aug. 1865) by which Prussia was to administer Schleswig and Austria Holstein. However, friction between these two German powers continued over the future of the duchies. A Prussian Crown Council meeting (28 Feb. 1866) decided if necessary to risk war in the pursuit of its aims against Austria. Prussia helped to secure its strategic position through an alliance with Italy, which had territorial aims against Austria and would tie down Austrian forces in the south. In return, Prussia promised to support Italian claims to Austrian-ruled Venetia.

Austria, responding to the growing tension, asked the Diet of the German Confederation to decide the issue of the future of Schleswig-Holstein (1 June), thereby hoping at least to gain the support of the smaller German states. This move breached the Austro-Prussian agreement of 1864 that the future of the duchies would only be decided by their common consent. In response, Prussia terminated the Gastein Convention, thereby restoring the Austro-Prussian condominium control established by the Treaty of Vienna (1864) which had ended the Second Schleswig-Holstein War. Exercising its rights under this treaty, Prussia sent forces into Holstein (7 June), but Austrian troops avoided a confrontation. Austria proposed to the Diet that the confederal army be mobilized against Prussia for its breach of the Gastein Convention (to which the Confederation had not in fact been party) (11 June). Prussia threatened the Diet members that support for the motion would be taken as a declaration of war against Prussia. The motion, however, was passed (14 June) with the support of nine members, and Prussia responded at once by announcing that it considered the Confederation dissolved. The Prussian army now took action, first against Austria's smaller German allies and then against Austria itself. Italy declared war on Austria on 20 June.

Course of War

In a remarkably quick war, the speed of which surprised even the Prussians, Austria and her allies were defeated. The critical engagement was the Battle of Königgrätz (Sadowa) (3 July), where 220,000 Prussians defeated an Austrian force of 215,000. The Prussians benefited from their excellent organization, created by their chief of staff, Helmuth von Moltke, and enjoyed the superior firepower of their new breech-loading needle rifle against the Austrians' muzzle-loading variety. The French emperor, Napoleon III, intervened at this point to act as a mediator (5 July). A preliminary peace was signed at Nikolsburg (26 July), with a final treaty being signed at Prague (23 Aug.).

Political result

The Treaty of Prague (23 Aug. 1866) restored peace between Austria and Prussia, while a series of peace treaties was signed at Berlin with the south German states (Aug.–Sept. 1866). Prussia annexed Hanover, Hesse-Cassel, Nassau, Frankfurt and Schleswig-Holstein and an indemnity was levied on the remaining defeated states. In time of war Prussia was to be allowed to take control of the railways and military of Bavaria, Württemberg and Baden. A North German Confederation was established, encompassing all the German states north of the Main, as well as Saxony. Separate peace treaties were signed at Berlin with Württemberg (13 Aug. 1866) and Baden (17 Aug. 1866).

Remarks

This step in the consolidation of Prussian power in Germany was followed by German unification under Prussian predominance, excluding Austria, after the Franco-Prussian War of 1871. Austria entered a period of domestic reorganization which resulted in the creation of the dual monarchy of Austria-Hungary by the *Ausgleich* of 1867. Austria's interests, now that it was excluded from Germany, turned more towards the Balkans, which would eventually involve it in the crisis that would spark the outbreak of the First World War.

Franco-Prussian War 1870–1

Belligerents: **France**
                     Prussia, North German Confederation, Bavaria,
                     Württemberg, Baden, Hesse-Darmstadt

Cause

France had long been the single greatest military power in Europe, but the rise of Prussian power began to threaten this supremacy. Bismarck, the architect of German unification under Prussian leadership, believed that France would be unwilling to see any increase in German strength and would block any further steps towards unification. He therefore considered that German unification could not be achieved without the prior defeat of France.

Occasion

The incident which finally brought about war was the candidature in 1870 of a German prince, Leopold of Hohenzollern-Sigmaringen, for the vacant Spanish throne. He was a member of the Roman Catholic branch of the Prussian ruling family and the prospect of his election as king of Spain aroused concern in France about possible encirclement by Prussia and its allies. After much French diplomatic activity the prince's candidature was withdrawn. Despite this considerable diplomatic triumph the French ambassador was instructed to demand of the Prussian king, Wilhelm I, a guarantee that the candidature would not be renewed, which the king politely refused to give. Bismarck released an edited version of this encounter to the press, in what became known as the Ems Telegram (13 July 1870), aimed at exciting public anger in both France and Germany by giving the impression that both sides had been insulted by brusque behavior. Bismarck correctly predicted that the resultant public outcry would force the unprepared French government into war, while simultaneously rallying the other German states to the Prussian cause. France duly declared war on Prussia (19 July 1870).

Course of War

The poorly-prepared French army under Emperor Napoleon III faced well-organized German forces, directed by Field Marshal von Moltke and his general staff. The Germans, who had well-prepared war plans (unlike the French), enjoyed a string of early successes. The German assault was so successful that the entire war was fought on French soil. At the Battle of Sedan (1 Sept. 1870), a Prussian army of 200,000 defeated a French army of 130,000, which was forced to surrender. The Prussians took captive the French emperor, 39 of his generals, 2,700 officers and 84,000 men. When news of the disaster reached Paris, Napoleon was declared dethroned and a republic was proclaimed. The new government was determined to continue the war, but the German army advanced and laid siege to Paris (19 Sept. 1870–28 Jan. 1871). After a heroic defence, the city surrendered because of the heavy Prussian bombardment. The fall of Paris marked the effective end of the war.

Political result

By the Treaty of Frankfurt (10 May 1871), France ceded most of the area of Alsace-Lorraine to Germany and was forced to pay a heavy indemnity. German unification had meanwhile been completed by the proclamation of the Prussian king as German emperor in the Hall of Mirrors at the Palace of Versailles outside Paris (18 Jan. 1871). The date chosen was the anniversary of Prussia becoming a kingdom in 1701; it was in this same room in 1919 that defeated Germany would sign the peace treaty following the First World War.

Remarks

Bismarck's aim of German unification had been achieved and there was a significant shift in the European centre of power, from France to Germany. The annexation of Alsace-Lorraine remained an issue that embittered Franco-German relations in the following decades and was one of the contributory causes of the First World War, after which the territories reverted to France. They were again annexed to Germany during the Second World War, returning to French control in 1945.

3 Wars of Italian Unification

Austro-Piedmontese War 1848–9

Belligerents: **Austria**
                      Piedmont

Cause

The unification or *Risorgimento* (resurrection) of Italy into a single state was accomplished in a series of wars in the mid-nineteenth century. Italy in the early part of the century was composed of several states: the Kingdom of Sardinia (Piedmont); the Austrian-ruled provinces of Lombardy-Venetia; the Austrian client-states of Tuscany, Modena and Parma; the Papal States; and the Kingdom of Naples (Two Sicilies). The Kingdom of Sardinia, often referred to by its mainland section, Piedmont, was ruled by the House of Savoy. It became the focus of unification attempts directed against Austrian domination of the peninsula.

Occasion

The year 1848 saw revolutions across Europe, beginning with a reformist-separatist rising in Sicily (Jan.) and followed by revolutions in France (Feb.) and Vienna (March). Reports of the events in Austria, which led to the fall of Metternich (13 March), sparked uprisings in Austrian-controlled northern Italy. Milan, the chief city of Lombardy, rose in the famous Five Days' revolt (18 March), forcing the Austrian Marshal Radetzky to retreat into the Quadrilateral, a fortified area which controlled the alpine passes between northern Italy and southern Austria. The Piedmontese king, Charles Albert, taking advantage of Austria's weakness, entered the war (23 March). He later received support from the other Italian states, although none of them officially declared war.

Course of War

The war was fought in two phases (March–Aug. 1848 and March–Aug.

3 Italian unification

1849). Radetzky's force numbered no more than 70,000 men and reinforcements were hampered by general Italian resistance. At first Charles Albert's army was delayed (most of it being deployed on the Franco-Piedmontese border) and his initial force was only 45,000 strong. Radetzky avoided a direct confrontation until reinforcements reached him under General Nugent (25 May). Charles Albert had meanwhile annexed Lombardy, Venetia, Modena and Parma after a plebiscite. This aroused suspicions that his prime interest was the aggrandizement of his own kingdom. Such distractions allowed the Austrians to regroup under the brilliant Radetzky, who assumed the offensive at the end of May. In a series of battles around Custozza (23-7 July) Charles Albert, although holding the hilly ground and with a force now of 75,000, was defeated by Radetzky with 60,000 men. The Piedmontese king, hoping to save the remnants of his army, then abandoned Milan, which fell to Radetzky (4 Aug.), and a truce was concluded at Vigevano (9 Aug.). Charles Albert returned to his capital at Turin, where a new ministry wished to renew the struggle.

A revolution in Hungary had meanwhile distracted the Austrians. When the armistice expired (12 March 1849) the Piedmontese government denounced it and hostilities resumed (20 March). The Piedmontese army, under Charles Albert and his chief of staff, the Polish General Chrzanowski, was defeated by Radetzky at the Battle of Novarra (28 March). An armistice was immediately agreed and Charles Albert abdicated in favor of his son, Victor Emmanuel II.

Political result

The Treaty of Milan (6 Aug. 1849) imposed a heavy indemnity on Piedmont, while the territorial settlement of 1814 was restored.

Remarks

The Piedmontese defeat spelled disaster for the republics established in the cities of Venice, Rome and Florence. Venice held out until 22 August 1849, while the Roman republic, after an epic defence led by the nationalist leaders Mazzini and Garibaldi, fell on 2 July 1849 to the combined armies of Austria, France and Naples. The Pope was restored by these powers as the temporal ruler of Rome.

Austrian War with France and Piedmont 1859

Belligerents: **Austria**
                    France, Piedmont

Cause

Cavour became premier of Piedmont in 1852 and over the next nine years engineered the unification of Italy. Attempting to redress Charles Albert's mistakes in the Austro-Piedmontese War of 1848–9, he ensured that in another conflict Piedmont would have essential foreign support and adequate military preparation. By 1856 Cavour had adopted a clearly anti-Austrian policy. Major reforms to the army were completed by 1858, a naval base was constructed at Spezia and railways were built with military objectives in mind. Cavour in particular saw the need for a French alliance, and relations were strengthened when Piedmont entered the Crimean War as an ally of France and Britain. This policy culminated in the secret Plombières Agreement (20 July 1858), by which the French emperor, Napoleon III, agreed to support an anti-Austrian policy provided that a war could be justified as being defensive and thus obtain French popular support. This agreement was formalized by the Treaty of Turin (10 Dec. 1858). It was agreed that on the defeat of Austria Piedmont would gain Lombardy-Venetia, while France would receive Nice and Savoy from Piedmont.

Occasion

Having concluded the Turin Treaty, Cavour set about goading the Austrians into taking action, including using the Italian National Society (Società Nazionale Italiana) to generate anti-Austrian agitation. Austria sent an ultimatum to the Piedmontese government (23 April 1859), telling it to disarm within three days, and when this was refused the Austrians invaded (29 April). The same day France declared war on Austria.

Course of War

The main events of the war were the battles at Magenta and Solferino. The Battle of Magenta (4 June 1859) was fought between about 55,000 French and 58,000 Austrians, with the Piedmontese army absent. Both sides suffered from poor generalship, with MacMahon leading the French and Gyulai the Austrians. The French victory forced Gyulai to retreat towards the fortified area between northern Italy and southern Austria known as the Quadrilateral and Victor Emmanuel II and Napoleon III entered Milan in triumph (8 June). The Austrian emperor, Franz Joseph, then took personal command of his army. The Battle of Solferino (24 June) pitted an Austrian army of 120,000 against a Franco-Piedmontese army of equal strength. Here the French used new rifled artillery with great effect. This engagement saw an allied victory, although the Austrians withdrew in good order and casualties were high on both sides (22,000 Austrians and 18,000 allied). Franz Joseph now sought a negotiated settlement. The French emperor was doubtful of his ability to crack the Austrian Quadrilateral, concerned about the possibility of Prussian support for Austria and worried about the implications of a powerful new north Italian kingdom. As a result of these concerns Napoleon III agreed to Franz Joseph's request and offered moderate terms, with an armistice being agreed at Villafranca (11 July 1859).

Political result

By the Treaty of Zurich (10 Nov. 1859), Austria ceded most of Lombardy, but not Venetia, to Napoleon III, who in turn gave it to Piedmont. This procedure was adopted to reduce Austria's humiliation and heighten Napoleon III's prestige. Italian nationalists were angered by this, given Italian sacrifices, particularly that Venetia was to be denied them. Under the Treaty of Turin France received as its reward the districts of Nice and Savoy (May 1860). However, the Italian states of Tuscany, Modena and Parma, which had overthrown their royal houses, had meanwhile voted for union with Piedmont, thereby creating a great north Italian kingdom. Moreover, the events in north Italy helped cause a revolution in Naples (April 1860), which was supported by an irregular army under Garibaldi. With the capture of the Neapolitan royal stronghold at Gaeta (13 Feb. 1861) Naples was absorbed into the new Kingdom of Italy. At the same time a Piedmontese army occupied most of the Papal States, although Rome was defended by a French army (Sept. 1860) and remained under the Pope. The Kingdom of Italy was proclaimed (17 March 1861), but Rome itself was not acquired until 1870.

Remarks

The bloodshed of the war led to the founding of the Red Cross by the Convention of Geneva (1864).

Italo-Austrian War 1866

Belligerents: **Italy**
                    Austria

Cause

The period 1859–61 saw most of the aims of Italian unification achieved, but Venetia remained outside the kingdom. As in the 1850s, before the

Franco-Piedmontese War against Austria, the need for a strong ally was perceived. Italy therefore made an alliance with Prussia, which was hoping to break Austrian power inside the German Confederation (8 April 1866). By this treaty Italy pledged to support Prussia in a war with Austria. Prussia was not bound by a reciprocal obligation, but it was agreed that Italy would receive Venetia in return for creating this second front.

Occasion

The Austro-Prussian Seven Weeks' War began on 16 June 1866 and Italy declared war on Austria on 20 June. The Austrians had meanwhile signed a secret neutrality agreement with the French emperor, Napoleon III (12 June), which it was hoped would prevent French involvement, as had occurred in the 1859 war. By its terms Austria, having concluded that its position in Venetia was untenable, promised to cede Venetia to France on the understanding that it would be given to Italy.

Course of War

The war was a military disaster for Italy. The main engagement was the Second Battle of Custozza (24 June), where a force of 80,000 Italians was defeated by 74,000 Austrians. The Austrians, however, then had to rush north to protect Vienna from the Prussians, but before they could do this the Prussians defeated the Austrians at the Battle of Königgrätz (3 July). The one naval engagement of the war occurred at the Battle of Lissa (20 July), where Admiral Persano, having finally been coaxed from harbour by his government, led his Italian fleet of ten ironclads to disaster, witnessing the loss of three ironclads and 620 men to the Austrians under Admiral Tegetthoff, who commanded seven ironclads. Prussia's conclusion of a separate armistice with Austria left the latter free to turn its forces against Italy. The Italians hurriedly agreed to an armistice (12 Aug.).

Political result

As agreed earlier, Austria surrendered Venetia to Napoleon III (5 July), who turned it over to Italy. This was confirmed by the Austro-Italian Treaty of Vienna (3 Oct. 1866).

Remarks

The unification of Italy was now virtually complete. The city of Rome itself would be added after the collapse of French power in the Franco-Prussian War of 1870–1, which brought about an end to French protection of the Pope's temporal sovereignty. Some further territory in the north was acquired from Austria after the First World War.

4 Decline of the Ottoman Empire

Greek War of Independence 1821–32

Belligerents: **Ottoman Empire**
                     Greece, France, Great Britain, Russia

Cause

Greece had been under Ottoman Turkish control for four centuries, when the spread of nationalism in the wake of the French Revolution, together with an intellectual revival and Ottoman misrule, combined to generate a powerful national movement in Greece.

Occasion

An opportunity to eliminate Ottoman rule occurred when the Ottoman army became involved in suppressing Ali Pasha, the sultan's troublesome vassal in Epirus. Ethnic Greeks living in Russia had formed a secret society, the Philiki Etairia, committed to a restoration of Greek independence. Under the leadership of a Greek serving in the Russian army, Alexander Ypsilanti, the Philiki Etairia mounted an invasion of the Ottoman-ruled Danubian Principalities (Romania) (March 1821). It was hoped that this would persuade Russia to intervene, while also sparking a revolt among the inhabitants. The invasion was a failure, being crushed at the Battle of Dragashani (19 June 1821). These events, however, did spark an uprising in the Peloponnese, where the standard of revolt was raised at Patras (25 March 1821, old style, still celebrated as Greece's national day).

Course of War

The Greeks enjoyed some initial successes, as the Ottoman army was still busy with Ali Pasha. Greek privateers gained control of the sea, making particularly good use of fireships. The Greeks also benefited from widespread sympathy, philhellenism, in Europe. Writers such as Shelley, Goethe, Schiller and Victor Hugo avidly supported the Greek cause, while

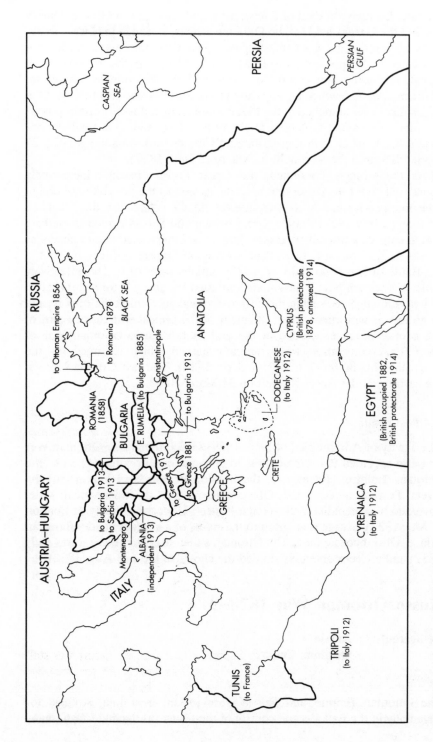

4 Decline of the Ottoman Empire

the poet Lord Byron died of a fever after going to fight in Greece. During 1822–3 the Greeks held off the Ottoman armies, although they were weakened by internecine political struggles. The Ottoman sultan turned for assistance to his powerful vassal, Mehemet Ali, the pasha, or viceroy, of Egypt, promising him control of Crete and the Peloponnese in return. Mehemet Ali dispatched an army under his son Ibrahim, together with the largest fleet ever launched in the Mediterranean by a non-European power. Ibrahim's forces first took control of Crete, before landing in the Peloponnese (1825). After long sieges, Ibrahim's forces took Missolonghi (22/23 April 1826) and the Acropolis in Athens (5 June 1827).

As the struggle continued, the Great Powers became increasingly concerned about the disruption to trade, as well as the possibility of one of their number furthering its own interests in the region. By the Treaty of London (6 July 1827) France, Great Britain and Russia agreed to mediate and to enforce a truce if necessary. When Ibrahim refused to end hostilities a joint Anglo-French-Russian fleet, already off Greece, engaged his fleet in the Battle of Navarino (20 Oct. 1827), sinking most of it. This effectively ended the war, although the sultan continued the struggle for a further two years. The Russians, seeing the Ottomans weakened, took the opportunity to go to war with them. The settlement of the Greek War formed part of the overall peace concluded at the end of the Russo-Ottoman War of 1828–9. A convention was eventually agreed which arranged for the evacuation of Ibrahim's troops (7 Sept. 1828). The last Ottoman forces, the garrison at the Acropolis, left on 31 March 1833.

Political result

The Treaty of Adrianople (14 Sept. 1829) settled the Russo-Ottoman War and also specified that Greece was to become an autonomous part of the Ottoman Empire. However, in the London Protocols (3 Feb. 1830) the Great Powers agreed that Greece should be an independent state, governed by a hereditary 'Sovereign Prince'. Under the Treaty of London (7 May 1832) Greece was raised to the status of a kingdom and a Bavarian prince, Otto, became king. The Ottoman sultan accepted these terms (July 1832) and a Greek assembly ratified the choice of Otto (8 Aug. 1832).

Russo-Ottoman War 1828–9

Belligerents: **Russia**
                     Ottoman Empire

Cause

The Ottoman Empire and Russia were locked in a long struggle for hegemony in the Balkans and control of the Caucasus, having fought many wars since the seventeenth century. For the most part this period saw the gradual erosion of Ottoman power, with occasional Russian reverses. This war was but one more instalment in a struggle that would only end during the First World War with the collapse of both empires.

Occasion

Russia again turned its attention towards the Ottoman Empire during the 1821–9 Greek War of Independence. Russia concluded the Convention of Akerman with the Ottomans (7 Oct. 1826), who were distracted by the war in Greece. Through this Russia achieved its demands for the autonomy of the Danubian Principalities (Romania) and Serbia, the recognition of Russian sovereignty over disputed districts in the Caucasus and the right of transit for Russian merchant ships through the Straits. Russia, however, hoped to gain even more. After Great Britain, France and Russia had destroyed the Ottoman fleet at Navarino (20 Oct. 1827), relations between Russia and the Ottomans deteriorated even further. Before the former could attack the Ottoman Empire, however, it had first to end its war with Persia (1826–8). In 1828 Russia took the opportunity of the sultan's denunciation of the Convention of Akerman in the aftermath of Navarino to attack the Ottoman Empire, declaring war (26 April 1828) and invading the Danubian Principalities (June).

Course of War

The three-pronged Russian invasion met tough Ottoman resistance and a siege of the Ottomans at Varna on the Black Sea lasted three months (July–Oct. 1828). The Russian forces in the Caucasus were successful in taking the important fortress of Kars (5 July 1828). A new Russian offensive in 1829 succeeded in pushing back the Ottoman forces and by the end of August 1829 the Russians were within a few miles of Constantinople. In the face of this threat, despite still having a large army in the Balkans and although the Russian army was weakened by disease, the Ottoman sultan sued for peace.

Political result

By the Treaty of Adrianople (14 Sept. 1829), Russia annexed the mouth of the Danube and the Black Sea littoral of the Caucasus, and also received an indemnity. The Ottomans recognized Russian gains in Persia and Russian sovereignty over Georgia, accepted the right of free passage of Russian merchant ships through the Straits and granted Serbia autonomy. The treaty also dealt with the settlement of the Greek War of Independence.

First Ottoman-Egyptian War 1831–3

Belligerents: **Ottoman Empire**
                    Egypt

Cause

Mehemet Ali, the powerful pasha (viceroy) of Egypt, was dissatisfied with his reward for assisting the Ottoman sultan in the Greek War of Independence. Greek independence had deprived him of his promised reward of the Peloponnese, leaving him only with the island of Crete. He wanted more and unsuccessfully demanded control of Syria for his son Ibrahim. In comparison with the sultan's army, Mehemet Ali's forces were modern, his army having been organized by a French officer and his fleet having been rebuilt after the disaster at Navarino in 1827 during the Greek war. He now hoped to achieve full independence from Ottoman rule.

Occasion

Mehemet Ali found an excuse for war when the Ottoman pasha of Acre refused to surrender some Egyptian refugees. This was followed by an invasion of Syria, led by Ibrahim (1831).

Course of War

Ibrahim rapidly captured Jerusalem, Acre, Damascus and Aleppo. Having gained control of Syria, he then crossed the Taurus mountains into Anatolia. At the Battle of Konya (21 Dec. 1832) Ibrahim defeated the sultan's army and took its commander, Reshid Pasha, prisoner. He was now poised to attack Constantinople itself. The sultan, in desperation, finding Britain preoccupied by the Belgian Revolution and France sympathetic to Mehemet Ali, turned to Russia for salvation. The Russians responded by sending a fleet to protect Constantinople (20 Feb. 1833). This caused Mehemet Ali to come to terms with the sultan.

Political result

Under the Convention of Kiutayeh (Kutahiya) (14 May 1833), Mehemet Ali also became pasha of Syria. This temporarily satisfied the Egyptian ruler, but he still nurtured ambitions of a greater role, which would lead to a second war in 1839. The Treaty of Unkiar Skelessi (8 July 1833) gave Russia its reward for saving the sultan from the Egyptian army. Russia pledged itself to provide troops to protect the Ottoman Empire if necessary; in return the sultan agreed to close the Straits to all warships in the event of a war against Russia. Russia now hoped to exercise a virtual protectorate over the Ottoman Empire.

Second Ottoman-Egyptian War 1839–40

Belligerents: **Ottoman Empire**
                    Egypt

Cause

Despite the settlement of the First Ottoman-Egyptian War in 1833, the sultan still hoped to suppress his unruly Egyptian vassals, Mehemet Ali and his son Ibrahim.

Occasion

After a series of revolts in Syria against the administration of Ibrahim, the sultan took the opportunity to attack the Egyptians (21 April 1839).

Course of War

The sultan's forces invaded Syria across the Euphrates (21 April 1839), but Ibrahim annihilated them at the Battle of Nezib (Nizib) (24 June). The Ottoman defeat was due, in part, to the fact that their commander, Hafiz Pasha, ignored the advice of the young Helmuth von Moltke, later to be the architect of Prussian victory in the Franco-Prussian War of 1870–1. The commander of the Ottoman fleet then switched sides and turned the fleet over to Mehemet Ali (1 July). The Ottoman Empire seemed on the verge of collapse and the Great Powers (except France, which favored Mehemet Ali) intervened to save the sultan. By the Treaty of London (15 July 1840), concluded by Austria, Great Britain, Prussia and Russia, Mehemet Ali was offered the hereditary viceroyship of Egypt and the governorship of southern Syria for his lifetime. An Anglo-Austrian fleet was sent to Beirut to apply pressure on the Egyptians. Mehemet Ali, however, rejected these terms, which led to the British bombardment of Beirut and the landing of British forces (9 Sept.). At the same time, a revolt against Egyptian rule broke out in Lebanon. Mehemet Ali, after losing Beirut (10 Oct.) and Acre (3 Nov.), agreed to a settlement.

Political result

By the Convention of Alexandria (27 Nov. 1840) Mehemet Ali became hereditary pasha of Egypt, renounced any further claims against the Ottoman Empire and returned its fleet. His family remained the rulers of Egypt until 1952. The sultan, after some delay, agreed to this settlement (13 Feb. 1841). By the Straits Convention (13 July 1841) the Great Powers agreed that the Straits would be closed to all warships during peacetime.

Montenegrin-Ottoman War 1852–3

Belligerents: **Montenegro**
                          Ottoman Empire

Cause

In 1851 Danilo II ascended to the throne of the independent principality of Montenegro and, wishing to marry, ended the system dating from 1516 of a combined prince-bishop (*vladika*) by separating the offices. These changes were approved in 1852 after agreement from the Russian tsar, the only other Orthodox monarch in the world and a traditional protector of Montenegro. Austria was also consulted.

Occasion

The Ottoman government, however, was suspicious of the tsar's role, being sensitive to any hint of a Russian protectorate over Montenegro. The Ottoman governor of the neighboring province of Bosnia, Omar Pasha Latas, who was strengthening Ottoman rule in the region, now attempted to weaken Montenegro by detaching a portion of the country by offering the inhabitants land grants. This was followed by the seizure of Zhablyak, their ancient capital, by some Montenegrins. Danilo prudently ordered the evacuation of the city but the Ottomans were not assuaged and invaded Montenegro.

Course of War

Five separate Turkish armies attacked Montenegro, causing Danilo to ask Austria and Russia for support. Austria, although wary of traditional Russo-Montenegrin friendship, was angry with the Ottomans for receiving Hungarian and Polish refugees after the 1848–9 revolution. As a result, both Austria and Russia applied diplomatic pressure on the Ottoman government and in the face of such opposition the Ottomans ended hostilities, Omar was recalled and all captured territory was restored.

Political result

A peace treaty was signed (3 March 1853) restoring the prewar status quo.

Crimean War 1853–6

Belligerents: **Russia**
                    Ottoman Empire, France, Great Britain, Piedmont

Cause

The growing weakness of the Ottoman Empire during the nineteenth century made it an area of expansion for the Great Powers. This led to conflict between Russia, which hoped in general to expand its regional influence and in particular to gain control of the Straits, France, which was developing an interest in the Middle East, and Britain, which preferred to maintain the status quo.

Occasion

The immediate background to the war was a dispute over the guardianship of the holy places in Jerusalem, which the Ottoman government had traditionally allowed to certain European states. Russia claimed a broad role as protector of the Orthodox Christians, who were the chief pilgrims to Jerusalem and who controlled the most important holy places. France had in the past exercised protective rights for Roman Catholics, but these had lapsed from disuse. Renewed French involvement was evident from the time of the Second Ottoman-Egyptian War of 1839, and the new French government of Louis Napoleon Bonaparte decided to reclaim its former rights. Ottoman reluctance to alienate the Russians on this issue was overcome by a display of French military power. The Ottoman government agreed to the French demand for possession of the key to the Church of Bethlehem and the right to place a silver star on Jesus' birthplace in the Church of the Nativity (Dec. 1852). This success coincided with Louis Napoleon's assumption of the title of Emperor Napoleon III.

Russia responded to French ambitions with an ultimatum to the Ottomans (May 1853) demanding recognition not only of Orthodox control of the holy places but also of Russia's right to act as protector of the Ottoman Empire's 12 million Orthodox subjects, a demand which threatened Ottoman sovereignty. An Anglo-French fleet anchoring in the Straits was sent to support the Ottomans (13–14 June). When the Ottomans rejected the Russian demands, a Russian army invaded the Danubian Principalities (Romania) (2 July). Diplomatic efforts failed to resolve the dispute and the Ottoman Empire declared war on Russia (4 Oct. 1853).

Course of War

The early Russian defeat of an Ottoman flotilla in the Battle of Sinope (30 Nov. 1853) helped to inflame Anglo-French public opinion and Britain and France declared war on Russia (28 March 1854), after Russia had ignored their ultimatum to withdraw from Ottoman territory. They were later joined by Piedmont (Sardinia) (26 Jan. 1855), which hoped to win the allies' goodwill in its claims against Austria (as pursued in the 1859 Franco-Piedmontese War with Austria). Prussia and Austria remained neutral and called on Russia to restore the status quo. Austria also moved an army to its border with Russia. In the face of such opposition the Russians evacuated the Danubian Principalities (July 1854). The Austrians then occupied the principalities, with Ottoman permission, thereby tying down a sizeable Russian force.

There were three theatres of action, the Balkans, the Crimea and the Caucasus, as well as secondary theaters in the Baltic and the Far East. An allied force of 62,000 men landed in the Crimea (7 Sept. 1854), the main arena, and soon defeated the Russians at the Battle of Alma (20 Sept.), although they suffered heavy casualties themselves. The Russians fell back on their great fortress at Sebastopol, which the allies besieged. Russian attempts to break the siege were defeated at the Battle of Balaklava (25 Oct.), which saw the suicidal British charge of the Light Brigade, and at the Battle of Inkerman (5 Nov.). There followed a prolonged winter siege of Sebastopol, in which the allied powers, ill-prepared for such a campaign, suffered badly from disease. When Sebastopol finally fell (9 Sept. 1855), it was estimated that the siege had cost 600,000 lives through fighting and disease.

In the Caucasus the Russians met with more success, capturing the Ottoman fortress of Kars (28 Nov. 1855). The major action in the Baltic Sea was the Battle for the Åland Islands (7–16 Aug. 1854), which were captured by an Anglo-French force and their fortress destroyed. Anglo-French operations in the Baltic forced Russia to tie down a large force to defend its capital, St Petersburg. There were also some skirmishes in the Far East. It was finally due to an Austrian threat to enter the war after the fall of Sebastopol, when the Russians showed signs of continuing the war, that hostilities were finally ended (Dec. 1855).

Political result

By the Treaty of Paris (30 March 1856), all occupied territory was restored; Russia lost a small strip of Bessarabia to the Ottoman Empire to help guarantee the security of the Danube; the Black Sea was declared a neutral zone; the Ottoman Empire was explicitly admitted to the Concert of Europe, and all parties agreed to respect the territorial integrity of the Ottoman Empire.

Remarks

The British and French benefited from vastly superior equipment, in particular the deployment of screw-propelled ships against the Russian sailing ships. The war also saw the first use of ironclads. Russia suffered from logistical problems, there being no railways south of Moscow. The war was also the first to be subject to rapid press coverage, which in Britain helped bring about popular disillusionment with its conduct and led to the fall of Lord Aberdeen's government. The Crimean War was notable too for the nursing work of Florence Nightingale, which led to an improvement in military medicine. It was the first war for several centuries in which Britain and France were on the same side.

Montenegrin-Ottoman War 1858

Belligerents: **Montenegro**
                    Ottoman Empire

Cause

Following the hostilities of 1852–3, Montenegrin-Ottoman relations remained turbulent in the face of rising nationalism in the Balkans. Tension again began to build after the murder of a Montenegrin priest, whose head was subsequently displayed on the Ottoman fortress of Spuj. In response to the Montenegrin government's protest, Ottoman forces were moved to the frontier.

Occasion

The war began with a border incident in 1858 when some villages on the Adriatic coast proclaimed their union with Montenegro and a Montenegrin senator briefly seized the key fortress of Spizza on the Bay of Antivari. Prince Danilo of Montenegro appealed to the Great Powers for support and French and Russian ships were accordingly deployed off Ragusa (Dubrovnik).

Course of War

Most of the military activity occurred in the Grahovo district, which had been declared a neutral zone by an 1842 agreement. It was initially seized by an Ottoman general, Husein Pasha, but he was defeated by Prince Mirko, 'the Sword of Montenegro', in a battle (12–13 May) known as the Marathon of Montenegro.

Political result

A Conference of Ambassadors at Constantinople in 1858 agreed to border rectifications which gave Grahovo and surrounding districts to Montenegro.

Montenegrin-Ottoman War 1861–2

Belligerents: **Montenegro**
                     Ottoman Empire

Occasion

Montenegrin victories in the Montenegrin-Ottoman War of 1858 helped to encourage their ethnic kinsfolk in Herzegovina to revolt against Ottoman rule. A rising there in 1861 led to the defeat of Omar Pasha, although Montenegro did not intervene because of pressure from the Great Powers. The revolt was finally suppressed and Omar proceeded to turn on Montenegro, which he saw as a continual source of trouble in the region, invading the principality in the winter of 1861–2.

Course of War

Omar's forces succeeded in cutting Montenegro in two, by severing the narrow (12 mile) neck connecting the eastern and western halves of the country. The futility of proceeding with the war led the Montenegrins to agree to a settlement.

Political result

In the Convention of Scutari (31 Aug. 1862), the Ottoman Empire agreed to a very generous peace settlement, in the hope of ending Montenegrin hostility by removing the main sources of grievance. The frontiers of 1859 were restored and the Montenegrins were allowed to import any goods, except arms, through Ottoman territory and to rent agricultural land in the Ottoman Empire.

Montenegrin-Serbian-Ottoman War 1876

Belligerents: **Montenegro, Serbia**
                     Ottoman Empire

Cause

During the early 1870s Ottoman control in the Balkans began to erode rapidly, with a series of uprisings by local peoples. In 1875 a revolt occurred in Herzegovina, a majority of whose inhabitants were ethnic Serbs. The Great Powers intervened, fearing the effects of further instability in the region, and demanded reforms from the Ottomans. Austria in particular was concerned about the possibility of a large Slav state to its south which might act as a magnet for its own Slavic subjects. In 1876, soon after Abdul Hamid II became sultan, a revolt began in Bulgaria and was savagely suppressed. In Britain Gladstone, then Liberal opposition leader, made the 'Bulgarian atrocities' a major political issue.

Occasion

Montenegrin-Ottoman relations had begun to worsen with the murder in 1874 of some Montenegrins by Ottomans at Podgoritsa. The revolt in neighboring Herzegovina further exacerbated relations, with Prince Nicholas of Montenegro protesting to Britain that this put him in an intolerable position. Both Britain and Russia advised the Ottomans to placate Nicholas by ceding a seaport and some territory to Montenegro. The Ottomans did not act on this advice and in June 1876 a Montenegrin-Serbian alliance was concluded. Serbia then declared war on the Ottoman Empire (1 July 1876) and Montenegro did so the following day.

Course of War

Montenegrin forces were markedly successful, in contrast to the poor performance of the Serbian army. A Montenegrin army striking north under Prince Nicholas defeated the Turks at Vuchidol and advanced to the outskirts of Mostar, the Herzegovinan capital, where it halted after a threat of Austrian intervention. In the south the Montenegrins won victories at the battles of Milovgrad and Medun. The poorly-organized Serbian army fared badly. Commanded by the Russian General Cherniaev, the conqueror of Tashkent and a pan-Slav, it was defeated by Suleiman Pasha at Alexsinatz and Cherniaev's headquarters at Deligrad was captured. Prince Milan of Serbia now arranged for an armistice, which ended abruptly when, in an ill-timed gesture (16 Sept.), he proclaimed himself king of Serbia (a dignity he finally achieved in 1882). This was followed by a defeat at Djunis (29 Oct.), leaving the way to Belgrade open to the Ottoman army and forcing Prince Milan again to seek an armistice. A Russian ultimatum to the Ottomans resulted in an armistice being arranged within 48 hours (1 Nov.).

Political result

In the peace talks the Montenegrins hoped to gain territory, including the seaport of Spizza. The Ottomans were willing to agree to this, but both Austria and Italy objected, fearing that such a port would become a Russian Adriatic base. The Ottomans did, however, refuse to give up Nikshich. Negotiations collapsed and Montenegro prepared to renew the war. The British vainly attempted to prevent this by proposing a compromise formula. These moves were overtaken by the Russian declaration of war on the Ottoman Empire in April 1877, leading Nicholas to resume hostilities. Meanwhile, an Ottoman-Serbian peace protocol signed at

Constantinople (28 Feb. 1877) had restored the prewar status quo on that front. After the fall of Plevna (Dec. 1877) during the Russo-Ottoman War, when Russian victory was assured, Serbia again declared war.

Russo-Ottoman War 1877–8

Belligerents: **Russia, Montenegro, Romania, Serbia, (Greece)**
Ottoman Empire

Cause

As the Balkans became increasingly inflamed by nationalism, a powerful pan-Slav faction in Russia pressed Tsar Alexander II to take advantage of the situation. It was also hoped that territory lost in the Crimean War could be regained.

Occasion

Russia began to prepare for the possibility of war and, after intervening diplomatically (Oct. 1876) to save Serbia from defeat in the 1876 Montenegrin-Serbian-Ottoman War, began partial mobilization (13 Nov.). An agreement with Romania (16 April 1877), still technically under Ottoman suzerainty, allowed Russian troops transit across that country. Russia then declared war (24 April), and Romania declared its independence (21 May). Romania was not at first asked to join in the war, but as Russian reverses developed it was invited to participate. Serbia joined the Russians after the fall of Plevna (Dec. 1877) had assured a Russian victory. Montenegro, which was already at war with the Ottomans, likewise joined the Russian effort.

Course of War

The war was fought simultaneously on two fronts: the Danube-Balkan front and the Transcaucasian front. On the former, a Russian army under Grand Duke Nicholas numbered 190,000 men against an Ottoman army of 300,000, of which 170,000 were deployed in Bulgaria. In the Transcaucasus, a Russian army of 60,000 under Grand Duke Michael faced an Ottoman force of 70,000–100,000. The Russian army suffered from a shortage of reserve officers, poor equipment, antiquated rifles and artillery, and the inept leadership of the grand dukes. Conversely, the Ottoman army had reasonably modern arms, although it was badly organized. Early Russian successes and advances were checked by the Ottomans (July 1877). The Russians now became bogged down in a siege of the fortress of Plevna (19 July–10 Dec.), losing 30,000 men in three unsuccessful assaults. However, with the Russian capture of Plevna the Ottoman lines finally broke and the Russian army raced towards Constantinople, reaching the city by 30 Jan. 1878. The following day an armistice was agreed. Russia's allies had also performed well, with Montenegro capturing Nikshich and the coastal areas of Spizza, Antivari and Dulcingo, while the Serbs took Nish. Greece, which had hesitated too long, joined the war the day after the armistice but was forced to withdraw by the Great Powers.

Political result

The Treaty of San Stefano (3 March 1878), which ended the war, almost led to a major European conflict. In the Caucasus Russia acquired Kars, Ardahan and Batum. Montenegro's independence was again recognized by the Ottomans and it acquired its long-sought aims of Spizza, Nikshich, Podgoritsa and Zhablyak, which tripled its size. The independence of Romania and Serbia was recognized, and a vast autonomous Bulgaria was created, including Macedonia and an Aegean seaport. A large indemnity was also levied on the Ottomans. The other Great Powers were alarmed at this great extension of Russian power, with Bulgaria being perceived as a virtual Russian satellite. This resulted in a Great Power congress held at Berlin which modified the San Stefano treaty. The Treaty of Berlin (13 July 1878) reduced the size of Bulgaria, the province of Eastern Rumelia being created to its south, under Ottoman sovereignty but with a Christian governor. Under other provisions, Romania ceded Bessarabia to Russia, receiving in return northern Dobrudja from Bulgaria; Montenegro lost Spizza to Austria but acquired other territory, as did Serbia; Austria was allowed to occupy and administer the Ottoman provinces of Bosnia-Herzegovina; international recognition was accorded to the independence of Serbia, Montenegro and Romania; and Greece was promised further territorial additions, which were finalized in 1881. Beyond the Balkans, Russia was confirmed in possession of the Caucasus, while Cyprus became a British protectorate under nominal Ottoman rule.

Remarks

This compromise peace, intended to retain an equilibrium between the Great Powers, was disliked by the Balkan states. The arrangements for Bulgaria proved to be impractical and were soon altered by events, beginning with the 1885 Serbo-Bulgarian War, while Bulgarian governments up to the Second World War attempted to regain the San Stefano frontiers. Austria's control of Bosnia-Herzegovina spawned later crises, such as the Annexation Crisis of 1908 and the assassination of the Austrian heir in its capital, Sarajevo, in 1914 – the action which sparked off the First World War.

Serbo-Bulgarian War 1885

Belligerents: **Bulgaria**
                    Serbia

Cause

The Congress of Berlin (1878), as part of the settlement of the 1877–8 Russo-Ottoman War, created a principality of Bulgaria, notionally under the suzerainty of the Ottoman sultan, and an autonomous Ottoman province of Eastern Rumelia under a Christian governor-general. Alexander of Battenberg, a German prince related to the Russian tsar, was chosen as prince of Bulgaria. Russian influence in the country was strong and all officers in the army above the rank of lieutenant were Russian. In 1885 the inhabitants of Eastern Rumelia revolted and proclaimed their union with Bulgaria. Prince Alexander accepted the union and made preparations for the expected Ottoman invasion, while carefully continuing to recognize Ottoman suzerainty. The Ottomans, however, decided against action, fearing at that time a revolt in Macedonia. But the king of Serbia, Milan I, was concerned by the shift in the regional balance of power caused by the enlargement of Bulgaria and he demanded compensation. Other Serbian motivations were a bitter tariff war and a border dispute after the Timok river had changed course. Serbia was financially in straitened circumstances, having spent heavily on a new rail network, and felt it had little to lose. As one Serbian official observed, 'a naked man will jump far'.

Occasion

The Serbian army was militia-based, while the Russian-trained and officered Bulgarian army was organized on the German model. The Russians, however, refused to support Bulgaria's absorption of Eastern Rumelia and withdrew its officers, leaving Prince Alexander to rely on the junior officers. Seeing Bulgaria thus weakened, Serbia declared war (14 Nov. 1885).

Course of War

The Serbian declaration of war found most of the Bulgarian army deployed along the Ottoman frontier. Alexander hurriedly redeployed his army in a series of remarkable forced marches and centered his forces on Slivnitza. In the Battle of Slivnitza (17–19 Nov. 1885) a Serbian army of 28,000 met a Bulgarian force of 10,000 (later reinforced by 5,000 men). The Bulgarians were victorious, although they suffered 3,000 casualties to the Serbs' 2,000. Prince Alexander then carried the war into Serbia and at the Battle of Pirot (26–27 Nov.) he again defeated the Serbs. Only the diplomatic intervention of Austria, which threatened military action, brought about an armistice (28 Nov.).

Political result

The Treaty of Bucharest (3 March 1886) restored the prewar status quo.

Remarks

Bulgaria's victory did much to forge a sense of Bulgarian national unity. Serbia lost nothing but prestige, a factor which contributed to its participation in the Balkan War against Bulgaria in 1913. Russia did not forgive Prince Alexander and was instrumental in his subsequent deposition (7 Sept. 1886). The war provided the backdrop for George Bernard Shaw's play, *Arms and the Man.*

Graeco-Ottoman War 1897

Belligerents: Greece
Ottoman Empire

Cause

The origins of this war lay in Greek irredentist desires. The island of Crete was under Ottoman control, although by the Pact of Halepa (Oct. 1878) the sultan had allowed its people a large measure of autonomy. Communal unrest continued, however, and in 1889 the sultan abrogated most of the earlier guarantees. The Greek government was anxious to intervene and gain control of the island but was prevented from doing so by the Great Powers, who wanted to maintain the status quo established by the Congress of Berlin (July 1878) after the Russo-Ottoman War of 1877–8.

Occasion

A revolt by the Cretans (24 May 1896) caused the sultan hurriedly to restore the Halepa Pact. This action proved ineffective and the revolt was renewed, with an independent government being proclaimed (Feb. 1897) at Akrotiri, across from the capital at Canea. The Greek government dispatched a torpedo-boat flotilla under King George's second son, Prince George, to prevent Ottoman reinforcements from landing. When Great Power intervention rendered this action ineffective, the Greek government landed a force under Colonel Vassos on the island (15 Feb.). Great Power intervention continued, however; a combined force from Austria, Britain, France, Germany, Italy and Russia occupied Canea and proceeded to bombard the rebel government. In Greece, popular support for their kinsfolk in Crete was further fanned by the National Society (Ethniki Etaria) and armed bands invaded Ottoman territory on Greece's northern frontier (9 April). The Ottoman government then declared war on Greece (12 April 1897), having first secured the neutrality of Bulgaria and Serbia.

Course of War

The Greek army in the north, commanded by Crown Prince Constantine, was soon defeated by the German-trained Ottoman army under Edhem Pasha. The final defeat of the Greek army at Domokos (17 May) opened the pass to Lamia to the Ottomans. The Russian tsar, a nephew of the Greek king, intervened diplomatically to rescue Greece and an armistice was signed (19 May).

Political result

Under the Treaty of Constantinople (4 Dec. 1897), Greece was forced to agree to small border rectifications in the north which gave the Ottomans a more defensible frontier. An indemnity was levied against Greece of four million Turkish pounds, to be collected by an international commission. In a separate settlement, four of the Great Powers (France, Great Britain, Italy and Russia) assumed de facto control of Crete, which remained formally under Ottoman suzerainty, and Ottoman forces were withdrawn. These four powers then appointed Prince George of Greece as their high commissioner, to meet the inhabitants' desire for a Greek ruler.

Remarks

The Greek campaign was spontaneous, with little preparation, and badly organized. It revealed that Greece could not hope to defeat the Ottoman Empire alone, eventually leading it in 1912 to join in the Balkan League for this purpose. Crete was finally annexed to Greece in 1913 during the Balkan Wars.

Italo-Ottoman War (Tripolitanian War) 1911–12

Belligerents: **Italy**
                     Ottoman Empire

Cause

Italy had long harbored ambitions to control the coast of the Mediterranean opposite Italy, then usually referred to as Tripoli, later as Libya. The Italian patriot Mazzini had exclaimed in 1838: 'North Africa belongs to Italy.' With the weakening of the Ottoman Empire, the European imperial powers began to seize control of Ottoman territories in North Africa. Franco-Italian tension had risen when France pre-empted Italian aspirations in Tunis (1881), but this was resolved by a 1901 agreement by which France gave Italy a free hand in Tripoli and in return Italy promised not to interfere with French aims in Morocco. Britain subsequently acquiesced in this.

Occasion

In 1911 the Agadir Crisis erupted between the Great Powers over the French role in Morocco. Taking advantage of the distraction of the Great Powers over this issue, Italy attacked the Ottoman Empire with the aim of acquiring a North African foothold directly to its south, to counterbalance France's possessions in Morocco, Algeria and Tunis, and Britain's control of Egypt. During September 1911 Italy sent a series of ever-more extreme ultimatums to the Ottoman government over Italian rights in Libya, finally declaring war (29 Sept. 1911).

Course of War

An Italian squadron landed a force which took Tripoli (5 Oct.), although the poorly-prepared logistics meant that no troop transports arrived until 11 October. This delay allowed the Ottomans to organize an effective resistance. The war continued in a desultory manner, with the Italians defending their coastal seizures, until the Ottomans, facing the crisis in the Balkans which resulted in the First Balkan War in 1912, sued for peace. Some naval fighting took place off Beirut and in the Aegean Sea, while Italian forces occupied (April–May 1912) and retained the Greek-populated Dodecanese islands in the Aegean.

Political result

In the early stages of the war the Italian government had optimistically issued a royal decree (5 Nov. 1911), annexing the provinces that comprised Libya. At the end of the war two documents were signed by the belligerents in a complicated settlement. By the secret Treaty of Ouchy (15 Oct. 1912), the Ottomans evacuated Libya (i.e. the provinces of Tripolitania and Cyrenaica), but the sultan, while allowing local autonomy, did not formally renounce sovereignty and retained the right to appoint religious officials. In the same agreement the Italians asserted their complete sovereignty over Libya, but recognized the sultan's rights in his religious capacity as caliph.

The public Treaty of Lausanne (18 Oct. 1912) agreed the Ottoman evacuation of Libya followed by the Italian evacuation of the Dodecanese as soon as the Ottoman move was completed. The outbreak of the First World War, however, left Italy in possession of these islands until the Second World War, after which they passed to Greece. Italian authority was accepted in Tripolitania by 1914, but in Cyrenaica it was faced with a revolt by a coalition of remaining Ottoman soldiers and the Islamic Senussi confraternity, aided by Egyptian nationalists. Attempts at negotiations failed and an Italian campaign was launched (April 1913), which delayed Italian entry into the First World War. On the Italian declaration of war against Austria (23 May 1915), a general Arab rising occurred throughout Libya, with Italian forces retreating to coastal enclaves. Under the terms of the secret Treaty of London (26 April 1915), Britain and France promised Libya to Italy. It was not until 1931, however, that Italian rule was firmly established in Libya, only to be destroyed during the Second World War.

Balkan Wars 1912–13

Two wars fought in the Balkan peninsula which eliminated the Ottoman Empire from Europe, except for a small area around its then capital of Constantinople (later Istanbul).

FIRST BALKAN WAR 1912–13

Belligerents: **Bulgaria, Greece, Serbia, Montenegro**
                     Ottoman Empire

Cause

The states of southeast Europe which had formerly been under Ottoman rule still had a number of outstanding irredentist claims against the empire. While the Ottomans had fought well against individual states, it was perceived that a collective action might break the Ottoman grasp on their remaining Balkan territories.

Occasion

In the aftermath of the Ottoman defeat in the Italo-Ottoman War, Bulgaria, Greece, Serbia and Montenegro formed the anti-Ottoman Balkan League (March 1912), a complex series of bilateral agreements. Montenegro inaugurated the fighting (8 Oct. 1912), precipitating declarations of war by Bulgaria and Serbia (17 Oct.) and Greece (18 Oct.).

Course of War

The Ottoman forces were driven back by this combined onslaught and suffered a string of defeats. The Bulgarians defeated the Ottoman army at the Battle of Lule Burgas (28–30 Oct.), allowing them to advance as far as the Chatalja Line which defended Constantinople. In the Battle of Monastir the Serbs defeated an Ottoman force of 40,000, with the Ottomans suffering 20,000 dead or captured (5 Nov.). Salonika fell to the Greeks (9 Nov.), pre-empting its capture by the Bulgarians, who also coveted it, by one day. In the face of these disasters the Ottoman government gladly accepted an armistice (3 Dec.) proposed by the Great Powers, who met at the London Conference to discuss the crisis. The situation altered, however, when the Ottoman government was toppled in a coup and the new government, headed by Enver Pasha, refused peace terms.

GERMANY

AUSTRIAN   EMPIRE

RUSSIA

Vienna

Budapest

KINGDOM OF HUNGARY

BESSARABIA

MOLDAVIA

To Moldavia 1856
To Russia
1878

To Serbia 1833

BOSNIA–
HERZEGOVINA
Austro–Hungarian
Occupied 1878
Annexed 1908
Sarajevo

Belgrade
SERBIA Independent
1878

ROMANIA

WALLACHIA   Bucharest

DOBRUDJA

To Romania
1878

Ceded to
Romania 1913

To Serbia 1833

To Serbia
1878

BULGARIA
Independent 1908

Sofia

To
Montenegro
1878

MONTENEGRO

Cattaro   Cetinje

To Montenegro
1913

To Serbia
1912–13

EASTERN RUMELIA
United to Bulgaria 1885

To Bulgaria
1913

To Bulgaria
1913

Adrianople

To Bulgaria
1913

To Montenegro
1878

ALBANIA
Independent
1912–13

To Greece 1913

Salonika

Constantinople

ITALY

To Greece
1881

Islands to Greece 1913

OTTOMAN
EMPIRE
(TURKEY)

Ionian Islands
To Greece 1863

GREECE

Athens

Independent 1830

DODECANESE
ISLANDS

To Italy 1912

CRETE
Autonomous 1898
United to Greece 1913

5 Balkan Peninsula to 1913

Hostilities were resumed (3 Feb. 1913), with disastrous consequences for the Ottomans. The Greeks took the chief city of Epirus, Ioannina (3 March), a Bulgarian-Serb force took Adrianople (26 March) and the remaining Ottoman positions in Albania and Macedonia also fell. The Ottomans now agreed to make peace.

Political result

A preliminary peace was agreed by the Treaty of London (30 May 1913). The Ottoman Empire ceded to the allies all territory beyond a line drawn from Enos on the Aegean Sea to Media on the Black Sea. Greece received Crete, several Aegean islands and southern Epirus; Serbia, Bulgaria and Greece were to divide Macedonia; and Albania became independent.

SECOND BALKAN WAR 1913

Belligerents: Greece, Serbia, Montenegro, Romania, Ottoman Empire
Bulgaria

Cause

The preliminary peace treaty in London which ended the First Balkan War in May 1913 had left open the future division of the Balkan lands surrendered by the Ottoman Empire. In particular, the problem of the future of Macedonia led to a break-up of the Balkan League and a realignment of the states against Bulgarian ambitions. The Great Powers, in overseeing the settlement of the First Balkan War, had blocked some of the aspirations of the Balkan League's members. The powers had forced Bulgaria to cede part of the Dobrudja as compensation to Romania, which had not participated in the war as it did not border the Ottoman Empire. Serb hopes for access to the Adriatic were blocked by Austria-Hungary, leading Serbia to look for compensation in territory it had not received under the Treaty of London. This led to a secret Greek-Serb alliance envisaging a common border in Macedonia at the expense of Bulgarian claims (June 1913).

Occasion

Dissatisfied with the progress of negotiations, and concerned about a possible Greek-Serb attack, Bulgaria opted for a pre-emptive war to achieve its aims, invading Greece and Serbia without a declaration of war (30 May 1913).

Course of War

The initial Bulgarian offensive was halted by the Greeks and Serbs. A Greek-Serb counteroffensive (2 July) began to roll back the Bulgarian armies. With Bulgaria on the defensive, Romania declared war on that country (15 July) and Romanian forces moved swiftly on the Bulgarian capital of Sofia. The Ottomans also took the opportunity to regain lost territory, attacking and retaking Adrianople (22 July). The war was a disaster for Bulgaria, which sued for peace. A peace conference was convened on 30 July.

Political result

By the Treaty of Bucharest (10 Aug. 1913), Bulgaria accepted the division of most of Macedonia between Greece and Serbia, although it retained a small port on the Aegean Sea at Dedeagatch (Alexandropoulis). Bulgaria also ceded southern Dobrudja to Romania. Both Serbia and Montenegro were doubled in size by the settlement, while Greece also did well, increasing its territory by 70 per cent. In the Treaty of Constantinople (29 Sept. 1913) between Bulgaria and the Ottoman Empire, the Ottomans regained Adrianople and part of eastern Thrace (most of the western part having gone to Greece).

Remarks

The fluid situation in the Balkans was the immediate prelude to the outbreak of the First World War in 1914. The growth of Serbian power as a result of its victories caused concern in neighboring Austria-Hungary, whose subsequent moves to crush Serbia resulted in the crisis which led to the start of that war.

5   World Wars and Related Conflicts

First World War 1914–18

Main belligerents: **Central Powers – Germany, Austria-Hungary,
Ottoman Empire
Allied and Associated Powers – France, Great
Britain and Dominions, Russia, United States,
Japan, Italy**
(see Appendix A for full list)

Cause

The causes of the outbreak of the First World War remain an issue of significant debate among historians. Among the contributory factors often cited are the growth of German power disproportionate to other European states after unification (1871); Anglo-German naval rivalry; Franco-German tension over France's loss of Alsace-Lorraine after the 1870–1 Franco-Prussian War; the interlocking alliance systems of Europe; and growing economic pressures.

Occasion

The spark which ignited the growing tensions in Europe was the assassination of the heir to the Austro-Hungarian throne, the archduke Franz Ferdinand, at Sarajevo (28 June 1914) by a Serbian nationalist. The Austro-Hungarian government suspected official Serbian complicity and seized on this opportunity to crush the Serb nationalist threat to its empire with a harsh ultimatum. Serbia's partial rejection of the ultimatum was used as an excuse for Austria-Hungary to declare war on Serbia (28 July). This activated the complex alliance system of Europe: Russia mobilized (30 July), causing Germany to declare war on Russia (1 Aug.) and on France (3 Aug.). In accordance with the Schlieffen Plan, Germany attacked France via Belgium, which brought Britain and its dominions into the war (4 Aug.) in defence of Belgian neutrality, as guaranteed by the 1839 Treaty of London.

43

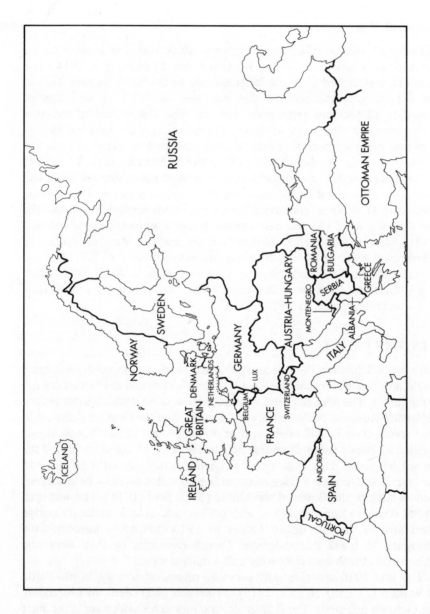

6 Europe in 1914

The Central Powers were joined by the Ottoman Empire (29 Oct. 1914) and Bulgaria (11 Oct. 1915), while the Allies were joined by, among others, Japan (23 Aug. 1914), Italy (23 May 1915) and the United States (6 April 1917).

Course of War – overview

Virtually all military planners expected a quick war, but it soon settled down to one of attrition. On the Western Front, by November 1914 a line of trenches stretched from the Belgian coast to the Swiss frontier. One of the notable characteristics of this war was the high casualty figures, exceeding all previous experience. The war also saw significant technical innovations, with the use of airplanes, the invention of the tank and the use of poison gas – all increasing general destructiveness to a level not reached by previous wars. As the war dragged on the belligerents moved to a state of 'total war' with the full mobilization of national resources, including mass conscription and the introduction of government-planned economies, which would become characteristics of twentieth-century conflicts. The social upheaval of the war also caused political unrest: Ireland revolted (1916), Russian and French soldiers mutinied and two Russian revolutions overthrew the tsar and brought the communists to power (1917). The war of stalemate finally ended with the American entry in April 1917, which tipped the scales in favor of the Allies. What became known as the Great War cost an estimated six million lives.

WESTERN FRONT

Germany's Schlieffen Plan assumed that the more developed French army would mobilize faster than the Russian forces and would therefore pose the initial threat. The plan required a decisive blow to be struck against France before the Russians could be fully mobilized, when the German army could then concentrate its full might against them. To defeat the French, it was decided to invade through neutral Belgium in order to come up behind the French left flank. This violation of Belgian neutrality brought Britain into the war. The German armies came within 20 miles of Paris before being thrown back in the Battle of the Marne (5–10 Sept. 1914). The war then settled down to trench warfare, with neither side able to make a decisive breakthrough. In four major battles in 1915 the Allies unsuccessfully attempted to break this stalemate. French casualties by then were two million and British casualties were half a million men.

The year 1916 saw Germany adopt an offensive strategy. In the Battle of Verdun (21 Feb.–18 Dec. 1916) the French succeeded in withstanding the German offensive. The British also attempted an offensive, in the First Battle of the Somme (24 June–13 Nov. 1916), in which they advanced eight miles at the cost of over half a million men, with the Germans suffering somewhat higher casualties. During 1917 the Germans withdrew slightly to consolidate their lines, but Allied offensives were no more successful than previously. The French General Nivelle attempted an offensive, but gained little ground at great sacrifice. The Nivelle offensive (16–20 April) resulted in 120,000 French losses over five days. In the Battle of Passchendaele (31 July–10 Nov. 1917), the British advanced five miles at the cost of 300,000 casualties.

The American entry and build-up of forces in Europe helped to turn the tide of battle in 1918. The Germans attempted one last great offensive in the west under Ludendorff. In five separate offensives Ludendorff made some advances, but failed to break the Allied lines. A series of Allied counteroffensives then took the initiative and finally began to push back the exhausted German forces. After the most important of these, the Meuse-Argonne offensive (26 Sept.–11 Nov.), the Germans were finally forced to request an armistice (11 Nov. 1918). The German understanding was that a peace treaty would be concluded on the basis of the Fourteen Points enunciated by President Wilson of the USA (8 Jan. 1918).

EASTERN FRONT

The Russians initially advanced into Germany while the Germans were occupied on the Western Front. However, at the Battle of Tannenberg (26–31 Aug. 1914) the German commander, Hindenburg, defeated the Russians. The Russians lost 125,000 men to the Germans' 10,000 and the Russian commander committed suicide during the retreat. Russia had, however, forced Germany to commit more troops to the east, thereby lessening its ability to deploy soldiers against France. The Russians performed better against the Austrians, occupying most of Galicia. In 1915 the Germans followed up their success with an offensive which cleared the Russians from Galicia, captured Warsaw (5 Aug.) and took the front 200 miles east of Warsaw. During 1916 the Germans again focused their energies in the west. The Russian Brusilov offensive (4 June–20 Sept. 1916) proved important in that it forced the Germans to withdraw critical forces from the Battle of Verdun and decisively weakened the Austrians.

Russian casualties were high, over one million, and this contributed to the outbreak of revolution. The tsar was deposed (March 1917), but the new provisional government attempted to fight on until it was ousted by the Bolsheviks under Lenin, who removed Russia from the war. Lenin concluded a peace with Germany, the Treaty of Brest-Litovsk (3 March 1918). Under its terms Russia lost one third of its population, including Finland, the Baltic Provinces, Poland, the Ukraine and territory in the Caucasus. The Russian negotiator, Trotsky, at first refused to sign such harsh terms, but they were finally agreed to at Lenin's insistence. Lenin accepted that Russia had lost and wished to concentrate on consolidating the Bolsheviks' power within Russia. After the collapse of the Central Powers the terms of Brest-Litovsk were cancelled by the Versailles Treaty.

BALKAN FRONT

The Austrians took the first military action of the war, bombarding the Serbian capital of Belgrade (29 July 1914). This was followed by an Austrian invasion of Serbia, which after some initial success was driven out by December through the determined fighting of the Serbs. After the failure of the Allies at Gallipoli, Bulgaria entered the war on the side of the Central Powers (11 Oct. 1915), hoping to regain the lands won in the First Balkan War but lost in the Second Balkan War. A renewed Austro-German-Bulgarian invasion of Serbia eventually forced the Serbian army to retreat to Corfu (Nov. 1915). The Central Powers were now in control of most of the Balkans. In 1916 the Allies intervened in Greece, establishing their forces at Salonika and eventually bringing to power a pro-Allied government (June 1917). During 1918 an offensive under French command succeeded in defeating the Bulgars, who formed the backbone of the Central Powers' forces in the region, leading Bulgaria to agree to an armistice (29 Sept. 1918).

OTTOMAN FRONT

The Ottoman Empire entered the war on the side of the Central Powers (29 Oct. 1914), threatening the western Allies' lines of communication with Russia. The major engagement of the war here was the Gallipoli campaign, conceived by Winston Churchill, the First Lord of the Admiralty, as a means to capture Constantinople, knock the Ottoman Empire out of the war, reopen the lines to Russia, help free the Balkans and encircle the Central Powers. The Allied landing at Gallipoli, near Constantinople (April 1915), was successful, but poor leadership failed to follow up the advantage gained and allowed the Ottoman army to surround the landing area. The Allies were unable to break the Ottoman lines and eventually withdrew (Jan. 1916), by which time the Allies and Ottomans had each lost about a quarter of a million men.

The Ottomans were less successful in fending off British attacks in their Arab possessions. An Arab national revolt (June 1916), combined with a British attack from Egypt, drove the Ottomans out of the Middle East. Jerusalem fell to the British (9 Dec. 1917), the Ottomans were defeated at the Battle of Megiddo (19–21 Sept. 1918) and an armistice was arranged (30 Oct. 1918). Ottoman power was finally broken after centuries of predominance.

COLONIAL AND NON-EUROPEAN FRONT

This was a subsidiary area of operations where the Allies took the opportunity to seize the German colonial empire. The Allies met the greatest opposition in German East Africa, where a brilliantly-led German force resisted until the end of the war.

WAR AT SEA

Unlike the Second World War, there were few major naval engagements. At the outbreak of war the British navy imposed an effective blockade of Germany, which in the long term did much to weaken Germany and bring about its final collapse. The major sea engagement was the Battle of Jutland (31 May 1916), where the German High Seas Fleet of 16 dreadnought battleships, 5 battle cruisers and 5 pre-dreadnought battleships, on emerging from harbor, met the British fleet of 37 dreadnoughts. Only bad weather allowed the Germans to escape from what would have been a disastrous engagement. As it was, the Germans did not seriously threaten British naval supremacy again. The Germans turned to submarines (U-boats) as commerce raiders in the hope of cutting off seaborne supplies to the Allies. The indiscriminate sinking of merchant shipping helped to bring the United States into the war on the Allied side.

Political Result

The Treaty of Versailles (28 June 1919), concluded with Germany, was much harsher than the Germans had expected on the basis of the armistice agreements. By its terms Germany lost 13 per cent of its European territory and all its overseas colonies and was limited to an army of 100,000, a navy of six battleships and no airforce. The Rhineland region bordering France was demilitarized and any union with Austria prohibited. Germany was also to pay reparations, but the Allies were unable to agree upon the amount, which was therefore left open at that time and was later set by a Reparation Commission in 1921 at $33,000 million. Germany also admitted responsibility for having caused the war. The treaty was severely criticized almost from the first as harsh and impractical. The reparations were clearly fantastic and had to be revised by the Dawes Plan (see below). Attempts to meet the reparations payments condemned Germany to an almost perpetual state of financial crisis. Hitler later frequently cited the treaty's harshness and promised to overturn it, in order to gain support. Others, however, have cited Brest-Litovsk (see above) as the kind of treaty the Germans would have imposed if victorious. The unsatisfactory nature of the Versailles treaty is often cited as a contributory factor to the political instability which helped bring about the Second World War.

The Treaty of St Germain (10 Sept. 1919) was concluded with Austria. Under its terms the new Austrian republic retained only 27 per cent of imperial Austria, was limited to an army of 30,000 and was required to pay reparations. One of the most controversial clauses was that forbidding an Austro-German union, which seemed to contradict the general Allied principle of peace treaties based on national self-determination. Despite popular support for such a union in both countries, the Allies did not wish to see Germany strengthened or enlarged in any way. (Germany and Austria were later unified by Hitler in the *Anschluss* of 1938.) Italy's

0 ———— 250 Miles

Stockholm

Leningrad
(St Petersburg)

Talinn

ESTONIA

SWEDEN

DENMARK

Riga   LATVIA

NORTH SLESVIG

Copenhagen

Memel   LITHUANIA

DANZIG
(Free City)

Kaunas

Vilna
(seized from
Lithuania)

Minsk

HOLLAND

Königsberg

EAST PRUSSIA
(GERMANY)

BELGIUM

Berlin

Thorn

Gradno

GERMANY

Posen   P O L A N D

Malmedy

Warsaw   Brest
Litovsk

Paris

SAARLAND (L. of N.)

Prague

UPPER SILESIA

Kiev

Metz
LORRAINE

ALSACE

Strasbourg

CZECHOSLOVAKIA

Cracow   Lvov

GALICIA

FRANCE

Munich

SWITZERLAND

Vienna

Czernowitz   BUKOVINA

SOUTH
TYROL

AUSTRIA

Budapest

HUNGARY

SLOVENIA

Trieste   Fiume

Zagreb

TRANSYLVANIA

R O M A N I A   BESSARABIA   Odessa

Marseilles

MONACO

SAN MARINO

CROATIA

Zara
(Ital.)

BOSNIA

Y U G O S L A V I A

VOJVODINA

Belgrade

SERBIA

Bucharest

CORSICA (Fr.)

ITALY

MONTE-
NEGRO

Sofia

Rome

BULGARIA

SARDINIA (Ital.)

Naples

Tirana

ALBANIA

Salonika

Adrianople

Constantinople
(Istanbul)

GREECE   TURKEY

Post-war settlements
Territory lost by

Germany

Russia

Bulgaria

Austria and Hungary

From Turkey to Greece 1920
Recovered 1923

Frontiers of new states

SICILY

Athens

Smyrna

DODECANESE
(Ital.)

Rhodes

CRETE

7 First World War: postwar settlements

acquisition of the Trentino, South Tyrol and Istria completed the *Risorgimento* begun in the Italian Wars of Unification.

The Treaty of Neuilly (27 Nov. 1919) was the treaty concluded with Bulgaria. By its terms Bulgaria lost four small but strategic salients on its frontier with Yugoslavia, and its Aegean coastline to Greece. Bulgaria was limited to an army of 33,000 and was to pay reparations.

The Treaty of Trianon (4 June 1920) was the peace treaty concluded with Hungary. By its terms Hungary lost 71 per cent of its territory and 60 per cent of its population, was limited to an army of 35,000 and had to pay reparations. As a result of the new borders Hungary, like Austria, lost its outlet to the sea. Resentment was caused by the fact that the new frontiers placed 1.8 million Hungarians just outside the country, particularly in Transylvania (which was assigned to Romania). The chief aim of Hungary's alliance with Hitler in the 1930s was to regain these lands and peoples, which was temporarily achieved by the Vienna Awards (1938, 1940).

The Treaty of Sèvres (10 Aug. 1920) was the abortive peace treaty concluded with the Ottoman Empire. By its terms Greece received significant territorial gains in Thrace and Asia Minor and the Ottoman Empire's Arab provinces became League of Nations mandates (Britain receiving the mandates for Palestine and Iraq, France those for Lebanon and Syria). The Straits were internationalized and opened to all shipping at all times. A Turkish national movement under Kemal Atatürk prevented the implementation of the Sèvres treaty, which was signed by the sultan's government. Atatürk's defeat of the Greek army in the Graeco-Turkish War of 1920–2 led to Sèvres being superseded by the Treaty of Lausanne.

The Treaty of Rapallo (16 April 1922) was a German-Soviet friendship treaty, providing for a mutual exchange of diplomatic recognition, increased trade and a reciprocal cancellation of financial claims, including reparations. It also opened up the possibility of the German army training on Soviet soil with weapons prohibited by the Versailles treaty. The agreement was concluded during the Genoa Conference which was discussing reparations and international economic problems, where Germany and the Soviet Union were ignored by the other powers, which had not yet extended de jure recognition to either government. The result was to draw the two pariah states of Europe together in an agreement of mutual benefit, ending their diplomatic isolation, much to the irritation of the Allied powers.

The Dawes Plan (April 1924) was agreed in the aftermath of the French occupation of the Ruhr, following Germany's default on its reparations payments under the Versailles treaty. The Americans proposed an international committee to investigate Germany's capacity to pay. This committee, headed by the American banker Charles Dawes, called for the evacuation of the Ruhr and adjusted the annual payments to a flexible rate determined by German economic prosperity. The Dawes Plan, combined with currency reform and the Locarno Pact, inaugurated a new period of German prosperity.

The Young Plan (7 June 1929) was a revision of the Dawes Plan, which had only scheduled the payments, without specifying the termination date or final sum of reparations to be paid. The original sum of $33,000 million set in 1921 was recognized as unrealistic. An international committee of experts under the chairmanship of the American, Owen Young, was established to settle the matter. The countries represented were Belgium, France, Germany, Great Britain, Italy, Japan and the United States. The solution arrived at was to reschedule the debt to run until 1988, while the final sum payable would be less than one third of the original $33,000 million. Payments were to be made through a new Bank of International Settlements. The onset of the world depression in 1929 caused a suspension of payments and in 1933 Hitler denounced the reparations clause of the peace settlement.

The Locarno Pact (1 Dec. 1925) was a set of bilateral treaties guaranteeing Germany's western frontiers. Following the Ruhr Crisis (1923), which was resolved through the Dawes Plan, a conference met at Locarno in Switzerland to attempt to reduce political tension. The moving spirits were the German foreign minister, Stresemann, the French premier, Briand, and the British foreign secretary, Austen Chamberlain. Under the Locarno treaties, the Franco-German and Belgo-German frontiers were mutually guaranteed by these states, together with Britain and Italy. Germany also agreed to settle border disputes with Poland and Czechoslovakia by arbitration. By their guarantee Britain and Italy were bound to intervene in the event of a violation of the western frontiers, but not of the eastern frontiers, which Germany did not fully accept as definitive. For a while the 'Spirit of Locarno' gave a feeling of stability to European affairs. Some of the eastern states were suspicious, however, that the Great Powers were trying to point any German expansion eastwards, away from themselves.

Polish-Soviet War 1920

Belligerents: **Poland**
                     Soviet Russia

Cause

Poland had disappeared as an independent state, following three partitions (1772, 1793 and 1795), by which Russia, Prussia and Austria had divided all Polish territory among themselves. With the collapse of these empires at the end of the First World War, Poland re-emerged as an independent state. The Paris Peace Conference (1919) proposed as the new country's eastern frontier a line, known as the Curzon Line, which included within Poland all those districts of a definitely Polish character. The Polish government, however, claimed a frontier much further east on historical grounds.

Occasion

The German evacuation of the contested district, combined with Russia's preoccupation with its civil war, provided an opportunity for Poland to implement its claims. The Russians also attempted to occupy the evacuated districts and hostilities followed (April 1920).

Course of War

The war began well for the Poles, who under Marshal Pilsudski occupied Kiev (7 May 1920), before a Russian counterattack drove them back to the outskirts of Warsaw. In the Battle of Warsaw (16–25 Aug.), the westward advance of the Russian army was checked, the Poles took 100,000 prisoners and again began to advance. The war also saw the last great cavalry charges in European warfare. An armistice was agreed to in October.

Political result

By the Treaty of Riga (18 March 1921), Poland received a frontier substantially to the east of the Curzon Line. Poland had also seized the city of Vilna (Vilnius) (Oct. 1920), although Lithuania also claimed this city and had established its capital there. This crisis soured relations between these states between the two world wars, preventing any security cooperation.

Graeco-Turkish War 1920–2

Belligerents:　Greece
　　　　　　　　Turkey

Cause

Greece had long harbored aspirations of reuniting the historic Greek lands, many of which were still under Ottoman rule in 1914. The Megalia Idea, as it was known, looked to be within sight after the First World War, when Ottoman power collapsed. The Greek government, led by Prime Minister Venizelos, seemed likely to obtain most of its irredenta in the peace settlement.

Occasion

The Great Powers meeting at Paris (1919) were in some dispute over the future division of the Ottoman Empire. It seemed possible that Italy might try to pre-empt any decision by landing forces to take control of part of Anatolia. To prevent this, Great Britain, France and the United States authorized the Greeks to land at Smyrna on their behalf, as it was envisaged that in any case Greece would in some form control this area in the future. Greek forces landed at Smyrna (15 May 1919), an action which enflamed Turkish opinion and ironically gave added impetus to the Turkish nationalist movement led by Kemal Atatürk, who established a new government at Ankara (Angora).

Course of War

The Greeks moved rapidly inland to consolidate their hold on the region. The unexpected death of King Alexander of Greece (25 Oct. 1925) led to the downfall of the architect of Greece's wartime achievements, Venizelos, and the return to power of the exiled King Constantine I (19 Dec. 1920). The king had poor relations with the Allies, who now withdrew their active support for Greece. The new Greek government was determined to maintain its position in Anatolia and a series of offensives was mounted against Atatürk's forces (Jan.–Aug. 1921), pushing them back to the Sakkaria river. The Turkish line here was the last obstacle before Ankara, some 40 miles away, but as events proved this was also the high-water mark of the Greek advance. The Battle of the Sakkaria River (24 Aug.–16 Sept.) saw Atatürk brilliantly envelop the Greek army, which, however, managed to disengage in good order. A Turkish counteroffensive (Aug.– Sept. 1922) shattered the Greek army, which fled towards Smyrna, where inadequate planning trapped many of the soldiers. Smyrna fell to Atatürk's army (9–11 Sept.) and most of the Greek sections of the city were burned, with many Greek deaths. This effectively ended the war. The débâcle sent over one million refugees fleeing to Greece. King Constantine abdicated and subsequently the new Greek government tried and executed five ex-ministers for their part in the catastrophe (Nov. 1922).

Political result

The Treaty of Lausanne (24 July 1923) superseded the earlier Treaty of Sèvres. By its terms Turkey gave up the Arab portions of the Ottoman Empire, but regained control of the strategic Aegean islands of Imbros and Tenedos and part of Thrace from Greece. The Straits remained open to all commercial traffic, the number of naval vessels of non-riparian states in the Black Sea at any one time was restricted and it was stipulated that if Turkey was at war only neutral ships would be allowed to pass. The application of these regulations was entrusted to an International Commission of the Straits, reporting to the League of Nations. Greece and Turkey agreed to an exchange of populations, with 400,000 Turks being sent to Turkey in exchange for 1.3 million Greeks.

The Montreux Convention (20 July 1936), negotiated by Turkey, Britain, France and the Soviet Union, created a régime for the Straits that superseded the provisions of the Lausanne treaty. The International

Commission of the Straits was abolished. In times of war Turkey, if neutral, was to prevent the passage of belligerent ships.

Second World War 1939–45

Main belligerents: **Axis–Germany, Italy, Japan**
Allies (United Nations) – China, France, Great
Britain and Dominions, Soviet Union, United
States
(see Appendix B for full list)

The war had distinct origins in both Europe and Asia. There is a significant historical debate on the origins of the European war, but the immediate background was certainly the rise to power in Germany of Adolf Hitler (1933), who led Germany in a calculated bid to subjugate Europe. The Asian war likewise centered around Japan's bid for regional domination. The Second World War can be seen as a series of interlocking wars; and each will be dealt with separately, while the postwar settlement will be dealt with as a whole.

POLISH WAR 1939

Belligerents: **Germany, Soviet Union**
Poland

Cause

Hitler, through a successful diplomatic campaign, had increased German power in Europe by a series of aggressive actions which included the re-militarization of the Rhineland (7 March 1936), the *Anschluss* (union) with Austria (12 March 1938), the annexation of the Sudetenland from Czecho-slovakia (29 Sept. 1938) and the annexation of the rump of Czecho-slovakia (15 March 1939). Hitler, however, was now determined on war, his next target being Poland, which received a unilateral Anglo-French guarantee of its security (31 March and 6 April 1939). Germany secured its military position through an agreement with the Soviet Union, the Molotov-Ribbentrop Pact (23 Aug. 1939), which arranged for the partition of Poland and led to the Soviet annexation of the Baltic republics of Estonia, Latvia and Lithuania.

Occasion

Germany fabricated a *casus belli*, claiming a Polish violation of its borders, and invaded Poland (1 Sept. 1939). In accordance with their guarantees, Britain and France declared war on Germany (3 Sept.), but provided no real assistance to Poland.

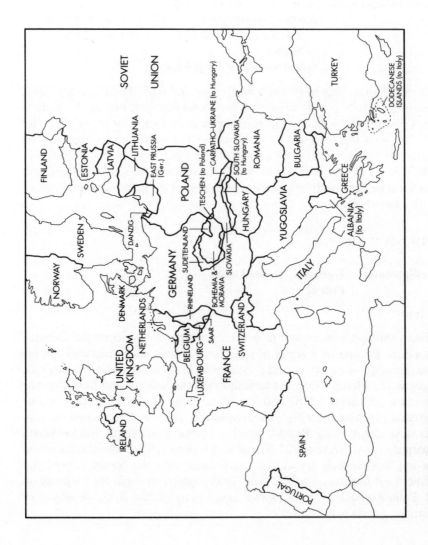

8 Second World War: Europe in 1939

Course of War

The Polish War lasted four weeks and ended with the defeat of the Poles. The German campaign of *Blitzkrieg* (lightning war) by 44 divisions, combined with aerial bombardment, rapidly pushed back the Polish army. Within two weeks Warsaw was surrounded. At this stage (17 Sept.) the Soviet Union entered the war in order to obtain the areas promised to it in the Molotov-Ribbentrop Pact. Polish forces now faced an impossible two-front war against two of the largest armies in the world. Warsaw fell to the Germans (27 Sept.) and the fighting ended with the surrender of the last Polish unit in the field (5 Oct.). The Polish army had fought tenaciously and inflicted 50,000 casualties on the German forces. Polish casualties were 60,000 soldiers killed and 140,000 wounded. Many Poles escaped abroad and fought on the Western Front with the French and British armies. After the outbreak of the German-Soviet War in 1941, Polish units were formed within the Soviet Union.

Political result

By a German-Soviet Convention (28 Sept. 1939) Poland was divided between the two countries along the Bug and San rivers. Parts of northern and western Poland were annexed to Germany, while the remainder of the area under German control was organized into a *General-Gouvernement.* In the Soviet sector the northern portion was given to Lithuania, itself soon to be annexed by the Soviet Union, while the remainder was annexed directly to the Soviet Union. Both sections of Poland were treated with the greatest brutality. Most of the Polish officers captured by the Soviet army were later killed in what became known as the Katyn Massacre. After the German invasion of the Soviet Union (June 1941), the Soviet section of Poland came under German control, until the Soviet army in turn drove back the German armies during 1944. The Soviet Union then placed a pro-Soviet government in power in Warsaw and the country remained under effective Soviet control until late 1989. As part of its 1939 agreement with Germany, the Soviet Union also annexed the Romanian territories of northern Bukovina and Bessarabia (June 1940) and the Baltic republics of Estonia, Latvia and Lithuania (Aug. 1940). Under the postwar settlement, the Soviet Union retained the areas seized when it was an ally of Germany, while Poland received as compensation an equivalent area from eastern Germany.

WAR IN THE WEST 1939–45

Main belligerents: **Germany, Italy**
Great Britain and Dominions, France, Denmark,
Norway, Belgium, the Netherlands, Luxembourg,
United States, Canada

Cause

As German aggression under Hitler increased during the 1930s, so Western concerns grew. At the Munich Conference (Sept. 1938) Hitler pledged that the Sudetenland was his final territorial demand in Europe. This pledge was violated, however, by the German annexation of Czechoslovakia (March 1939). Britain and France reacted by issuing a guarantee of the territorial integrity of Poland, which was correctly assumed to be Hitler's next target.

Occasion

The German invasion of Poland (1 Sept. 1939) activated the Anglo-French guarantee. Beyond declaring war and mobilizing their forces, however, Britain and France did very little. While the Germans conducted *Blitzkrieg* in Poland, the British and French conducted a *Sitzkrieg* in the west. With the defeat of Poland and the coming of spring, however, Germany turned its forces westward. In order to protect its northern flank Germany invaded Denmark and Norway, while to expedite the invasion of France it invaded the Low Countries, thus enabling German forces to by-pass the French fortifications on the German border known as the Maginot Line.

Course of War

In the spring of 1940 Germany launched its western offensive, overrunning Denmark (9 April), Norway (9 April–9 June), the Netherlands, Belgium and Luxembourg (10–15 May), and finally forcing the surrender of France (21 June). A pro-German government was established in France, which moved its seat to Vichy. A Free French government was set up in London, which was also the seat of governments-in-exile from Belgium, Czechoslovakia, Greece, Luxembourg, the Netherlands, Norway, Poland and Yugoslavia. Italy joined Germany in its campaign just before the collapse of France (10 June). There followed the Battle of Britain, when Germany attempted to subdue the country through aerial bombardment (Aug. 1940–May 1941). The leadership of British Prime Minister Winston Churchill during this period was central in obtaining essential supplies from the United States and in maintaining British morale. The American entry into the war (11 Dec. 1941) and the Allied build-up of forces in Britain laid the basis for the subsequent invasion of Europe.

The first defeat for the Axis powers occurred in North Africa, where Germany had sent forces to support the Italians in Libya, with the hope of threatening the Suez Canal. In the Battle of El Alamein (23 Oct.–4 Nov. 1942), the Germans were defeated by a British army in the east. An Anglo-American force landed at the opposite end of North Africa (8 Nov. 1942) and by May 1943 the Axis forces had been driven from North Africa.

The next stage was the Allied invasion of Sicily (July 1943), which helped bring about the overthrow of Mussolini (24 July) and the conclusion of an armistice with Italy (3 Sept. 1943). The Germans in the Italian peninsula, however, continued the war and the Allies conducted two amphibious landings, at Salerno (9 Sept. 1943) and at Anzio (22 Jan. 1944). In tough fighting the Allies slowly pushed the Germans back up the Italian peninsula and Rome was liberated (4 June).

Two days later (6 June 1944) the Allies launched the largest amphibious invasion in history, the D-Day landings. An Allied fleet of 4,000 ships conveyed an army of 176,000 men to a 30-mile stretch of the Normandy coast in northern France, opposite Britain. After initial resistance to some of the landings, the Allies pushed inland. Massive Allied aerial bombardment of Germany had already done much to weaken German power. The D-Day invasion led to the rapid liberation of Western Europe and the invasion of Germany. The Allies liberated Paris (25 Aug. 1944) and Brussels (3 Sept.), and as Allied forces entered Germany from the west (11 Sept.) the Soviet armies were simultaneously advancing in the east. The Germans were rolled back and their armies in the west surrendered (7 May 1945).

Political result

The German surrender was unconditional and the territorial frontiers of Western Europe were restored. An Allied army occupied Germany.

WINTER WAR (RUSSO-FINNISH WAR) 1939–40

Belligerents: **Soviet Union**
            Finland

Cause

Finland had formed part of the Russian Empire between 1809 and 1917, when it achieved independence under the leadership of the brilliant Marshal Mannerheim, who would also command the Finnish forces during the Winter War. A secret protocol of the Molotov-Ribbentrop Pact (Aug. 1939) between Germany and the Soviet Union placed Finland within the Soviet sphere. Following Germany's unexpectedly rapid successes in the opening weeks of the Second World War, Stalin moved to consolidate the

Soviet position in the Baltic region, occupying the republics of Estonia, Latvia and Lithuania (Oct.–Nov. 1939). He then moved to complete his control of the areas promised to the Soviet Union in the pact by turning against Finland.

Occasion

Soviet moves against the Baltic republics were followed immediately by demands for Finland to cede territory on the Karelian isthmus, where the frontier came within 20 miles of Leningrad (St Petersburg), and an area near the ice-free Arctic port of Petsamo (Pechenga); also demanded was a lease on the Hanko peninsula at the southern tip of the country. In return, the Soviet Union offered territorial compensation along the central border. The Finns refused these demands, although they were willing to make some concessions. Without awaiting further negotiations, the Soviet army invaded Finland (30 Nov. 1939). Stalin clearly intended to make Finland into at least a puppet state, creating on the first day of the war a 'Democratic Government of Finland' at the captured border town of Terijoki.

Course of War

A Soviet force totalling a million men was pitted against a Finnish army of 300,000. Despite such odds the Finns, making excellent use of ski forces, consistently beat back the Soviet army. The initial Soviet assault was a three-pronged attack. The first, an amphibious attack across the Gulf of Finland, was repulsed. The second, in the far north, succeeded in seizing Petsamo before being halted. The largest force invaded across the Karelian isthmus, but was halted at the line of fortifications known as the Mannerheim Line. The largest single engagement of the war was the Battle of Suomussalmi (11 Dec. 1939–8 Jan. 1940), in which two ill-equipped Soviet divisions were encircled by one, smaller, Finnish division. In freezing weather, the Finns annihilated the Soviet forces (27,500 Soviet and 900 Finnish dead). In February the Soviets threw in 54 divisions (one million men) against the Mannerheim Line and, despite huge losses, finally broke through. In the face of such an onslaught the Finns were forced to capitulate (12 March 1940). The Finns had suffered a total of 25,000 dead (including civilians), compared to the Red Army's 200,000.

Political result

By the Treaty of Moscow (12 March 1940), the Soviet Union obtained all the areas demanded before the war, as well as a large portion of southeast Finland (running along the 1721 frontier), the Salla district on the northeast frontier and a 30-year lease on Hanko for use as a Soviet naval base. As a result of this treaty 11 per cent of the Finnish population

(420,000) lost their homes and left the ceded area. In the wake of the German attack on the Soviet Union (June 1941), Finland again went to war with the Soviets.

Remarks

The war aroused much sympathy for Finland in the West, but no practical aid. The deficiencies of the Soviet military leadership, still suffering from the losses inflicted upon it during the Great Purge, were observed by Hitler and his generals, who assumed that the Soviet Union would rapidly collapse if attacked by Germany.

BALKAN WAR 1940–5

Main belligerents: Germany, Italy, Bulgaria, Romania, Hungary
Yugoslavia, Greece, Great Britain and Dominions

Cause

The origins of this war lay in the Italian dictator Mussolini's plans for a new Roman empire. Under his leadership, Italy had defeated and taken control of Ethiopia in the Third Italo-Ethiopian War (1935–6) and the king of Italy had been proclaimed emperor of Ethiopia. This was followed by the invasion of Albania (7 April 1939), which met with only token resistance. A puppet régime was established and the Italian king was proclaimed king of Albania. The Italian conquest of Albania made the Adriatic in effect an Italian sea. On the outbreak of war in Europe in 1939, the Greek dictator, Metaxas, attempted to remain neutral, but Mussolini hoped to continue his imperial expansion with the conquest of Greece. Mussolini was also irritated that Hitler had not first consulted him on war policy and therefore hoped to show his independence with an attack on Greece. This would establish Italy's position as a Mediterranean power.

Occasion

Italy embarked on a series of provocations of Greece, which included torpedoing the Greek cruiser *Elli* off the island of Tinos (15 Aug. 1940). Mussolini, looking for a *casus belli*, finally sent an ultimatum to Metaxas, which was delivered at 3 a.m. on 28 October. Metaxas refused the humiliating demands and Italy invaded Greece at 5.30 a.m. the same day.

Course of War

Metaxas had done much to improve the Greek army, and in the face of the Italian threat the nation rallied behind him. The initial Italian offensive launched from Albania was thrown back (Oct.–Nov. 1940), and a Greek counteroffensive carried the fighting into Albania. Hitler's plans to invade the Soviet Union, with preparations to be completed by May 1941, were disrupted by the fiasco of the Italian invasion of Greece. In order to secure his Balkan flank, Hitler decided to rescue Mussolini's army from imminent defeat, but to do so necessitated crossing Yugoslavia. The Yugoslav government at first decided to ally itself with Germany (25 March 1941), but anti-Axis figures overthrew this government (27 March). Germany then decided on the invasion of Yugoslavia. Bulgaria willingly participated in these plans, still hoping to redress its defeat in the Second Balkan War of 1913. The German army invaded Yugoslavia (6 April 1941) and quickly overran the country, capturing the key cities of Zagreb (10 April), Belgrade (12 April) and Sarajevo (15 April). Hungary, Romania and Bulgaria joined in the invasion of Yugoslavia, which was forced to surrender unconditionally (17 April 1941). Simultaneously with the Yugoslav invasion, the German army operating from Bulgaria invaded Greece, which likewise was soon overrun. Britain moved to support the Greeks and the most notable engagement was the Battle of Crete, in which the Germans succeeded in capturing the island with the first airborne assault in history (31 May). The delay caused to the German invasion plans against the Soviet Union is considered one of the key contributory factors to its eventual failure, as it caused the Germans to fail to reach their objectives before the Russian winter set in.

Political result

Yugoslavia was partitioned between the victorious Axis countries. Italy, Bulgaria, Hungary and Romania all annexed territory and a pro-Axis Croatian state was established. Greece was occupied by German, Bulgarian and Italian forces. In both countries strong resistance movements soon emerged and conducted a guerrilla war against the invaders. This was complicated by a split in the resistance between communists and non-communists. In Yugoslavia the communist Partisans and the non-communist Chetniks were engaged in a virtual civil war. In Greece a similar rivalry resulted in the outbreak of the Greek Civil War immediately after the evacuation of the Axis armies (Dec. 1944). In liberated Yugoslavia a communist government took power under Josef Tito, while in Greece, after a lengthy and bloody conflict (1944–9), a non-communist government was left in control.

As the tide of war turned against Germany, its allies in the Balkans began to switch sides: Italy (Sept. 1943), Romania (Aug. 1944), Bulgaria (Sept. 1944) and Hungary (Jan. 1945). Athens was liberated (14 Oct. 1944), followed by Belgrade, which was liberated by Tito's Partisans with Soviet assistance (20 Oct. 1944). As a result of the leading role played by the Soviet army in the defeat of the Axis in the Balkans, the Soviet Union largely determined the future forms of government there, imposing communist régimes on all states except Greece.

GERMAN-SOVIET WAR 1941–5

Main belligerents: Germany
Soviet Union

Cause

Germany and the Soviet Union had formed an alliance of convenience in 1939, the Molotov-Ribbentrop Pact. With their victory in the 1939 Polish War and the elimination of Poland, together with the Soviet Union's other territorial acquisitions, the utility of such cooperation began to diminish. German military power was now at its zenith, while the Soviet Union after its initial drubbing in the 1939–40 Winter War with Finland seemed to be at its nadir. It therefore appeared to be the optimum time for Germany to defeat the Soviet Union, before Stalin could rebuild a military establishment decimated by his purges. By November 1940 German-Soviet co-operation was in rapid decline.

Occasion

Hitler took the decision to invade the Soviet Union (18 Dec. 1940) and gave orders for preparations to be made for an invasion in mid-May 1941. As a by-product of its anti-Soviet plans, and in order to protect its flank, Germany became involved in the Balkan War in April 1941. Up to this point Germany had tried to avoid the problem it had faced in the First World War of fighting on two fronts. Hitler, however, dismissed the possibility of any threat being posed by his only surviving West European enemy, Britain, while it was assumed that the Soviet Union would be defeated in a lightning campaign before the onset of winter. Both these assumptions proved inaccurate. German forces invaded the Soviet Union (22 June 1941) without a declaration of war, as soon as the Balkans had been secured.

Course of War

After initial successes the German invasion proved disastrous following the onset of the harsh Russian winter. In their initial advance, the Germans came within 30 miles of Leningrad and Moscow before being halted by the winter weather (5 Dec. 1941). The Soviets had rushed reinforcements from Siberia under Zhukov, who had previously been fighting the Japanese in the Nomonhan Incident. Zhukov then launched a counteroffensive which regained some ground (6 Dec. 1941). Soviet forces withstood great

German sieges of Leningrad (Oct. 1941–Jan. 1944) and Stalingrad (Aug. 1942–Feb. 1943). In the greatest tank battle fought up to that time, the Battle of Kursk (5–13 July 1943), the Germans were finally halted and the Soviet army began slowly to push back the German forces.

As the Soviet army advanced across Eastern Europe it also brought Soviet domination to the countries it occupied. Soviet armies took Bucharest (1 Sept. 1944), Belgrade (20 Oct. 1944), Warsaw (17 Jan. 1945) and Budapest (13 Feb. 1945), before finally capturing Berlin (2 May) and receiving the surrender of the German armies in the east (8 May).

Estimates vary on Soviet casualties; the approximate figures of deaths are often given as between 10 and 15 million civilians and 8 million military personnel.

Political result

Soviet armies occupied the eastern portion of Germany. As a result of the postwar settlement, the Soviet Union annexed half of East Prussia, giving the southern half and other German territory to Poland as compensation for Polish land taken by the Soviet Union while it was an ally of Germany. Germany itself was divided, with a pro-Soviet communist régime being established in the east under the name of the German Democratic Republic. This pro-Soviet government remained in power until 1989, when the collapse of communist rule opened the way for German unification a year later (3 Oct. 1990).

SINO-JAPANESE WAR 1931–45

Belligerents: **Japan**
                        China

Cause

Japan was hard hit by the world economic crisis that began in 1929. Factions, particularly within the army, saw a solution in the acquisition of a large continental area which could provide needed raw materials and act as an area for colonization. The prime target was the northern Chinese province of Manchuria, which bordered Japanese-ruled Korea and where Japan already had substantial interests, acquired following the Russo-Japanese War of 1904–5.

Occasion

An excuse to intervene in Manchuria was arranged in the Mukden Incident (19 Sept. 1931). Members of the Japanese Kwantung Army, who were

9 Second World War: Asia

responsible for guarding the Japanese-owned South Manchurian Railway, exploded a bomb on the line near the city of Mukden (Shenyang), which they then blamed on the Chinese. This was used as the pretext for occupying Manchuria.

Course of War

The Japanese army, claiming that it was acting to protect Japanese interests, moved rapidly to occupy all Manchuria. China was unable to do much to oppose Japanese aggression, as it was itself embroiled in a complex civil war. Japan established a puppet state in Manchuria, known as the Empire of Manchukuo, which was placed under the notional rule of the old Manchu dynasty overthrown in China in 1911 (18 Feb. 1932). Japanese control was extended by the invasion of the Chinese Inner Mongolian province of Jehol, which Japan claimed belonged to Manchukuo (Jan.–March 1933). When Japanese forces seemed about to threaten Peking (Beijing), the Chinese government agreed to an armistice at Tangku (31 May 1933). By its terms the Chinese were forced to evacuate the port city of Tientsin (Tianjin) and to demilitarize eastern Hopeh (Hebei) province.

Japan embarked on a full-scale invasion of China in July 1937 and the conflict became known as the China Incident. On this occasion fighting began with a clash near the Marco Polo bridge near Peking (7 July 1937). The modern, well-equipped Japanese army did well against the poorly-trained and badly-equipped Chinese army. Japanese forces took Peking (28 July) and Tientsin (29 July) and by the end of 1937 had taken control of most of China north of the Yellow river (Huang He). Shanghai fell after a long struggle (8 Aug.–8 Nov. 1937), followed by Nanking (Nanjing) (13 Dec.), whose inhabitants were treated with great brutality by the Japanese victors. Japan continued to extend its control during 1938, taking Canton (Guangzhou) with amphibious forces (21 Oct.), but it was unable to gain control of the country as a whole or to defeat the Chinese army decisively. The war now settled down to one of attrition and the Japanese established a puppet Chinese government at Nanking (30 March 1940).

Following the collapse of France (June 1940), Japan established effective control of French Indochina (July 1940). It was, however, coming under increasing pressure from the United States, which was tightening its restrictions on the sale of natural resources to Japan. In order to obtain these essential war materials and to eliminate the American threat Japan attacked the United States (Dec. 1941), as well as the British and Dutch colonies in the Pacific region. This expanded the conflict into the Pacific War. Meanwhile the war of attrition continued in China, but the end was finally brought about by the surrender of Japan due to its defeat in the Pacific War (Aug. 1945). The number of Japanese troops and resources tied down in China, however, was a major contributory factor to its defeat in the Pacific.

Political result

At the end of the Second World War China regained all territories previously lost to Japan. Throughout the war, tense relations had existed within China between the nationalist government led by Chiang Kai-shek (Jiang Jieshi) and the communist movement headed by Mao Tse-tung (Mao Zedong). It was often a three-cornered war, with the communists and the nationalists fighting each other as well as the Japanese. With the defeat of Japan, China again dissolved into civil war (1946–9), which ended with a communist victory. The nationalist followers of Chiang took refuge on the island of Formosa (Taiwan), where they maintained the Republic of China, while the communists under Mao established the People's Republic of China with its capital at Peking.

CHANGKUFENG INCIDENT (KHASAN INCIDENT) 1938

Belligerents: **Japan**
                                Soviet Union

Cause

The Sino-Soviet border had been a matter of dispute for many years, the Chinese claiming that Russia had seized territory from China during the nineteenth century through 'unequal treaties'. Japan inherited this border dispute when it invaded the northern Chinese province of Manchuria and established the puppet state of Manchukuo there in February 1932. Several border skirmishes occurred in the area during 1935–8. Particularly heavy fighting occurred in June 1937 over two islands in the Amur river (Heilong Jiang), which formed part of the boundary between China and the Soviet Union. One area of dispute lay on the Manchukuo-Soviet border near its juncture with the Korean border (Korea then being a Japanese province). The area was known to the Japanese as Changkufeng and to the Russians as Khasan.

Occasion

In early July 1938 the Soviet army occupied a strategically important part of the disputed area, which could give them command of the vital Korean-Manchurian railway. This in turn led to a Japanese decision to dislodge the Soviet force.

Course of War

The initial confrontation was no more than a small border skirmish (29 July), but fighting soon escalated. A larger Japanese assault drove the

Soviets from their hilltop emplacement at Changkufeng (31 July). The Soviets responded by committing more forces, including over 200 aircraft, and fighting ensued for about ten days before a ceasefire came into effect (11 Aug.). Japanese casualties are estimated at over 500 dead, while the Soviets may have suffered about twice that number.

Political result

After the ceasefire the Japanese, having made their point as to their claim to the district, withdrew their forces and the Soviets reoccupied the area. The Soviet army, however, had learnt important lessons during the Changkufeng Incident and would apply them with great effectiveness the following year in the Nomonhan Incident with Japan.

Remarks

The Sino-Soviet border remains an issue and was a factor in the Sino-Soviet Dispute of 1969.

NOMONHAN INCIDENT (KHALIN GOL) 1939

Belligerents: **Japan, Manchukuo**
                     Soviet Union, Mongolia

Cause

The Nomonhan Incident or, as the Soviets call it, Khalin Gol, is one of the least-known wars of the twentieth century but also one of the most significant. Its obscurity is due to the isolated location in which it was fought, the lack of publicity at the time, its concurrence with the outbreak of the Second World War and the subsequent fate of the Japanese officers involved. Ostensibly, Japan and the Soviet Union were acting on behalf of their client states, Manchukuo (Manchuria) and Mongolia respectively, over a disputed piece of desert on the Manchurian-Mongolian border in the vicinity on Nomonhan, a place so obscure that it failed to appear on most of the Japanese army's maps. This war continued the test of strength of the previous year which had occurred during the Changkufeng Incident of 1938.

Occasion

The Japanese army in Manchuria, known as the Kwantung Army, was frequently troublesome and often acted independently of the wishes of the Japanese government. It perceived the opportunity finally to prove the superiority of the Japanese army over the Soviet army, which had been seriously weakened by Stalin's recent purges of its officer ranks.

Course of War

Border skirmishing occurred (May 1939) with the recently-deployed and untried Japanese 23rd Division. A Japanese reconnaissance party was ambushed, leading to an escalation in hostilities. The Japanese launched an offensive into Mongolia (early July), but were repulsed. All Japanese attempts to gain the initiative failed and a Soviet counteroffensive (20–31 Aug.) cleared the Japanese from the disputed zone. The day after this offensive ended the Second World War began in Europe.

Political result

Soviet-Japanese diplomatic relations were not broken during the fighting. An oral agreement between the Japanese and the Soviets was reached in talks in Moscow (15 Sept. 1939) leading to a cessation of hostilities (16 Sept.). It was agreed to turn the border demarcation over to a joint Soviet-Japanese Commission (19 Nov.). A border was finally agreed (15 May 1942), with Mongolia gaining all but token portions of the disputed area.

Having resolved the Japanese problem, the Soviet Union turned its attention on Poland, which it invaded (17 Sept. 1939), thereby entering directly into the European theater of the Second World War. The Soviet army at Nomonhan was commanded by General Zhukov, later one of the greatest commanders of the Second World War. The fighting at Nomonham must count as one of his most important battles, where he learnt the value of massive joint operations involving armor and air power, with a central emphasis on firepower. It was a technique he would apply with deadly effectiveness in Europe in 1941–5.

The Japanese defeat at the hands of the Soviets contributed to Japan's fateful decision in 1941 to 'strike south' against the United States rather than to 'strike north' for a final showdown with the Soviet Union. Several of the Japanese officers who fought in and survived the Nomonhan campaign were subsequently pressurized into committing suicide, so preventing them from teaching the Japanese army the lessons of Nomonham.

PACIFIC WAR 1941–5

Belligerents: **Japan**
United States, Great Britain, Australia, New Zealand, Netherlands, France, China

Cause

The causes of the Pacific War were similar to those behind the Sino-Japanese phase of the conflict and centered on the problems caused by

Japan's lack of natural resources. As Japan's military efforts in China dragged on, so it required ever greater imports of essential war materials. As late as 1940–1 Japan was receiving four fifths of its petroleum requirements from the United States. The United States was also an important source of scrap iron. It was the threat posed to the continuance of these supplies by growing American opposition to Japanese war aims that convinced Japan to 'strike south' in search of the vital petroleum and natural rubber resources of the Dutch East Indies (Indonesia) and the British colony of Malaya.

Occasion

After the collapse of France in June 1940, Japan took the opportunity to establish effective control of French Indochina (July 1941) while leaving it under French colonial administration (until 1945). The United States, Britain and the Dutch government-in-exile responded to this action by freezing Japanese assets. This had the effect of removing Japan's ability to continue purchasing the raw materials it required for its war effort. For Japan the alternatives now were either to disengage from its aggressive policies or to go to war with these states. A new Japanese government, led by General Tojo, decided on war (Oct. 1941), which began soon afterwards with a surprise attack on the American Pacific Fleet at Pearl Harbor in Hawaii (7 Dec. 1941); simultaneously, assaults were initiated against British and Dutch possessions.

Course of War

The attack on Pearl Harbor succeeded in neutralizing the American Pacific Fleet for some months. The initial Japanese offensive was remarkably swift and successful, capturing Hong Kong (25 Dec. 1941), Singapore (15 Feb. 1942), Mandalay (1 May 1942), the Dutch East Indies (9 March 1942) and the Philippines, where the last American fortification to fall was at Corregidor (6 May 1942). By July 1942 Japan had pressed as far west as the Burma-India border area and as far south as Papua, where it seemed poised to invade Australia. This, however, was the highpoint of its success. The Pacific War came to center on a series of sea battles between the American and Japanese fleets, fought at long range with aircraft, without the fleets themselves being in view of one another. The most notable were the Battles of Midway (4–6 June 1942) and Leyte Gulf (23–6 Oct. 1944) which together saw the destruction of Japanese naval power. Simultaneously, the Americans and their allies began to push northward toward Japan in an island-hopping campaign under the leadership of General MacArthur. Meanwhile a British army pushed the Japanese out of Burma. By the spring of 1945 the Allies were poised for an invasion of the Japanese home islands, but this was avoided by the use of the newly-invented atomic bomb, which was dropped on the cities of Hiroshima (6 Aug.) and Nagasaki (9 Aug.). Japan surrendered on 10 August 1945 (signed 2 Sept.).

Political result

Japan was occupied by the United States. Subsequently, most Western powers concluded a peace settlement with Japan under the Treaty of San Francisco (*see below*). The Japanese withdrawal from Indochina set in train the events which resulted in the Franco-Vietminh War and the Vietnam War, while its withdrawal from Korea set the stage for the Korean War. The collapse of the Japanese military power left the United States as the predominant Pacific state.

POLITICAL RESULT OF THE SECOND WORLD WAR

(*For signatories of the agreements referred to, see Appendix C.*)

After its unconditional surrender, Germany was divided into four zones of occupation, which were allocated to Great Britain, the United States, France and the Soviet Union. These four powers agreed in the Berlin Declaration (5 June 1945) that they were to determine the future borders and status of Germany. Berlin, though lying in the Soviet Zone, was to be occupied by all four powers. At the Potsdam Conference (17 July–2 Aug. 1945), the United States, the Soviet Union and Great Britain agreed to the Soviet annexation of the northern half of East Prussia, and to allow Poland, pending a final settlement, to occupy and administer the area east of the Oder-Neisse rivers (Pomerania, Silesia and southern half of East Prussia). Germany thus lost 23 per cent of its post-1918 territory.

Repeated meetings between the Allied powers (1945–7) failed to achieve any agreement as to the future of Germany. The United States and Great Britain finally merged their zones (1 Jan. 1947), so beginning the creation of a West German state. The Soviet Union withdrew from the Allied Control Council (20 March 1948), and after the Western powers had implemented currency reforms in their sectors the Soviets imposed a blockade on Berlin (20 June 1948–May 1949). This caused one of the greatest crises of the postwar period, as the United States and Britain kept West Berlin supplied by a massive airlift. In 1949 the Western zones were merged to form the Federal Republic of Germany, while the Soviets established the German Democratic Republic in their zone. Berlin remained under four-power occupation. This division continued until the unification of Germany in 1990 (*see below*).

The Treaties of Paris (10 Feb. 1947) were signed by the Allies with Italy, Romania, Bulgaria, Hungary and Finland. Italy lost its colonial empire, whose territories became United Nations' mandates, and it renounced all claims to Ethiopia. Italy also lost some territory on the Adriatic Sea to Yugoslavia, and the Dodecanese islands in the Aegean Sea to Greece. Romania accepted its loss of northern Bukovina and Bessarabia to the Soviet Union (taken in 1940 as part of the Soviet-German Molotov-Ribbentrop Pact) and of the southern Dobrudja to Bulgaria. Romania, however, regained northern Transylvania, lost in 1940 to Hungary. Hungary also ceded a strip of territory opposite Bratislava to Czechoslovakia. Finland ceded the northern province of Petsamo (Pechenga) and part of the Karelian isthmus to the Soviet Union. All Axis powers were required to pay reparations.

The Treaty of San Francisco (8 Sept. 1951) was concluded with Japan by most (48) of the Allies. The Japanese loss of all territory acquired in its wars since 1895 was agreed. The Soviet Union did not sign the treaty, but later agreed a declaration ending its state of war with Japan (19 Oct. 1956).

The Austrian State Treaty (15 May 1955) re-established Austrian independence. Austria had been united with Germany in 1938 and after the war it, like Germany, had been divided into four zones of occupation. By the 1955 treaty the occupying forces were withdrawn and Austria was declared a neutral state. After the collapse of Soviet power in Eastern Europe the Austrian government unilaterally declared obsolete several articles of the State Treaty (7 Nov. 1990), while reaffirming its obligation to ban nuclear, chemical and biological weapons.

The Helsinki Accords (1 Aug. 1975) were in effect a recognition of the existing European status quo, in the absence of a German peace treaty. The Final Act of the Conference on Security and Cooperation in Europe (CSCE) was signed by 33 European states, the United States and Canada. The agreement was divided into three 'baskets'. Basket One outlined ten principles, including an endorsement of human rights, together with a series of confidence-building measures on European military security; Basket Two concerned economic, scientific and environmental cooperation, including the development of East–West trade; Basket Three dealt with humanitarian cooperation and advocated the free movement of people and information.

The Treaty on the Final Settlement with Respect to Germany (12 Sept. 1990) was signed by the four Allied powers and East and West Germany after the collapse of Soviet influence in Eastern Europe during 1989. The treaty opened the way for German unification (implemented 3 Oct. 1990). It fixed Germany's borders at their prevailing position, prohibited Germany from manufacturing, possessing or controlling nuclear, biological and chemical weapons, agreed that the withdrawal of Soviet forces should take place by the end of 1994 and terminated the Allies' role in Berlin and the two Germanies. Linked to this treaty were four German-Soviet bilateral treaties: (1) on Good Neighborliness, Partnership and Cooperation; (2) a 20-year agreement on economic cooperation; (3) a treaty on the

German monetary contribution towards the Soviet forces in eastern Germany; and (4) a treaty regulating the position of these Soviet troops and the timing of their removal. A German-Polish treaty (14 Nov. 1990) confirmed the Oder-Neisse line as the frontier between the two countries.

6 Central Asian Wars

Russo-Persian War 1826–8

Belligerents: **Russia**
                  Persia

Cause

The gradual expansion of Russia into the Caucasus brought it into conflict with Persia (present-day Iran). The Caucasian kingdom of Georgia had for centuries been under the suzerainty of Persia, until it was annexed by Russia in 1801. This led to a prolonged Russo-Persian war (1804–13), in which the Persians were defeated. In the Treaty of Gulistan (12 Oct. 1813) Persia recognized the Russian annexation of Georgia, as well as of three border districts (Derbent, Shirvan and Karabash). However, the Persian shah, Fath Ali, did not give up hopes of redressing this defeat.

Occasion

Fath Ali used the vague wording of the Treaty of Gulistan to lay claim to the control of the three border districts, but negotiations broke down and the Russians occupied them. Pressure from military and religious quarters forced the shah to break the treaty and a Persian army under the heir to the throne, Abbas Mirza, crossed the Aras (Araxes) river into Russia (16 July 1826).

Course of War

At first the Persian army did well, occupying all of Russian Armenia and Azerbaijan and almost reaching Tiflis (Tblisi), the Georgian capital. The Russians, however, conducted a brilliant counteroffensive which threw back the Persians, defeating them at the Battle of Ganja (26 Sept. 1826). Although it had numerical superiority (30,000 Persians to 15,000 Russians), the Persian cavalry fled before the Russian artillery and the Persians withdrew south of the Aras. The miserly shah refused to pay his

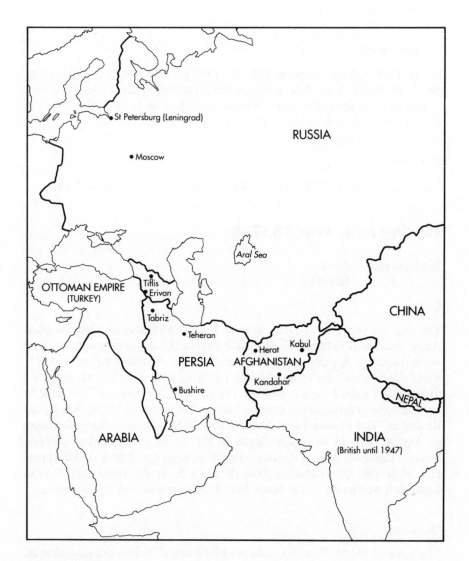

10 Central Asia

soldiers during the winter months and so the army dispersed, thereby assisting the Russians' advance. The Russians captured Erivan (1–13 Oct. 1827) and occupied without resistance Tabriz (19 Oct. 1827), the capital of Persian Azerbaijan, where they captured the entire artillery park. This effectively ended the war.

Political result

By the Treaty of Turkmanchai (22 Feb. 1828), Persia lost its two remaining provinces north of the Aras river, Erivan and Nakhichevan, and it agreed to pay an indemnity. No armed Persian vessels were to be allowed on the Caspian Sea, while Russia was allowed to maintain a navy there.

Remarks

This war increased British fears of a growing Russian menace to India.

Persia-Herat War 1837–8

Belligerents: **Persia**
                     Herat

Cause

The city and province of Herat have changed hands several times between Afghanistan and Persia (present-day Iran). In the eighteenth century they again passed to Afghanistan, at the height of the Afghan Empire. In 1818, when the Sadozai, the ruling Afghan dynasty, were overthrown, they fled to Herat to establish an independent principality. Afghanistan now came to be divided into three states, centered around the cities of Herat, Kabul and Kandahar. The Persian ruler, Mohammed Shah, hoped to take advantage of Afghan disarray to regain Herat. In this he enjoyed Russian support, Russian influence having increased in Persia since the Treaty of Turkmanchai after the Russo-Persian War of 1826–8, in the hope that Persian expansion westwards would block British penetration into Afghanistan.

Occasion

The amir of Herat, Kamran, refused Mohammed Shah's demand that he acknowledge Persian suzerainty. The British supported Kamran in this decision. Kamran's refusal led to a Persian invasion.

Course of War

The Persian army marched to Herat through Khorasan at a leisurely pace, taking four months, and on arriving they laid siege to the city (1 Dec. 1837–29 Sept. 1838). The Heratis, however, had burned all buildings within 12 miles of the city and brought in all the animals and grain, while the city's defences were ably organized by the British India Company officer, Eldred Pottinger. The one serious attempt to storm the city cost the Persians 1,700 casualties (24 June 1838). The siege was finally raised after a threat of British intervention by the foreign secretary, Lord Palmerston. British resolve was indicated by its seizure of Kharg Island in the Persian Gulf to use as a possible base of operations against Persia.

Political result

The British concluded a treaty with Kamran (9 June–13 Aug. 1839) making Herat an exclusively British sphere of influence. The British expedition in the First Anglo-Afghan War of 1839–42 in support of Shah Shuja was a consequence of British concern to retain Afghanistan as a buffer zone for its Indian empire.

First Anglo-Afghan War 1839–42

Belligerents: Great Britain
**   Afghanistan**

Cause

British fears were alive to Russian expansion in Central Asia, which it was thought might threaten India. The Russian-instigated Persian siege of Herat in the Persian-Herat War of 1837–8 worried Britain, as Herat was seen as the key to India.

Occasion

A British mission was sent to Kabul under Captain Alexander Burnes to negotiate with the Afghan leader, Dost Mohammed, who hoped for British help in regaining Peshawar, which had been seized by the Sikhs in 1823. The fact that Dost Mohammed was also negotiating with the Russians for support, however, helped cause a breakdown in his talks with Burnes. The governor-general of India, Lord Auckland, then decided to replace Dost Mohammed with Shah Shuja, a former ruler who had taken refuge in India.

Course of War

The British invasion came in March 1839 when the 21,000-man Army of the Indus under General Keane crossed into Afghanistan. In a rapid campaign he captured Kandahar (25 April) and Kabul (7 Aug.). Shuja was crowned after the fall of Kandahar. After the fall of Kabul Dost Mohammed fled to Bokhara, where he was detained, later escaping to lead an insurrection until he was captured (Nov. 1840) and sent to India. Meanwhile Keane, after installing Shah Shuja at Kabul, returned to India, leaving behind a garrison of 8,000 men. Dissatisfaction among the Afghans erupted in revolt in Kabul (2 Nov. 1841), in which Burnes and other British officers were killed and the remaining garrison surrounded. The British envoy attempting to negotiate with the rebel leaders was also killed (23 Dec.) and the British garrison evacuated the city, making a winter retreat to the Indian frontier. They were continually attacked on the way, and of the 4,500 soldiers and 12,000 followers who started out only one reached Jalalabad (although 95 prisoners were later recovered). The British managed to hold Jalalabad until a relief expedition under General Pollock arrived (16 April 1842), marched on Kabul and recaptured the city (15 Sept.).

Political result

Shah Shuja had been killed when the British left Kabul and the British East India Company now saw little profit in retaining a presence in the country. Dost Mohammed was therefore released and returned to his throne, spending the last 20 years of his life in restoring his domains; just before his death he succeeded in regaining Kandahar and Herat. He remained neutral during the Indian Mutiny (1857–8), but the British invasion left a bitter legacy for future Anglo-Afghan relations.

Anglo-Persian War 1856–7

Belligerents: **Great Britain**
              Persia

Cause

This was a continuation of the struggle for control of Herat which had resulted in the Persia-Herat War of 1837–8. The ruler of Herat, Kamran, was overthrown and murdered in 1842 and replaced by Yar Mahommed, who was in turn succeeded by his son, Sa'id Mohammed, who followed a pro-Persian policy. In 1855 Herat was seized by Kamran's nephew, Mohammed Yusuf Sadozzi, and Sa'id Mohammed was killed, with a consequent decline in Persian influence in Herat. Simultaneously, Dost Mohammed of Afghanistan finally succeeded in taking control of Kandahar, which caused some of its leading citizens to flee to the protection of the shah of Persia. Mohammed Yusuf, fearing that he would be Dost Mohammed's next target, appealed to the Persian shah, Nasir ad-Din, for protection. The shah responded by dispatching an army to Herat (Feb. 1856).

Occasion

The Persian forces seized Herat after a long siege (Oct. 1856), while Britain, which had long protected Herat from foreign control as it was an important link in the defenses of India, was involved in the Crimean War. The Persian army acted like conquerors rather than rescuers and the people of Herat rose against Mohammed Yusuf in anger at his having allowed the Persians into the country. The rebels ousted Mohammed Yusuf from the city and requested British protection. As a consequence of this the governor-general of India, Lord Canning, issued a proclamation of war against Persia (1 Nov. 1856). An alliance agreement aimed against Persia was signed at Peshawar (26 Jan. 1857) by the British and Dost Mohammed of Afghanistan.

Course of War

The British had been preparing since July 1856 for the possibility of war with Persia and when war was declared they moved with commendable speed. Within three weeks an army left Karachi, while in January 1857 a second army set out under General Outram. Kharg Island (4 Dec. 1856) and the port of Bushire (Bushahr) (10 Dec.) were taken as bases of operation. Outram's army met with general success. The most interesting operation of the war was the capture of Muhammarah (Khorramshah), which provided an early example of a combined naval and army action (26 March 1857). However, Outram learned (5 April) that peace had already been concluded.

Political result

By the Treaty of Paris (4 March 1857), the shah recognized the independence of Herat and promised not to invade it again. It was a mild treaty against the defeated state, which lost no territory and was not forced to pay an indemnity. Britain evacuated the areas it had occupied, a move spurred by the outbreak of the Indian Mutiny (May 1857). Six years later Herat was finally united to Afghanistan by Dost Mohammed. While British policy had sought to keep Herat independent of Persia, it was not opposed to its reabsorption into Afghanistan if circumstances warranted. In 1863, after Herat had attacked the Afghan town of Farrah, Dost Mohammed's army defeated Herat and annexed it to Afghanistan (27 May). Having reunited Afghanistan, Dost Mohammed died shortly thereafter (9 June 1863).

Second Anglo-Afghan War 1878–80

Belligerents: **Great Britain**
                     Afghanistan

Cause

Russian and British interests were coming increasingly into potential conflict as their involvement in Central Asia increased. British annexation of the Punjab after the Second Sikh War of 1848–9 gave it a frontier with Afghanistan, while Russia's annexations of Bokhara (1868) and Khiva (1873) brought it perilously close to northern Afghanistan. The ruler of Afghanistan, Dost Mohammed, had died in 1863 and was succeeded as amir by his son, Sher Ali, who turned vainly to Britain for support against the potential Russian threat to the north and the Persian threat to the west. This led the amir to tilt towards Russia.

Occasion

The outbreak of the Russo-Ottoman War of 1877–8 saw Russian forces poised to take the Straits, a move that Britain attempted to block. In order to divert the British, the Russians sent a mission to Kabul to conclude a treaty with the amir. An attempted counter-mission sent by the viceroy of India, Lord Lytton, was rejected. The refusal to allow this embassy to enter Afghanistan led the viceroy to declare war (Nov. 1878).

Course of War

British armies launched a three-pronged attack on Afghanistan (21 Nov. 1878), taking the frontier passes, defeating the amir's army at Peiwar Kotal (2 Dec.) and capturing Kandahar (8 Jan. 1879) and Jalalabad. Sher Ali left Kabul to seek aid from the Russians, who, however, urged him to make peace. He died soon thereafter (21 Feb. 1879) and was succeeded by his son, Yakub Khan. The new amir concluded peace with Britain. By the Treaty of Gandamak (26 May 1879) Yakub was recognized as amir, while some fringe areas of Afghanistan passed to Britain, which was to conduct Afghanistan's foreign relations, in return for Britain's offering a guarantee against aggression. A British envoy was to be allowed to reside at Kabul.

This seeming victory for Britain was disrupted when the first British resident, Sir Louis Cavagnari, and his escort were murdered (3 Sept. 1879). As a result, a British army again invaded Afghanistan, defeating the Afghans at the Battle of Charasia (6 Oct.) and taking Kabul (12 Oct.). Yakub Khan abdicated, whereupon his brother, Ayub Khan, claimed the throne from his base at Herat and marched on Kandahar. At the Battle of Maiwand (27 July 1880) Ayub Khan's army of 25,000 virtually annihilated a British force of 2,500. The British General Roberts, with 10,000 men, now moved against Ayub Khan. At the Battle of Kandahar (1 Sept.) Roberts, after a remarkable forced march of 334 miles in 23 days, defeated Ayub Khan, who returned to Herat. The British recognized Yakub Khan's cousin, Abdur Rahman, as amir.

Political result

Lord Lytton, who had advocated the interventionist policy in Afghanistan, was replaced as viceroy (May 1880) by Lord Ripon, who favored a rapid settlement. Britain returned to Abdur Rahman all of Afghanistan, retaining the mountain passes agreed in the Treaty of Gandamak (the Khyber Pass, the Kuram valley, Pishin and Quetta). With Abdur Rahman's accession Afghanistan entered on an unusually tranquil period, in which it maintained good relations with Britain and kept aloof from Russia, becoming in effect a buffer state. Ayub Khan made one last bid for power in 1881, when he captured Kandahar (27 July) after the withdrawal of British forces from Afghanistan. Abdur Rahman, however, defeated him (22 Sept.) and Ayub Khan fled to exile in Persia.

Third Anglo-Afghan War 1919

Belligerents: **Afghanistan**
                   Great Britain

Cause

Abdur Rahman was succeeded as amir in 1901 by his son Habibullah, who maintained good relations with Britain and followed a policy of strict neutrality during the First World War. His adherence to the treaty arrangements made with Britain in 1880, after the Second Anglo-Afghan War, helped lead to his assassination (20 Feb. 1919). Habibullah was succeeded by his son, Amanullah Khan, who was committed to the restoration of full Afghan sovereignty.

Occasion

The new amir proclaimed full Afghan sovereignty (13 April 1919), which the viceroy of India refused to recognize. Negotiations broke down and regular Afghan soldiers crossed the frontier with India, occupying strategic positions in the Khyber Pass (3 May).

Course of War

British forces quickly pushed back the Afghan invaders (11 May) and entered Afghanistan, while British planes bombed Jalalabad and Kabul, a type of warfare for which the Afghans were unprepared. The Afghans soon sued for peace (28 May).

Political result

The British Empire was exhausted after the First World War, strategically over-extended, and facing revolts in Ireland and Egypt. The Third Anglo-Afghan War also coincided with the events of the Amritsar Massacre, which threatened to provoke large-scale disturbances in India. As a result, Britain was willing to conclude a generous treaty with Afghanistan. By the Treaty of Rawalpindi (8 Aug. 1919), Britain recognized Afghanistan as fully independent and allowed it to resume the direct conduct of its foreign affairs.

Soviet-Afghan War 1979–89

Belligerents: **Soviet Union, Afghanistan (pro-Soviet government)**
Afghan resistance movements (*mujaheddin*)

Cause

The monarchy in Afghanistan was overthrown and a Republic of Afghanistan established (17 July 1973) which in turn was overthrown five years later in the Saur (April) Revolution, when the country was renamed the Democratic Republic of Afghanistan (April 1978). The new government was controlled by the (Marxist) People's Democratic Party of Afghanistan (PDPA), which was divided between two factions: the Parcham (Banner) faction, comprising mostly urban Dari-speakers, and the Khalq (Masses) faction, which consisted mostly of rural Pushtu-speakers. The new president, Nur Muhammed Taraki, and the other dominant member of the government, Hafizullah Amin, were both part of the Khalq faction.

Occasion

Taraki was overthrown and killed by Amin in a coup (Sept.–Oct. 1979). Meanwhile, an insurgency against the Marxist régime had been spreading throughout the country, supported by Moslem fundamentalists, royalists and anti-Russians. This led the Soviet Union to throw its support behind the Parcham faction. In accordance with the Brezhnev Doctrine, the Soviet government decided to intervene to maintain a pro-Soviet Marxist government in power and Soviet forces began to land in Afghanistan's capital, Kabul (24 Dec. 1979).

Course of War

Soviet forces attacked the presidential palace and captured President Amin, who was immediately executed (27 Dec. 1979). Babrak Karmal was named as the new president. The Soviet government justified its intervention on the basis of the new Afghan government's request for military assistance, and thousands of Soviet forces poured across the Oxus river into Afghanistan. By the summer of 1980 some 85,000 Soviet troops had been deployed, with the number eventually peaking at 120,000. The Afghan resistance, the *mujaheddin,* continued to fight, however. A Soviet offensive (March–May 1980) proved unable to cut off the rebels' support from refugee bases in Pakistan, which provided a safe haven and assistance for the *mujaheddin.* Although the Soviets and their Afghan allies controlled the cities and lines of communication, the countryside was open to the resistance groups. The *mujaheddin* received extensive support from the United States, China and Saudi Arabia. President Karmal was eventually replaced by Najibullah, a former head of the secret police, both as PDPA general-secretary (May 1986) and as president (Nov. 1987).

When Mikhail Gorbachev came to power in Moscow (March 1985), he instituted a policy change by which the Soviet Union sought to extricate itself from an increasingly costly, and probably unwinnable, war which had already cost it much support in the Third World. After he had announced the Soviet Union's intention to withdraw its military forces from Afghanistan (8 Feb. 1988), a settlement was quickly agreed at the Geneva talks sponsored by the United Nations.

Soviet losses were estimated at 15,000. The destruction to Afghanistan was on a vast scale and Afghan deaths were estimated at one million; up to a further five million Afghans fled as refugees to Pakistan and Iran.

Political result

The Geneva Accords (14 April 1988) were in fact four agreements, involving the Afghan government in Kabul, Pakistan, the Soviet Union and the United States. It was agreed that the Soviet Union would withdraw half its forces from Afghanistan by 15 August 1988 and the remainder by 15 February 1989. Both these deadlines were met. The *mujaheddin* formed a government-in-exile (23 Feb. 1989) but, to the surprise of many, President Najibullah managed to cling to power after the Soviet withdrawal.

Remarks

One result of the Soviet invasion was to cause President Carter to announce (3 Jan. 1980) that he would not submit to the US Senate the SALT-II treaty on arms limitation with the Soviet Union, much to the dismay of Moscow. A boycott of the 1980 Olympic Games in Moscow was also carried out by several Western states.

7 South Asian Wars

First Sikh War 1845–6

Belligerents: **Great Britain**
                     Sikhs

Cause

The eighteenth-century Sikh state was centered on the Punjab, stretching from the Sutlej river to the Afghan hills and from Multan to Kashmir. Sikh military capability was impressive, with a Western-style army possessing significant artillery. In the early nineteenth century the growing presence of the British across the Sutlej brought them into increasing contact with the Sikhs, leading to concern about future British intentions, while British military prestige suffered a setback due to the First Afghan War of 1839–42.

Occasion

After the death of Ranjit Singh (1839), one of the great leaders of the Sikh state, there followed several years of domestic turmoil, with the most powerful element being the 90,000-man army dominated by *punches* (committees). After a lengthy period without pay, some 50,000 troops under Lal Singh invaded British territory across the Sutlej (11 Dec. 1845), causing the British governor-general, Sir Henry Hardinge, to declare war (13 Dec.).

Course of War

The war was dominated by four major battles: Mudki (18 Dec. 1845), where the Sikh attack on the British under General Gough was repulsed with heavy casualties; Ferozeshah (21–2 Dec.), which proved inconclusive, although the Sikhs did retire beyond the Sutlej; Aliwal (28 Jan. 1846), where a renewed Sikh invasion was turned back and the Sikhs cleared from the south Sutlej; and Sobraon (10 Feb.), where Gough with 10,000 men attacked a Sikh army of 50,000 and defeated it. In the wake of Sobraon,

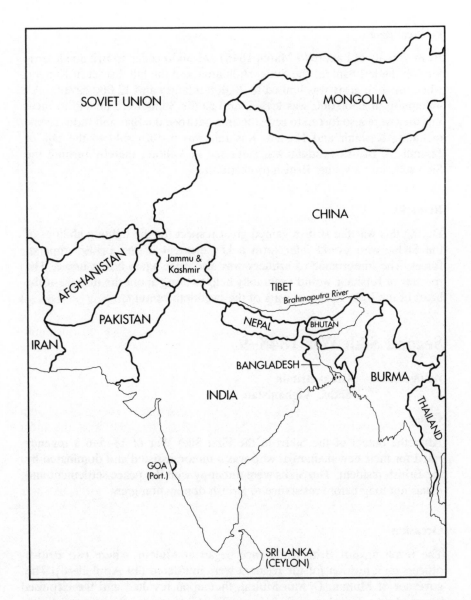

SOVIET UNION

MONGOLIA

CHINA

AFGHANISTAN

Jammu & Kashmir

TIBET

Brahmaputra River

PAKISTAN

NEPAL

BHUTAN

IRAN

BANGLADESH

BURMA

INDIA

THAILAND

GOA
(Port.)

SRI LANKA
(CEYLON)

11 South Asia

Gough marched on Lahore, the Sikh capital, and concluded a peace with the Sikhs. The Sikhs' tenacious fighting had inflicted higher than usual casualties on the British forces.

Political result

By the Treaty of Lahore (9 March 1846), the Sikhs ceded to Britain all territory on the left bank of the Sutlej, Jullundar and the hill district of Kangra, while the Sikh army was limited to 20,000 infantry and 12,000 cavalry. An indemnity of £500,000 was levied, and as the Sikhs were unable to meet this they were also forced to cede the area between the Bias and Indus rivers, including Kashmir and Hazara. Kashmir was in turn sold to the raja of Jammu. A British resident was stationed at Lahore, thereby turning the Sikh state into a virtual British protectorate.

Remarks

During this war the British gained great respect for the fighting abilities of the Sikhs, who would later form a key element of the British imperial forces. The importance of artillery was also once again borne home. The transfer of Kashmir would eventually help to bring about the dispute at the heart of the Indo-Pakistani wars of the twentieth century.

Second Sikh War 1848–9

Belligerents: **Great Britain**
                     Sikhs, Afghanistan

Cause

After the defeat of the Sikhs in the First Sikh War of 1845–6 a regency ruled for their new maharaja, who was a minor, assisted and dominated by the British resident. The Sikhs were unhappy with the peace settlement and it was not long before resistance to British domination grew.

Occasion

The revolt against British influence began at Multan, where two British officers on a mission for the resident were murdered (19 April 1848). The governor of Multan, Dewan Mulraj, thereupon revolted and the city was besieged by a British and Sikh force. The Sikh general then went over to the rebels, the local revolt turning into a national rising. The new governor-general, Lord Dalhousie, decided on immediate and decisive action.

Course of War

The war was dominated by two great battles. At Chilianwala (13 Jan. 1849) General Gough, with 12,000 men, unsuccessfully engaged an army of 40,000 Sikhs. Although Gough briefly won the field, he had to retreat due to lack of water. British casualties numbered 2,800. The outcry at the British losses was so great that it was decided to replace Gough with General Napier, but before this could be done Gough won the Battle of Gujrat (21 Feb. 1849). This was the first Anglo-Sikh battle in which the British had superiority in artillery. Here 24,000 men led by Gough defeated a Sikh force of 50,000 which was aided by Dost Mohammed of Afghanistan. In this engagement Gough lost only 96 men to the Sikhs' 2,000 dead. The Sikhs' leaders promptly surrendered (12 March 1849).

Political result

By an instrument agreed on 29 March 1849, the Sikh state was annexed to British India (and the famous Koh-i-Noor diamond was surrendered to Queen Victoria). The Treaty of Peshawar (30 March 1855) between Britain and Afghanistan finally resolved the issues raised by the Afghan role in the Second Sikh War. Britain was concerned about the imminent outbreak of the Crimean War and wished to ensure that Afghanistan would act as a barrier against any Russian move towards India. The treaty reopened diplomatic relations between Britain and Afghanistan, with the latter recognizing the British annexation of Peshawar in return for Britain promising support against Persian claims to Herat. This would be a factor in the Anglo-Persian War over Herat in 1856–7.

Kashmir Dispute (First Indo-Pakistani War) 1947–9

Belligerents: **India**
Pakistan

Cause

With the partition of India on its independence from Great Britain (15 Aug. 1947), into Pakistan and India, the 362 princely rulers were left to decide to which country they would accede. This was generally determined by geography, but Jammu and Kashmir, bordering both countries, proved a difficult case. This state had been created after the First Sikh War of 1845–6 when predominantly Hindu and Sikh Jammu was joined to predominantly Moslem Kashmir. At the time of partition the state had a large Moslem majority (1941 census: 77 per cent Moslem, 20 per cent Hindu), but the maharaja, who was a Hindu, remained undecided as to which country to join. (The first prime minister of independent India, Pandit Nehru, was himself a Kashmiri brahmin.)

Occasion

In October 1947 an uprising by Moslems was joined by thousands of Pakistani tribesmen armed by the Pakistani army. They marched on the capital of Jammu and Kashmir, Srinagar, and by 27 October were within 30 miles of their goal. On that day the maharaja acceded to India and Indian soldiers were flown to the state.

Course of War

By November 1947 Indian forces had cleared the Kashmir valley, relieving the pressure on Srinagar. In December the rebels launched a new offensive in the southwest, which resulted in heavy fighting until March 1948. In May 1948 Pakistani regulars entered the fighting in support of the rebels and a new offensive was conducted in the north and northwest. After several attempts, the United Nations was able to arrange a ceasefire (31 Dec. 1948, effective 1 Jan. 1949).

Political result

A final ceasefire line was agreed (29 July 1949) and this has in effect remained the boundary between India and Pakistan. India was left in control of Jammu and of the Kashmir valley. The dispute continues, however, and efforts at mediation have proved fruitless. The Kashmiri Constituent Assembly, elected in the Indian portion (Sept. 1951), ratified Kashmir's accession to India (15 Feb. 1954). The Moslems established a provisional government of Azad (Free) Kashmir (Oct. 1947), and Pakistan has never formally annexed the area under its control, arguing that the matter is still in dispute.

Remarks

The new boundaries left the headwaters of the old Punjab irrigation system in India, the system being critical to Pakistan's irrigation. India has made use of its control of the water supply to apply pressure on Pakistan.

Sino-Indian War 1962

Belligerents: China
                     India

Cause

This border war, following the Chinese absorption of Tibet (1959), hinged on two disputed areas in the far west and far east of the Sino-Indian frontier. China claimed to be reasserting the sovereignty it had historically enjoyed over Tibet, which it reorganized as the autonomous region of Xizang. The eastern dispute went back at least to the abortive Simla Convention on the status of Tibet (1913–14), when Sir Henry McMahon attempted to clarify the border between Assam and Tibet in an exchange of letters with the Tibetans. The proposed border was accepted by both the Tibetans and the British, and subsequently by independent India, but the entire Simla Convention was rejected at the time by China. The McMahon Line roughly followed the watershed of the Himalayas, giving Assam a secure mountainous northern frontier. The Chinese, however, claimed the more southerly Brahmaputra river as the border. The area in dispute was about 32,000 square miles and it originally fell within the North-East Frontier Agency during British rule, subsequently becoming part of the Indian state of Assam.

The second area of dispute was Ladakh on the Kashmir-Tibet border, which had never been demarcated. This otherwise barren area includes the strategically important Aksai Chin plateau, which provides the link between Tibet and Sinkiang (Xinjiang). The area had been effectively under Chinese control since 1950, and a road 1,200 km long had been constructed connecting the two regions (1956), of which 180 km fell within Indian-claimed territory. The Indian government in fact only learned of the road's existence after reading about it in a Chinese newspaper. Chinese proposals for negotiations were met with absolute refusal from India, leading to border skirmishes (1958–9).

Occasion

After the full Chinese occupation of Tibet (1959), the Tibetan leader, the Dalai Lama, fled to India. The Indian government under Prime Minister Nehru embarked on a more aggressive foreign policy, which led to the seizure of the remaining Portuguese colonial enclaves in the subcontinent (Dec. 1961). After this easy success, Indian forces increased their deployment on the Chinese frontier in support of this 'forward policy'. The Chinese premier, Chou En-lai, flew to India for talks (April 1962), but failed to reach an agreement. In June 1962 Indian forces started to move forward in both disputed areas to take control of the areas claimed. Despite Chinese protests, Indian forces began to establish a presence in these districts, although the Aksai Chin plateau proved too difficult to occupy. This then led China to take military action.

Course of War

China launched an offensive in both disputed areas (20 Oct. 1962). In the east the Chinese army moved rapidly 100 miles south of the McMahon Line, which exposed the Assam plains to attack. In the west the Chinese advanced 30 miles into Ladakh. Having proved their ability to dominate the disputed areas, the Chinese declared a unilateral ceasefire (21 Nov.). Indian dead numbered 1,383, while the Chinese dead were about half that figure.

Political result

The borders remain in dispute. Under its unilateral ceasefire, the Chinese army withdrew 12 miles (20 km) north of the McMahon Line and a similar distance in the west behind the 1959 line of control. China later returned all captured Indian equipment. Subsequent talks on the dispute have failed to reach a settlement. China has continued to offer recognition of the McMahon Line in return for Indian recognition of its sovereignty over Aksai Chin. In 1972 the disputed area south of the McMahon Line was separated from Assam and became the Indian union territory of Arunachal Pradesh (becoming a full state in 1987).

Remarks

The war dashed Nehru's hopes of creating a powerful non-aligned group of states with India and China as the nucleus. The Soviet Union's diplomatic support for India in this war further damaged its relations with China.

Second Indo-Pakistani War 1965

Belligerents: **India**
                     Pakistan

Cause

After the Kashmir Dispute of 1947–9 Indo-Pakistani tension flared again during 1965 over the disputed Rann of Kutch, which lies on the border between the Indian state of Gujarat and the Pakistani province of Baluchistan. The border here was not finally demarcated at the time of partition in 1947. Fighting broke out (9 April 1965), followed by sporadic skirmishing. A ceasefire was negotiated by Great Britain (effective 1 July), restoring the status quo. The tensions engendered by this skirmishing led to a renewal of the Kashmir crisis.

Occasion

Armed groups began infiltrating into Indian Kashmir from Pakistani-controlled Azad Kashmir (5 Aug. 1965). The Indian army moved to halt this by occupying points on the Pakistani side of the ceasefire line (16 Aug.). Pakistan responded with a tank offensive into the Jammu area of Kashmir (1 Sept.).

Course of War

The Indian army, in response to the attack by Pakistan, launched 'Operation Grand Slam', aimed at Lahore, the capital of the Pakistani province of Punjab (6 Sept.). The war saw extensive tank engagements, but neither side was able to achieve a decisive victory. A ceasefire was agreed at the insistence of the United Nations Security Council (23 Sept.). The war cost the lives of about 20,000 people, mostly civilians.

Political result

The Declaration of Tashkent (10 Jan. 1966) restored the prewar status quo. The talks resulting in this settlement were arranged by the Soviet Union between the Indian prime minister, Lal Shastri, and the Pakistan president, Ayub Khan, and were held in the Soviet city of Tashkent (4–10 Jan. 1966). The mutual pull-back of forces was concluded by 25 February. Unsuccessful follow-up talks were held at Rawalpindi in Pakistan (March 1966).

Remarks

The issue remains a volatile one in Indo-Pakistani relations. Occasional skirmishing continues, always threatening a renewal of war. A particular flashpoint is the Siachin glacier in the far north, where the ceasefire line is in dispute and where occasional fighting occurs. During 1990 there was a significant fear that fighting might erupt again in this area.

Third Indo-Pakistani War (Bangladesh War of Independence) 1971

Belligerents: **India, Bangladesh**
Pakistan

Cause

At the partition of India (1947) the new Moslem state of Pakistan was formed by two areas, East and West Pakistan, separated by 1,000 miles of Indian territory. The new country was dominated by West Pakistan, while predominantly Bengali East Pakistan produced most of the exports. Elections in 1970 gave a parliamentary majority to the Bengali autonomist party, the Awami League, led by Sheikh Mujibur Rahman. West Pakistan refused to accept an Awami League government and President Yahya Khan postponed indefinitely the convening of parliament. This led to increasing tension in East Pakistan, culminating on Pakistan Day in 1971 when, after further protests, the president declared a state of emergency and Sheikh Mujib was arrested (23 March). A declaration of independence was then issued by Mujib's supporters in East Pakistan, with the new country being called Bangladesh (26 March).

Occasion

The Pakistani government responded to the Bangladeshi movement with a brutal campaign of military repression which impelled over 10 million Bengalis to flee to India. The Indian government was supportive of the Bengalis' struggle, partly because the creation of Bangladesh would remove the threat posed to its own security by the existence of two borders with Pakistan, but also because of the pressure caused by the vast number of Bengali refugees in India. India provided training for the Bengali guerrillas, the Mukti Bahini (freedom fighters). In the face of growing Indian involvement in the struggle, Pakistan opted for a pre-emptive strike.

Course of War

Pakistan launched an unsuccessful attempt to copy the Israeli success in the 1967 Six Days' War in knocking out the enemy airforce on the ground. But India, aware of the possibility of war, had taken preventive measures and the Pakistani air assault failed (3 Dec. 1971). The next day Pakistan launched an invasion of Kashmir. India, however, focused its efforts on the war in the east, launching a five-pronged attack into Bangladesh/East Pakistan. Indian forces were remarkably successful, reaching the outskirts of the capital, Dhaka, within nine days. The battle for Dhaka lasted two days before the Pakistani commander surrendered (16 Dec.). With the war in the east won, India turned its attention westward, fighting one of the largest tank battles since the Second World War (15–16 Dec.). India then announced a unilateral ceasefire (17 Dec.).

Political result

In the Simla Agreement (2 July 1972), India and Pakistan agreed to return to their prewar positions. On 22 February 1974 Pakistan formally recognized Bangladesh's independence. Sheikh Mujibur returned from Pakistan to become prime minister (Jan. 1972) and subsequently president (Jan. 1975). He was later assassinated by dissatisfied army officers (15 Aug. 1975).

Remarks

The war also concerned the superpowers. The United States was looking to reopen relations with China and this led it to lean towards Pakistan, which had good relations with China because of their similar border disputes with

India. This in turn caused India to conclude a 20-year Treaty of Peace, Friendship and Cooperation with the Soviet Union (Aug. 1971). The timing of the Indian intervention in the war coincided not only with the end of the monsoon season, making large-scale movements possible in Bangladesh, but also with the onset of winter weather in the north, so precluding Chinese intervention in support of Pakistan.

8 Anglo-Burmese Wars

First Anglo-Burmese War 1824–6

Belligerents: Great Britain
                   Burma

Cause

Burma was one of the predominant regional powers in the early nineteenth century and its expansionist policies brought it into conflict with the increasing power of the British East India Company in India. In 1785 Burma had conquered and annexed the coastal state of Arakan, which bordered British-ruled Bengal. A rebellion in Arakan (1811–15), during which the rebels operated from bases in Bengal, led to a serious deterioration in Anglo-Burmese relations. In 1819 Burma annexed Assam, so increasing its border with British territory. Burma had also long been interested in annexing Bengal and the great Burmese general, Bandula, was coordinating policy to achieve this end. This was based on a misperception of British power, which was seen as comparatively weak because until 1819 it had been seriously distracted by other crises in India. Now, however, Britain could turn its attention fully on Burma.

Occasion

Burmese forces attacked the British-protected state of Cachar (1824), where they came into conflict with British forces. Simultaneously, Bandula moved to threaten the Bengali port of Chittagong. This resulted in a declaration of war by the (British) government of India (5 March 1824).

Course of War

While Bandula attacked Chittagong, Britain attacked Burma by sea, sending a force of 11,000 up the Irrawaddy river and capturing Rangoon (then only a small fortified village). As the British had hoped, Bandula was forced to move away from the Bengal Front to defend Upper Burma. The

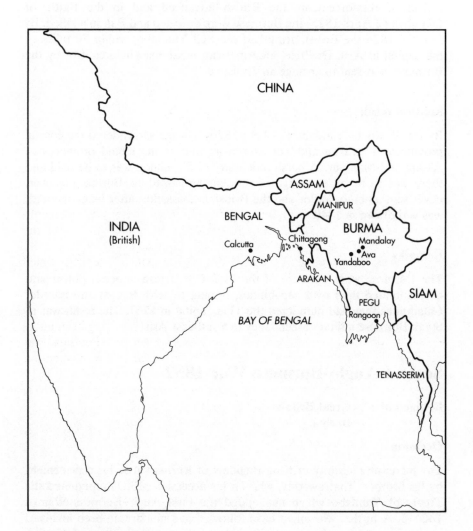

CHINA

INDIA
(British)

BENGAL

ASSAM

MANIPUR

BURMA

Calcutta

Chittagong

Mandalay
Ava
Yandaboo

ARAKAN

SIAM

BAY OF BENGAL

PEGU
Rangoon

TENASSERIM

12 Anglo-Burmese Wars

Burmese fell back, destroying supplies, and the British, with only a sketchy knowledge of the country, camped at Rangoon during the six-month rainy season and were soon decimated by disease. In December 1824 an attack by Bandula's army of 60,000 was nevertheless repulsed by a British force of only 4,000 effective soldiers under Sir Archibald Campbell. With the arrival of reinforcements the British advanced and in the Battle of Danubyu (2 April 1825) the Burmese were defeated and Bandula killed. By January 1826 the British army had reached Yandabo, within 70 miles of the capital at Ava. Dr Price, an American missionary held captive by the Burmese, was sent to arrange an armistice.

Political result

By the Treaty of Yandabo (24 Feb. 1826), Burma surrendered the coastal provinces of Arakan and Tenasserim as well as the inland provinces of Assam and Manipur. A harsh indemnity of £1 million was to be paid and there was to be an exchange of resident ambassadors. Burma, however, never sent an ambassador and the British ambassador, after being ignored, was withdrawn in 1840.

Remarks

The Burmese were unaware of the extent of British imperial power and overestimated their own capabilities, hoping to seize Bengal and plunder Calcutta as they had plundered the Thai capital in 1767. The result was to break Burmese military ascendancy in Southeast Asia.

Second Anglo-Burmese War 1852

Belligerents: **Great Britain**
                    Burma

Occasion

The increasing insanity of King Bagidaw of Burma led to his replacement by his brother, Tharrawaddy, who on his accession (1837) repudiated the Treaty of Yandabo which had ended the First Anglo-Burmese War of 1824–6. A further war might have followed had not Britain been involved in the First Afghan War of 1839–42, and the two Sikh Wars of 1845–6 and 1848–9. In 1846 the now insane Tharrawaddy died and was succeeded by his son, Pagan Min, whose two-year reign was notable for its cruelty. Central control rapidly collapsed and this instability helped to bring about another war with British India. In 1851 the governor of Pegu, Burma's remaining coastal province, acting independently, imposed fines on two British merchant ships with the intention of humiliating the British, as well as profiting from it. The governor-general of India, Lord Dalhousie, now free of other distractions, decided on action and sent a naval mission to Burma under Commodore Lambert, later known as the 'combustible commodore'. Lambert was insulted by the authorities at Rangoon and as a result initiated a blockade. Dalhousie sent an ultimatum to Rangoon, demanding compensation, together with an expeditionary force of 6,100 men. The ultimatum expired unanswered (1 April 1852) and British forces attacked (5 April).

Course of War

Dalhousie's careful preparations avoided the problems of the previous Anglo-Burmese war, with preventive health measures resulting in a mortality rate lower than the peacetime average in India. After a lull caused by the rainy season, Pegu province was occupied and its annexation to British India proclaimed (20 Dec. 1852). A revolution at the same time overthrew Pagan Min and brought to power his half-brother, Mindon. The new king refused to sign any treaty that explicitly involved the loss of Burmese territory, although he did not continue the war.

Political result

As a result of Mindon's refusal to conclude a peace treaty, Lord Dalhousie simply declared an end to hostilities. Britain retained Pegu province, together with a teak-rich strip to the north of Pegu. Burma now became entirely landlocked.

Third Anglo-Burmese War 1885

Belligerents: **Great Britain**
                    Burma

Cause

The latter part of the nineteenth century saw growing Anglo-French rivalry for dominance in Southeast Asia. Thibaw, who succeeded Mindon as king of Burma in 1878, decided to pursue a policy of closer links with France, much to the annoyance of Britain, which regarded Burma as falling within its sphere. Direct British negotiations with Thibaw were hampered by the 'shoe question'. Since 1875 British diplomats had ceased to have direct access to the king, having refused to remove their shoes in his presence in accordance with Burmese custom. In 1883 a commercial treaty was concluded between Burma and France, increasing British concerns about French penetration into the areas bordering India.

Occasion

In 1885 the Burmese government imposed a high fine on the British-owned Bombay-Burmah Trading Co., on clearly fabricated charges. Confiscation of the company's timber concessions was threatened. The British-Indian authorities now used this as a pretext to move against Thibaw. An ultimatum was delivered (30 Oct. 1885) demanding that a British minister be received and be allowed to wear his shoes, and that control of Burma's foreign affairs be entrusted to Britain. This was rejected and Britain took the decision to invade Burma (9 Nov.).

Course of War

The military department in Calcutta had long had contingency plans for an invasion, which began on 14 November. The Burmese were caught completely unaware by the speed of events. The British force of 9,000 men, together with 2,810 natives and 55 steamers and barges, moved directly on Mandalay, which fell within a fortnight with only four British dead. As the British approached Ava, the capital city, the king offered to surrender (26 Nov.) and the following day Thibaw ordered an end to fighting, although guerrilla warfare continued for some time.

Political result

It was at first thought to replace Thibaw with a more amenable king, but with no suitable candidate available the country was annexed to British India (1 Jan. 1886). Some resistance to British rule continued; the country was not pacified for another five years. At their height the British pacification forces numbered 32,000 men.

9   East Asian Wars

First Opium War 1839–42

Belligerents: **Great Britain**
                    China

Cause

Since 1750 European trading with China had been limited to one port, Canton (Guangzhou), located 2,000 miles from the capital at Peking (Beijing). In the early nineteenth century twin crises arose over the balance of payments and equality of treatment for foreigners. The balance of payments issue shifted dramatically in Britain's favor after it began selling opium, as well as cotton, which was the principle article of trade. This created not only a social problem for China but also an economic one, as silver flowed out of the country. In addition, Britain wished to force the Chinese government to treat its representatives on the basis of sovereign equality. As opium usage increased (in 1836 over 1,800 tons of the substance were imported into China), the Chinese government began a successful drive against the domestic opium trade. In 1838 this was extended to Canton, with the dispatch of a new imperial commissioner, Lin Tse-hsu, to the city.

Occasion

Lin demanded the surrender of the opium stocks held by the foreign merchants (March 1839), applying a blockade to their enclave for 47 days. The British government representative, Captain Charles Elliot, convinced the merchants to agree after promising them compensation. Over 20,000 chests of opium were turned over and destroyed and the blockade was lifted. Commissioner Lin demanded a pledge from the merchants to cease trading in opium, which they refused to give, fleeing instead to the Portuguese colony at Macao before being forced to take refuge aboard their ships. Eventually, desperate for supplies, Elliot held up a Chinese junk fleet at Kowloon (4 Sept.), the event which marked the beginning of hostilities.

Course of War

The Chinese believed in their military superiority and made little preparation for war. Elliot's request for action, however, was supported by the British foreign secretary, Palmerston, and in June 1840 he was joined by 16 warships and 4,000 soldiers under General Gough. They quickly seized Chusan (Zhousan) Island at the mouth of Hangchow (Hangzhou) Bay. This led to negotiations resulting in the ill-fated Convention of Chuenpi (20 Jan. 1841), by which Hong Kong was ceded to Britain. Britain also received an indemnity of $6 million and obtained the right of equal official contact and the promise that the Canton trade would be reopened. In return, Chusan was handed back to Chinese control. Both governments, however, disapproved of his arrangement, the unfortunate Chinese negotiator being taken away in chains, while Palmerston replaced Elliot with Sir Henry Pottinger.

The Chinese emperor now sent an 'Army of Extermination' south to defeat the British. Elliot meanwhile had resumed hostilities and captured the heights above Canton (24 May 1841), although he agreed to allow the city to ransom itself for $6 million to avoid needless slaughter. After Pottinger's arrival (Aug. 1841) with 25 ships of the line, 14 steamers and 10,000 soldiers, events moved rapidly with the capture of Amoy (Xiamen) (26 Aug.), Chusan (1 Oct.) and Ningpo (Ningbo) (13 Oct.). The Chinese attempted to take the offensive, while the British forces suffered from garrisoning duties which often left 50 per cent of them ineffective from disease. The Chinese conducted an assault of immense incompetence, attacking at the height of the rainy season on the basis of astrological advice and with over 60 per cent of their army of 61,000 tied down as bodyguards for the general staff. The Chinese offensive failed, while in the Yangtze campaign (7 May–20 Aug. 1842) the British took Shanghai and reached the Grand Canal, thereby cutting the grain supplies to Peking. After the fall (20 July) of Chingkiang (Zhenjiang), the key garrison on the Yangtze (Chang Jiang), had left Nanking (Nanjing) open to attack, the Chinese emperor decided to negotiate.

Political result

The Treaty of Nanking (21 Aug. 1842) was signed on board Pottinger's command ship, HMS *Cornwallis*. China agreed to pay an indemnity of $21 million, ceded Hong Kong to Britain, opened five ports to foreign trade – Canton, Amoy, Foochow (Fuzhou), Ningpo and Shanghai – and agreed to the appointment of British consuls. No explicit mention of opium was made. The supplementary Bogue Treaty (8 Oct. 1843), elaborating the arrangements agreed at Nanking, granted consular jurisdiction and extra-territorial rights to Britain, which also obtained most-favored-nation status. These terms were included in many subsequent treaties which contributed to a reduction of Chinese sovereignty.

Remarks

The power vacuum caused by the British invasion helped increase the strength of bandit gangs in China, leading in turn to the social disorder which erupted in the Taiping Rebellion. The Nanking treaty inaugurated the period of unequal treaties which were imposed upon a weakened China by foreign powers. The opium trade was not abolished until 1913.

Second Opium War 1856–60

Belligerents: **Great Britain, France**
                    China

Cause

From 1854 several Western powers were attempting to negotiate treaty revisions with China which would further broaden their opportunities for trade. Simultaneously, China was embroiled in the widespread Taiping Rebellion and in several regional insurrections. Anglo-French cooperation had reached a new highpoint with their collaboration in the Crimean War of 1853–6, which in turn led to closer agreement over China. With the appointment of Palmerston as prime minister in Britain (Feb. 1855), it was decided to follow a firm policy towards China.

Occasion

The notably anti-foreign Chinese governor at Canton (Guangzhou), Yeh Ming Ch'en, had proved successful in maintaining order in his region. In October 1856 the Canton police boarded a British-registered ship and removed 12 Chinese crewmen suspected of piracy and smuggling. The British complained and the prisoners were returned within a few days, but the level of apology offered was considered inadequate. In line with Palmerston's policy, action was taken and three warships were sent to Canton, seizing the surrounding forts and bombarding the city. In retaliation the inhabitants of Canton looted and burned the foreign trading area. Further military action was delayed by a general election in Britain, which confirmed Palmerston in power, and by the outbreak of the Indian Mutiny (May 1857), which diverted British forces. The French joined in the military expedition over the judicial murder of a missionary (Feb. 1856).

Course of War

An Anglo-French force of 5,700 men arrived off Canton and bombarded the city (28 Dec. 1857). Despite the lengthy interval between the initial hostilities and the follow-up action, the Chinese had made no military preparations. Canton fell quickly, Yeh was captured and sent to Calcutta, where he later died (1859), and a puppet administration was installed. The allies now sailed up the coast to Taku, which guarded the river entrance to Tientsin (Tianjin). The allies quickly took the Taku forts (28 May 1858) and were soon at the gates of Tientsin (31 May). The Chinese now agreed to a settlement. The Treaties of Tientsin (26–9 June 1858) were concluded with Britain and France, as well as with Russia and the United States, who also had representatives present. In these treaties the Chinese accepted the principle of diplomatic relations being conducted on the basis of equality; the opening of ten more treaty ports for trading; freedom of travel within China; and the payment of an indemnity.

The question of sovereign equality was unpalatable to the Chinese emperor, however, and when the allied representatives returned (June 1859) to exchange ratifications of the Tientsin treaties they found the river at Taku blocked. An Anglo-French force attempted to breach the obstruction, but was unexpectedly repulsed by the Chinese. The allies were saved when the commander of the otherwise neutral American Asiatic squadron, Commodore Tattnall, intervened, exclaiming, 'Blood is thicker than water.' A large Anglo-French force was now organized (10,000 British and 6,000 French). The Taku forts were taken (21 Aug. 1860) and the allies moved up the Peiho river to Peking (Beijing). A Chinese request for an armistice led to a meeting (18 Sept.) in which the allied representatives were seized, imprisoned and brutally treated, half of them being killed. The allied forces defeated the Chinese troops outside Peking (21 Sept.) and the emperor fled to the far north the following day. The imperial summer palace was taken and looted (6 Oct.). It was subsequently burned in retaliation for the treatment of the negotiators. The Chinese government then agreed to a settlement.

Political result

The Conventions of Peking (18 and 24 Oct. 1860) confirmed the earlier Tientsin treaties. The indemnity was increased and China ceded to Britain the Kowloon peninsula opposite Hong Kong, thereby increasing the size of this British crown colony.

First Franco-Indochinese War 1858–62

Belligerents: **France, Spain**
                    Vietnam

Cause

For centuries Vietnam had been under Chinese suzerainty, but with the decline of Chinese power in the nineteenth century the entire Southeast

Asian region became a focus of European colonial activity, particularly by France. French involvement in the Second Opium War of 1856–60 brought its forces into the region and provided it with an opportunity to expand its influence. The French emperor, Napoleon III, also hoped that a colonial victory would benefit his régime's domestic prestige. French attention turned to Vietnam, which was composed of three parts: from north to south, Tonking (Tonkin), Annam and Cochin China.

Occasion

Spanish and French missionaries had been active for many years in Vietnam, despite persecution by the government. Emperor (*Nguyen*) Tu Duc decided to follow a policy, in the face of increasing missionary activity, of isolation and dispersal of the Vietnamese Christians. For domestic reasons, Napoleon III had adopted the role of a protector of the church, while the death of a missionary in China (1856) had formed the pretext for French intervention in the Second Opium War. In 1857 the Spanish bishop of Tonking was murdered, and a joint Franco-Spanish expedition, which had the benefit of Manila in the Spanish Philippines as a base, was launched against Vietnam during a lull in the Second Opium War.

Course of War

A small force easily captured the port of Tourane (Danang) (2 Sept. 1858), south of the Vietnamese capital of Hué, only to find that the Vietnamese had stripped the town bare, rendering it useless. Nonetheless, a French garrison hung on here until, weakened by disease, it was finally evacuated (March 1860). The invaders, after taking Tourane, turned south toward Saigon, the key food-producing area of the country. Saigon fell (17 Feb. 1859), but a resumption of fighting in the Second Opium War caused France to divert its attention, while French involvement in the 1859 Austro-Piedmontese War prevented further reinforcements being dispatched.

Meanwhile a Franco-Spanish garrison of 1,000 was besieged in Saigon (March 1860–Feb. 1861). The end of fighting in China (Jan. 1860) allowed 3,000 reinforcements to be sent to the disease-weakened force in Vietnam. At the Battle of Chin Hoa (Ky Hoa) (25 Feb. 1861), the French defeated the besiegers of Saigon. The French now assumed the offensive and soon gained control of most of lower Cochin China, declaring its annexation to France (July 1861). After more fighting, Emperor Tu Duc, facing rebellion in the north, sued for peace (May 1862).

Political result

By the Treaty of Saigon (5 June 1862), France obtained the three eastern provinces of Cochin China (Bien Hoa, Dinh Tuong and Gia Dinh) and the island of Poulo Condore; the free exercise of Christianity was to be allowed throughout Vietnam; three ports were opened to trade; and an indemnity was to be paid. Spain received nothing except a share of the indemnity. This settlement gave France control of the mouth of the Mekong river and it began to spread its influence into the region. By the Treaty of Houdong (11 Aug. 1863), Cambodia became a French protectorate; moreover, in June 1867 France, through military force, seized the three western provinces of Cochin China (An Giang, Ha Tien and Vinh Long). This seizure was later confirmed by another Treaty of Saigon (15 March 1874).

Second Franco-Indochinese War 1881-3

Belligerents: **France**
                   Vietnam

Cause

France, after its defeat in the Franco-Prussian War of 1870-1, turned its energies with renewed vigor to its colonial empire. The premier, Jules Ferry, was a strong advocate of empire and it was hoped that southern China could be opened to trade through control of the Red river (Song-koi), which flowed through Tonking (Tonkin) in northern Vietnam. By the Treaty of Saigon (March 1874), France had obtained trading and extra-territorial rights in northern Vietnam. China, however, still claimed to have suzerain rights over Vietnam. Tonking at the time was suffering great unrest from rebels and from the Chinese Black Flags (Co Den), a combination of Chinese regulars and irregulars operating in northern Vietnam.

Occasion

France was determined to consolidate its position in Vietnam and in 1881 it claimed that French lives were at risk in Hanoi from the Black Flags. The real aim was to gain control of Tonking (northern Vietnam).

Course of War

In July 1881 the French parliament voted war credits and an expeditionary force was dispatched which captured Hanoi (25 April 1882). Emperor Tu Duc turned to the Black Flags for help; they in turn besieged Hanoi and in the fighting the French commander was killed. A powerful force was now sent to relieve Hanoi. In the meantime, however, Tu Duc had died and a succession crisis developed, leading the Vietnamese to request an armistice, which was quickly followed by a peace treaty.

Political result

By the Treaty of Hue (25 Aug. 1883), Annam (central Vietnam) and Tonking became a French protectorate (although the Vietnamese emperor was retained as a figurehead) and the French colony of Cochin China was enlarged. Vietnam surrendered all its warships and agreed to pay an indemnity. The large French empire which now existed in Southeast Asia was reorganized in 1887 as the Indochinese Union, encompassing the colony of Cochin China and the protectorates of Tonking, Annam and Cambodia, with Laos being added in 1893.

Sino-French War 1883–5

Belligerents: France
China

Cause

The Chinese were worried by the growth of French power, which was displacing traditional Chinese dominance in Indochina. The Chinese considered that the treaties concluded by France with Vietnam were invalid without their approval. An 1874 treaty between France and Annam had opened the Red river (Song-koi), together with the cities of Haiphong and Hanoi, to trade. France hoped thereby to open a trade route which would allow it to penetrate the southern Chinese provinces of Schezchuan (Sichuan) and Yunan (Yunnan). These areas along the Red river, however, were troubled by the activities of rebels, including the Chinese irregular forces, the Black Flags (Co Den). France dispatched forces to deal with this problem, causing China to protest, claiming that Annam was a vassal state to China. French forces also encountered Chinese regulars who had been sent to the area, whose key fortresses were Sontay, Bac-Ninh and Hung-Hoa.

Occasion

The French general, Bouet, moved on Sontay, but was held up by flooding. In a brutal campaign he treated all opponents as rebels and beheaded all prisoners. Bouet returned to France, however, after a quarrel with the civil commissioner and was replaced by Admiral Courbert. Sontay fell to Courbert's forces (17 Dec. 1883), and with the arrival of reinforcements the French moved inland in three columns, capturing Bac-Ninh (11 March 1884) and Hung-Hoa (12 April). Local agents of both countries, Li Hung-chang and Captain Fournier, reached an agreement (May) by which France would recognize Chinese suzerainty and guarantee China's southern frontier, and in return China would withdraw its forces from Vietnam. No date was set for this withdrawal, however. When French forces arrived to occupy the provincial capital of Langson (21 June 1884), the Chinese commander refused to leave, having no orders to do so. The French then attacked and were repulsed, with heavy losses. France demanded a heavy indemnity, while China was willing to consider paying a small one. France rejected the Chinese offer and hostilities resumed and escalated.

Course of War

Both sides technically acted as if no state of war existed. As a result, the French fleet was allowed to sail into Foochow (Fuzhou) harbor, and in the Battle of Foochow the French destroyed the Chinese fleet at anchor, together with the great arsenal there (23 Aug. 1884). The French went on briefly to take Formosa (Taiwan) and the Pescadores Islands. A French offensive in Tonking succeeded in capturing Langson (13 Feb. 1885), but shortly afterwards at the Battle of Langson the French suffered a severe defeat (28 Feb.). News of this disaster caused the fall of Jules Ferry's government in Paris (31 March). The new government rapidly concluded a peace which gave France its basic aims.

Political result

By the Treaty of Tientsin (Tianjing) (9 June 1885), China accepted the French protectorate over Vietnam (Tonking and Annam).

Sino-Japanese War 1894–5

Belligerents: China
                                 Japan

Cause

China had for centuries dominated Korea, which followed a policy of isolation which earned it the appellation of the 'hermit kingdom'. In the 1870s Japan determined to open Korea to the outside, much as it had itself been opened by the Americans earlier in the century. This led to a Sino-Japanese struggle for influence in Korea.

Occasion

Two incidents led to war. The first involved the murder of Kim Ok-Kiun, a Korean dissident with Japanese links, in a Japanese-owned hotel in Shanghai by another Korean acting with Chinese government connivance (March 1894). The Chinese returned both the body and the assassin to Korea, where the body of the dissident was hacked to pieces and the assassin was fêted. This action caused outrage in Japan. The second incident was the outbreak of the anti-foreign Tong-hak (Society of Eastern Learning) rebellion (May 1894). Unable to maintain order, the Korean government requested Chinese assistance. The Japanese in turn sent a large force to Korea, ostensibly to protect their own nationals. Although the rebellion was suppressed, the outside forces remained. The Japanese, having established their position, then made a bid for control, seizing the palace, kidnapping the king and appointing a regent (23 July 1894), who then requested Japanese assistance to expel the Chinese (27 July). This led to China and Japan exchanging declarations of war (1 Aug.).

Course of War

At the outbreak of war the Japanese already controlled the southern half of the country, while the most important northern town, Pyongyang, soon fell to them (16 Sept.). In a region without railways, control of the sea was essential to both sides for transporting troops. Chinese ships and troop transports were confronted by the Japanese in the Battle of the Yalu (17 Sept.). The Chinese Admiral Ting was in fact a cavalry officer; despite their slight superiority in numbers, his forces were defeated by the Japanese. The remnants of the Chinese fleet took refuge at Weihaiwei, where it was subsequently captured by the Japanese, whereupon Admiral Ting committed suicide (Feb. 1895). The Japanese had meanwhile crossed the Yalu river into China (24 Oct. 1894), while another force took Port Arthur (21 Nov.). The Japanese army proceeded into the Chinese province of Manchuria, and by mid-March 1895 they were only awaiting good weather before turning towards Peking (Beijing). As a result the Chinese were forced to sue for peace.

Political result

By the Treaty of Shimonoseki (17 April 1895), China abandoned suzerainty over Korea; China ceded to Japan the Liaotung peninsula in southern Manchuria, the island of Formosa (Taiwan) and the Pescadores Islands; four inland Chinese cities were opened as trading ports: Shasi, Chungking, (Chongqing), Soochow (Suzhou) and Hangchow (Hangzhou); and an indemnity was to be paid. Within eight days of the signature of the treaty Russia, France and Germany intervened to force Japan to reduce its gains (known as the Triple Intervention). In the face of such opposition Japan had to give up the Liaotung peninsula. Japan was then infuriated when these three powers themselves proceeded to grab bits of China, with Russia taking a 25-year lease on Port Arthur (Lushun), Germany a 99-year lease on Tsingtao (Qingdao) and France a 99-year lease on Kwangchow (Hangzhou) Bay (all in 1898).

Remarks

The shock of defeat helped bring about the Chinese Reform Movement, culminating in the Hundred Days of 1898, when a great many reforms were initiated. This reform attempt was stifled by a coup organized by the empress dowager. Japan recognized the necessity of strengthening its diplomatic position in order to forestall another Triple Intervention. It therefore sought an alliance with a European great power and this led eventually to the Anglo-Japanese Alliance of 1902.

Boxer Rebellion 1900

Belligerents: **China**
                              France, Germany, Great Britain, Japan, Russia,
                              United States, Austria-Hungary, Italy

Cause

This rebellion was a reaction by the Chinese against the increasing foreign domination of their country. The Boxers (The Fists of Righteous Harmony) were a grassroots, nationalist secret society. Originally aimed against the ruling Manchu dynasty, it shifted to an anti-foreign emphasis under the slogan 'Cherish the dynasty, exterminate the foreigners'. A focus of the group's anger was the activity of the numerous Christian missionaries. The ruling empress dowager hoped to use the Boxers as the vehicle for removing foreign influence and re-establishing the old order.

Occasion

Violence, first against Chinese Christians and then against missionaries and foreign workers, mounted during early 1900. Alarmed by these developments, the diplomatic legations at Peking (Beijing) requested increased protection from their governments, which had naval forces based down-river at the port of Tientsin (Tianjing). By early June the legations were reporting a fear of attack. Concerns were also expressed for the safety of the foreign community at Tientsin, leading to a demand by the foreign admirals for control of the commanding Taku forts. This was refused, but the forts were taken by storm by an allied force, with only the United States abstaining (17 June 1900). The Chinese government seized on this action as justifying a declaration of war (19 June) and sent imperial troops to join the Boxers. The German envoy, Baron von Kettler, was killed while attempting to see the Chinese government (20 June). The foreign powers, including the United States, ignored the Chinese declaration of war, preferring to state that they were merely acting to restore their treaty rights and to preserve peace.

Course of War

In Peking the foreigners were besieged both in the legation area (containing approximately 450 soldiers, 470 civilians and a few thousand Chinese Christians) and in the Pehtang cathedral compound (where there were 40 marines and 3,000 Chinese Christians). Massacres of Christians and foreigners were occurring simultaneously throughout much of China. The allied forces took control of Tientsin (23 July), and then proceeded with a combined force of 16,000 to march on Peking (4 Aug.), defeating a Chinese army of 10,000 at Yangtsu (5–6 Aug.). Peking fell to the allies (14 Aug.), and the empress fled to Sian (Xi'an) (15 Aug.). Peking suffered extensive looting, first from the Boxers, then from the imperial soldiers and finally from the allies. Meanwhile, when news of Kettler's death reached Germany, a force of 7,000 men was sent out under Field-Marshal Waldersee who acted as allied commander-in-chief. Allied cooperation soon declined into a general grab for influence, however, with Russia in particular taking the opportunity to occupy Manchuria (24 Sept.–10 Oct.).

Political result

The Boxer Protocol (7 Sept. 1901) was signed between China and France, Germany, Great Britain, Japan, Russia, the United States, Austria-Hungary, Italy, Belgium, the Netherlands and Spain. China agreed to the punishment of the leaders of the rebellion and of those who had committed atrocities; the forts between Peking and Tientsin were dismantled; permanent guards for the legations were established; and a large indemnity was levied. The United States later used its share of the indemnity to fund scholarships for Chinese students. This defeat helped precipitate the fall of the Manchu dynasty in 1911.

Russo-Japanese War 1904–5

Belligerents: **Japan**
            Russia

Cause

The collapse of Chinese power during the nineteenth century created a power vacuum in East Asia, which several states attempted to fill. Russian and Japanese encroachment on the fringes of China brought them into conflict at the turn of the twentieth century, with Japan becoming dominant in Korea and Russia in Manchuria. Russian influence in East Asia was enhanced by the construction of the Trans-Siberian railway (1891–1904). The shortest route for this railway to the Russian Pacific seaport of Vladivostok lay across the Chinese province of Manchuria, and this stretch was constructed by the Russian-controlled Eastern China Railway Co. A spur line was built down to Port Arthur (Lushun), on which city Russia obtained a 25-year lease (1898). During the Boxer Rebellion of 1900 Russia occupied all of Manchuria and began to extend its influence into Korea, to the dismay of the Japanese. Japan's position in Korea had been implicitly acknowledged by the Anglo-Japanese Alliance (1902), which provided for joint action if either was in conflict with more than one state. This gave Japan an assurance of benevolent British neutrality in the event of war with Russia, while guaranteeing assistance if Russia's ally, France, entered the fighting.

Occasion

Russo-Japanese negotiations to find a settlement of their conflicting interests ran through most of 1903, without success. Japan finally demanded that Russia evacuate Manchuria, as it was obliged to do under a 1902 treaty with China, and that it recognize Japanese predominance in Korea. Russia rejected these demands and Japan first broke off diplomatic relations (6 Feb. 1904) and then declared war on Russia (10 Feb.).

Course of War

The Japanese launched a surprise attack against Port Arthur, blockading the Russian fleet there (8 Feb.). Russian forces were crippled by extended supply lines, as the only link with Europe was the almost-completed single-track Trans-Siberian railway. After a lengthy siege, the surviving 10,000-man garrison at Port Arthur surrendered (2 Jan. 1905). The siege had cost 59,000 Japanese and 31,000 Russian lives. In a last desperate attempt to reverse the situation the Russians dispatched their Baltic fleet in a dramatic round-the-world voyage to the Pacific (Oct. 1904). Anglo-Russian relations plummeted after the Dogger Bank incident, in which the nervous Russian fleet mistook the British North Sea fishing fleet for a flotilla of Japanese torpedo boats and opened fire. After this inauspicious start the Russian and Japanese fleets met at the climactic battle of Tshushima in the straits between Japan and Korea (27 May 1905). Here the Japanese sank or captured almost the entire Russian fleet in the most decisive naval battle since Trafalgar in 1805. This marked the effective end of the war. Russia itself was now convulsed by political unrest and quite willing to negotiate.

Political result

The Treaty of Portsmouth (5 Sept. 1905) was mediated by the American president, Theodore Roosevelt, who subsequently received the Nobel Peace Prize for his work. By its terms Russia ceded to Japan Port Arthur and the southern half of Sakhalin Island, and recognized Japan's predominance in Korea. Manchuria returned to Chinese control, while Russian railway interests in southern Manchuria were transferred to Japan.

Remarks

Japan's victory was a turning point in history, marking the first defeat of a European great power by a non-European state. For Russia the war resulted in the outbreak of the October Revolution (1905), in which general discontent with the government's inefficiency led to the introduction of constitutional government for the first time. In East Asia Russia ceased to be an important factor until the Second World War brought about the collapse of Japanese military power. Some historians argue that the war led Russia to shift its attention to its European borders and to adopt a more assertive posture in the Balkans, thereby indirectly contributing to the outbreak of the First World War.

Franco-Vietminh War 1946–54

Belligerents: France
North Vietnam (Democratic Republic of Vietnam/ Vietminh)

Cause

The French colonial empire in Indochina consisted of Vietnam, Laos and Cambodia, acquired in part through the Franco-Indochinese Wars of the nineteenth century. During the Second World War the area came under the effective control of the Japanese (July 1941), although a puppet French colonial administration loyal to Vichy France was left nominally in power. As the war drew to a close, however, the Japanese replaced this régime with a Vietnamese government in order to prevent collaboration with the Allies (March 1945). The Vietnamese emperor, Bao Dai, officially proclaimed independence from France and appointed a pro-Japanese government. The communists in Vietnam, led by Ho Chi-minh, had meanwhile formed an effective anti-Japanese resistance movement, the Vietminh, which was strongest in the north, where it had the advantage of a base in China. When Japan surrendered (Aug. 1945), the Vietminh moved quickly to fill the power vacuum and proclaimed an independent Democratic Republic of Vietnam at Hanoi, the chief city of the north. Their control spread rapidly and helped to bring about Bao Dai's abdication (24 Aug.). France, however, hoping to reassert control over Indochina, reoccupied Saigon (later Ho Chi-minh City), the main southern city (22 Sept. 1945), and Hanoi (16 March 1946). Until early 1946 the French benefited from the presence of British soldiers who had originally been dispatched to the area to assist with the surrender of the Japanese forces.

Occasion

The first direct confrontation between the Vietminh and the French occurred when the Vietminh fired on a French warship which was attempting to block the delivery of arms to the main Vietnamese port of Haiphong (20 Nov. 1946). The French retaliated with an aerial attack in which 6,000 Vietnamese were killed. This was followed by a Vietminh offensive against the French, beginning at Hanoi (19 Dec.) and soon spreading across the country. France, in an unsuccessful attempt to assuage the Vietnamese, reorganized its possessions into the Indochinese Federation, which promised greater local autonomy. This was superseded by an agreement to create the Associated State of Vietnam (8 March 1949), which was to have independence in all but foreign and defence matters within the French Union. Most Western powers recognized this government. The Vietminh, however, were determined on full independence and embarked on a guerrilla campaign modeled on the techniques advocated by the Chinese communist leader, Mao Tse-tung (Mao Zedong). The Democratic Republic of Vietnam was recognized by the Soviet Union and the People's Republic of China.

Course of War

The initial phase of the conflict (1947–9) was primarily a guerrilla war which resulted in a stalemate between the combatants. The situation was altered, however, by the communist victory in China, which provided the Vietminh with a powerful ally to the north (Oct. 1949). During 1950 the Vietminh took a number of key places, forcing the French to retreat from most of north Vietnam and to concentrate their forces behind the de Lattre Line, a fortified perimeter controlling the Red river delta. Increasingly, French control throughout the country was being confined to the cities and the maritime fringe.

The financial strain of the war was becoming too great for the French economy, which had as yet not recovered from the Second World War. From 1952 the United States carried much of the financial burden. In a dramatic attempt to turn the tide of the war, the French adopted a plan to entice the Vietminh into an engagement in which they could be crushed. The site selected was Dien Bien Phu, 220 miles west of Hanoi near the border with Laos, to which 15,000 men were dispatched. The Vietminh under General Giap surrounded Dien Bien Phu and brought to bear a heavy concentration of artillery, estimated at 200 guns. The siege of Dien Bien Phu (20 Nov. 1953–7 May 1954) ended with the surrender of the French garrison. This marked the end of French power in Indochina. The war having become increasingly unpopular in France, the government now decided to extricate itself as best it could and agreed a ceasefire (21 June 1954).

Political result

The Geneva Accords (21 July 1954) in effect divided Vietnam into two zones along the 17th parallel. The north, with its capital at Hanoi, was to be ruled by the Democratic Republic of Vietnam (i.e. the Vietminh) and the south, with its capital at Saigon, was to be governed by the State of Vietnam. Officially Vietnam remained one country and the intention was for national elections to be held in July 1956, to be followed by political reunification. The elections were never held.

France's role in the region was slowly replaced by the United States, which became increasingly involved out of a concern to halt any spread of communist rule, viewing this as an extension of Soviet power. The question of the future control of Vietnam thereby became an aspect of the Cold War and led to American involvement in the Vietnam War of 1964–73.

Korean War 1950–3

Belligerents: **North Korea, People's Republic of China**
South Korea, United Nations (United States, Great Britain, Turkey, Canada, Australia, Thailand, France, Greece, New Zealand, Netherlands, Colombia, Belgium, Ethiopia, Luxembourg, South Africa)

Cause

Korea has been a pawn of the Great Powers for most of the twentieth century. After achieving independence from China in 1895 in the wake of the Sino-Japanese War, it was annexed by Japan in 1910 in the aftermath of the Russo-Japanese War. Liberated from the Japanese at the end of the Second World War, it was divided along the 38th parallel, with the north being occupied by Soviet forces and the south by American forces.

Occasion

It was intended by the victorious powers that the country should eventually be unified. By 1947, however, in the prevailing climate of the Cold War, the unification talks had collapsed and a communist Democratic People's Republic of Korea had been established in the north under Kim Il Sung, while a non-communist Republic of Korea was set up in the south under Syngman Rhee. In early 1949 both the United States and the Soviet Union agreed to withdraw their forces from Korea. The North Korean army then invaded across the 38th parallel (25 June 1950). The United Nations Security Council (which the Soviet Union was boycotting over the UN's refusal to admit the new communist Chinese government) condemned the invasion and voted that members should assist in restoring peace. The result was that eventually 15 of the UN's 60 members sent forces to South Korea, by far the largest number being provided by the United States.

Course of War

The tide of battle shifted greatly during the conflict. At first the North Koreans pushed their opponents to the southern end of the Korean peninsula into a pocket around Pusan, until General MacArthur retrieved the situation with his brilliantly-conceived landing at Inchon (15 Sept. 1950), which outflanked the North Koreans. In a successful offensive, MacArthur pushed north to the China-Korea border, formed by the Yalu river, but Chinese units, officially described as 'volunteers', then crossed the Yalu (25 Nov.), rolling back the UN forces to about the 38th parallel, where the front stabilized. Ceasefire talks began in July 1951 but were disrupted by sporadic fighting, an armistice not being agreed until July 1953. The battle toll for the UN forces was 118,000 dead (including 33,720 Americans and 70,000 South Koreans). Communist casualties were estimated at over one million.

Political result

By the terms of the Panmunjon Armistice (27 July 1953), the existing front line became de facto the new frontier. In effect the Korean peninsula was partitioned into two states, each dependent on an alliance with either the United States or the Soviet Union.

Remarks

The real war in Korea increased the international tensions of the Cold War. Although there was Great Power involvement in the conflict, attempts were made to avoid a direct confrontation. The United States fought as part of a UN-mandated action, while the Chinese were officially referred to as volunteers. Soviet ground forces were never directly involved, although they did supply the Chinese. The war also ended any possibility of a normalization of Sino-American relations, which remained antagonistic for the next 20 years.

Malaysian-Indonesian Confrontation 1963–6

Belligerents: **Indonesia**
                    Malaysia, Great Britain, Australia, New Zealand

Cause

Indonesia achieved independence from the Netherlands (1946) under the leadership of Sukarno, who adopted a belligerent foreign policy. During the period 1957–63 Indonesia carried out a policy of harassment of the Dutch in West New Guinea (now Irian Jaya) which finally culminated in its transfer to Indonesia. Almost immediately following this victory Sukarno initiated a similar policy of harassment aimed at Malaya, which had achieved independence from Britain, within the Commonwealth, in 1957.

Occasion

Britain's proposed solution for the future of its northern Borneo territories (Sabah, Sarawak and Brunei) was to join them with Malaya in a new Federation of Malaysia. An abortive revolt in Brunei by opponents of the federation (Dec. 1962) was suppressed by British forces. Indonesian support for the rebels was suspected, as Sukarno had made clear his opposition to the federation. In September 1963 the Federation of Malaysia was, nonetheless, established, including Sabah and Sarawak but not Brunei, which had opted out. As a result, Indonesian-Malaysian diplomatic relations rapidly collapsed, with Sukarno proclaiming that he would 'gobble Malaysia raw' or 'crush Malaysia'.

Course of War

The conflict never involved more than a few battalions of Malaysians and Indonesians, but did include 50,000 British, Gurkha and Commonwealth forces provided by Australia and New Zealand. The fighting was centered primarily in southern Sarawak (Borneo), with occasional Indonesian incursions being repulsed. The British introduction of helicopters was particularly effective. The confrontation dragged on into 1964, with Indonesia threatening intensification of the conflict. Indonesia meanwhile was dissolving into economic chaos and an abortive communist coup led to an army takeover (1 Oct. 1965), with Sukarno slowly being eased from power. The new military leaders began to wind down the conflict, in part because of the domestic fighting which had left between 500,000 and one million dead.

Political result

Peace talks were held in Bangkok (May–August 1966) and achieved a cessation of hostilities (1 June 1966). A pact ending the confrontation was signed at Jakarta (11 Aug.). Diplomatic relations were restored, with Indonesia in effect accepting Sabah and Sarawak's inclusion within Malaysia.

Remarks

Sukarno had claimed that the real enemy was British imperialism and neo-colonialism, which had created a puppet Malaysia. The economic and political strains of the confrontation exacerbated the situation within Indonesia and contributed to the unrest which led to Sukarno's downfall. The attempt to repeat the success of the earlier confrontation with the Netherlands failed because of British firmness. As a result, British prestige was enhanced by its effective support of Malaysia. The new Indonesian government moved rapidly to restore good relations with its neighbors, pursuing a policy of cooperation. Both Malaysia and Indonesia amicably joined in founding ASEAN (Association of South East Asian Nations) in 1967).

Vietnam War 1964–73

Belligerents: **United States, South Vietnam (Republic of Vietnam), Australia, New Zealand, Philippines, South Korea North Vietnam (Democratic Republic of Vietnam), Vietcong**

Cause

A strong anti-colonial movement developed in French Indochina during the 1930s, expanding through resistance work during the Japanese occupation in the Second World War and finally exploding in an uprising in Vietnam after the war's end. In the Franco-Vietminh War of 1946–54 France attempted to maintain its position by force against the rebels, the Vietminh, led by the communist Ho Chi-minh. The escalating struggle culminated in the siege of Dien Bien Phu (20 Nov. 1953–7 May 1954), where the Vietminh defeated a French force. This led to a French decision to withdraw from Indochina. A settlement was reached in the Geneva Accords (21 July 1954), by which Vietnam was divided at the 17th parallel, the north being left under communist rule, the south under a non-communist government. Laos and Cambodia were also recognized as fully independent states.

Occasion

The United States supported the French financially, out of concern that a Vietminh victory would lead to a communist-dominated, pro-Soviet Vietnam. After France's withdrawal, the United States filled the vacuum created, providing military assistance to the South Vietnamese government against the North Vietnamese-backed Vietcong guerrillas operating in the south. America's military presence also grew, from 950 men in 1961, to

15,000 in 1963 and 268,000 in 1966, finally peaking at over 500,000 in 1968–9.

The Tonkin Gulf Incident (2–4 Aug. 1964) brought about a direct confrontation between North Vietnam and the United States. It was reported (the incident is still disputed) that North Vietnamese boats had attacked an American destroyer. In response, the American Congress passed the Tonkin Gulf Resolution (7 Aug.), which authorized 'all necessary measures to repel any armed attack' on United States forces and the giving of assistance where requested under the Southeast Asia Collective Defence Treaty. There followed a dramatic escalation in American troop deployment and American bombing raids of North Vietnam. Several other states joined the American effort.

Course of War

The first American attack on North Vietnam was in retaliation for the Tonkin Gulf Incident (5 Aug. 1964). Bombing raids on the north continued (1965–8), but airpower proved ineffective in cutting off support for the Vietcong guerrillas and North Vietnamese regulars operating in South Vietnam. In the Tet Offensive (30 Jan.–26 Feb. 1968), timed to coincide with the lunar new year festivities, the communist forces attacked over 100 cities and towns. Although they were finally defeated and failed to spark a general uprising, the communists did shake their opponents. Tet forced the Americans to make a choice between undertaking the massive commitment required for victory or considering a negotiated peace. Public opinion in the United States turned against President Johnson, who opted not to seek re-election (31 March 1968). At the same time he suspended the bombing of North Vietnam above the 19th parallel and called for peace talks. These desultory talks were held in Paris (informal talks began 10 May 1968, formal talks 25 Jan. 1969). Much of the time was spent discussing the shape of the negotiating table. The new American president, Nixon, continued the war while a settlement was being considered.

The war expanded with an American invasion of neighboring Cambodia (1 May–29 June 1970) in an attempt to cut North Vietnamese supply lines to the south along the Ho Chi-minh Trail. The Americans were, however, simultaneously reducing their ground forces in Vietnam, thereby responding to growing domestic opposition to the war. The latter was the decisive factor bringing about the American withdrawal from Vietnam. Some have argued that the most important battle of the war was the New Hampshire primary election (1968), which brought about President Johnson's decision to leave office and showed the strength of public opinion about the war.

In 1972 there were hopeful signs in the peace talks, but when these broke down the Americans resumed their aerial bombardment of North Vietnam. This action helped to convince the North Vietnamese to agree to terms and a ceasefire was announced (23 Jan. 1973). Over one million Vietnamese on both sides, some 55,000 Americans and 5,000 other allied soldiers died in the war.

Political result

The Paris Peace Accords (27 Jan. 1973) provided for the withdrawal of all United States forces by the end of March. Under the terms of the ceasefire, both sides retained the ground they held, pending the implementation of vague clauses concerning elections. An international peacekeeping force was to oversee the arrangement. Some skirmishing continued, until a communist offensive (March 1975) toppled the South Vietnamese government and the country was united under a communist régime (30 April 1975). Communist régimes also seized power in Cambodia (April 1975) and Laos (Aug. 1975).

Sino-Soviet Dispute 1969

Belligerents: **China**
                   Soviet Union

Cause

After the Chinese communists took power in 1949 relations between the two great communist powers, the Soviet Union and China, appeared to be close. From 1956, however, relations began to deteriorate for a number of reasons, including the process of de-Stalinization in the Soviet Union initiated by Khrushchev in that year. This was followed by the suspension of Soviet nuclear technological assistance to China (1958). There was also personal rivalry between the Soviet rulers and the Chinese leader, Mao Tse-tung (Mao Zedong), for the leadership of the international communist movement. By 1960 China's relations with the Soviet Union were extremely strained, while it had no relations at all with the United States.

An element in the Sino-Soviet tension was a long-running border dispute. The Chinese government had denounced what it considered to be the 'unequal treaties' concluded in the nineteenth and twentieth centuries, by which various imperial states, including Russia, had obtained Chinese territory. Among the areas claimed by China was territory north of the Amur and Ussuri rivers, including the important Soviet Pacific port of Vladivostok. As part of the growing Sino-Soviet rift, border skirmishes began to occur in the region during 1960; thereafter, tension remained high in this area, as Sino-Soviet relations worsened.

Occasion

Fighting between China and the Soviet Union broke out (March 1969) over an uninhabited island in the Ussuri river, known to the Soviets as Damansky island and to the Chinese as Chenpao (Zhenbao). Each side claimed that this island lay within its frontier.

Course of War

Both participants have given differing accounts of the fighting for the island. It appears that an initial border skirmish (1–2 March 1969) was followed by large-scale fighting, including the use of tanks and artillery (15 March). While talks began on this crisis, sporadic fighting also occurred along the Sino-Soviet Central Asian border (April–Aug.), with a Soviet armored column entering the Chinese province of Sinkiang (Xinjiang) (2 May). The death of Ho Chi-minh of North Vietnam (3 Sept. 1969) provided an opportunity to end the hostilities as a token of respect. During the fighting the Soviet leadership apparently considered the possible use of nuclear weapons and approached the United States for its views. The Americans indicated their opposition to this, and such weapons were never used.

Political result

The Soviet Union, in a diplomatic note (29 March 1969), called for an end to military action. A joint Sino-Soviet commission on the navigation of the Far Eastern rivers met (18 June–8 Aug. 1969) and agreed on the steps to be taken to resume normal trade on the river. After the funeral of Ho Chi-minh, the Soviet premier, Alexei Kosygin, flew to Peking (Beijing) for talks, which led to the resumption of border talks. These were held intermittently during the period 1969–78. Discussions involving the border question have occurred at intervals since then, but no solution has been reached and it remains a possible source of further Sino-Soviet conflict. As a result of this dispute both countries have been forced to maintain vast armies on their 4,000-mile common frontier.

Remarks

The Chinese government under Mao had followed a radical foreign policy, opposed to both the Soviet Union (after 1960) and the United States, which was engaged in the 1964–73 Vietnam War to China's south. The Sino-Soviet split, however, forced China to focus its attention on the long Sino-Soviet frontier, preventing it from playing a significant role in the Vietnam conflict. While supportive of the communist régime in North Vietnam, China remained wary of its pro-Soviet attitude and was concerned by the possibility of strategic encirclement by the Soviet Union. This was a factor in the outbreak of the Sino-Vietnamese War of 1979.

Immediately after the Sino-Soviet Dispute of 1969 the United States sought to improve relations with China, which was now more amenable towards Washington in the light of its problems with the Soviet Union. The main obstacle here was American involvement in Vietnam, but as the United States began to disengage itself from that conflict, so Sino-American relations improved. Secret Sino-American talks began in 1971 and a rapprochement was achieved in 1972, symbolized by the visit of President Nixon to China in that year. Full Sino-American diplomatic relations were re-established in 1978. This dispute therefore provided the United States with an unexpected victory, in that the seeming Sino-Soviet communist monolith of the 1950s was replaced by a Sino-American relationship. It could be argued that the Americans were the only victors in this conflict.

Vietnam-Kampuchea War 1978-9

Belligerents: **Vietnam**
                    Kampuchea (Cambodia)

Cause

The crisis in Cambodia was a by-product of the general upheaval in Indochina which centered on the 1964–73 Vietnam War. With the communist victory in Vietnam, the Cambodian communists (known as the Khmer Rouge) also seized power (April 1975), renaming the country Democratic Kampuchea. Under the leadership of Pol Pot, the Khmer Rouge embarked on a program of radical social reform aimed at ruralizing society, while simultaneously exterminating any part of the population it considered to be contaminated by external ideas. This resulted in the deaths of millions of people in one of the greatest series of massacres in history. In 1978 Pol Pot extended these massacres to eastern Cambodia in the area bordering Vietnam, with the intention of ending what was perceived as Vietnamese influence in that region. Many Cambodians took refuge in Vietnam, leading the Khmer Rouge to launch a series of border raids, which in turn brought about Vietnamese counterattacks. The conflict also reflected Great Power tension, with China supporting Democratic Kampuchea and the Soviet Union backing Vietnam.

Occasion

The Khmer Rouge government broke off diplomatic relations with Vietnam (31 Dec. 1977), and as skirmishing increased Vietnam sponsored the creation of an opposition communist movement (2 Dec. 1978). This was followed by an invasion of Kampuchea by the Vietnamese, aided by the new opposition movement (25 Dec. 1978).

Course of War

The Vietnamese and their Cambodian allies achieved rapid military success, taking the now-depopulated capital of Phnom Penh (7 Jan. 1979) and occupying most of the remainder of the country by the end of January 1979. A new, pro-Vietnamese and pro-Soviet government was established under Heng Samrin, a former supporter of Pol Pot, and the country was renamed the People's Republic of Kampuchea (8 Jan. 1979). The Khmer Rouge continued to hold enclaves along the borders and, together with other opposition groups, continued to fight a guerrilla war against what they saw as a puppet régime. At its maximum deployment, the Vietnamese army in Kampuchea numbered 160,000.

Political result

The new government in Phnom Penh was recognized only by the Soviet Union, its allies and India. A loose grouping of anti-Vietnamese forces was organized under the leadership of Prince Sihanouk, the former ruler, known as the Coalition Government of Democratic Kampuchea (CGDK). The CGDK retained the Cambodian seat at the United Nations, enjoying both United States and Chinese support. Talks between the various sides were held, unsuccessfully, in July 1988. However, the Vietnamese government announced its intention to withdraw its forces (5 April 1989) by 30 September 1989, regardless of whether or not a settlement had been achieved. By that date Vietnamese forces appeared to have been withdrawn. An agreement was signed by the opposing Cambodian factions at Paris (23 Oct. 1991) which provided for UN supervised elections to a new national government, with an interim UN peacekeeping force.

Remarks

The struggle was not only a matter of regional power politics, but acted as a proxy for Great Power rivalry, with all important states playing some role.

Sino-Vietnamese War 1979

Belligerents: China
Vietnam

Cause

This war was partly the result of a long-standing border dispute and partly a product of Sino-Soviet antagonism. The Sino-Vietnamese border had been agreed during the period of French rule in Vietnam by the Peking Convention (1887, with a modification in 1895). Certain areas, however, had never been clearly delimited, and Vietnam subsequently accused China of having encroached on the frontier. The Vietnamese government only turned its attention to this area following Vietnamese unification after the end of the 1964–73 Vietnam War. At the same time, the Vietnamese communist government moved even closer to Moscow. During the Vietnam-Kampuchea War of 1978–9 China gave support to Kampuchea, which helped speed the decline in Sino-Vietnamese relations. In 1978 ethnic Chinese began to flee Vietnam, approximately 200,000 taking refuge in China. This was followed by Vietnam joining the Soviet-led Council for Mutual Economic Assistance (CMEA, or Comecon) (June), the ending of Chinese aid to Vietnam (July) and a Soviet-Vietnamese Treaty of Friendship and Cooperation (Nov.).

Occasion

Vietnamese success in Kampuchea resulted in the establishment of a pro-Vietnamese and pro-Soviet government at Phnom Penh (8 Jan. 1979). This probably triggered the crisis. China hoped to relieve the pressure on its Kampuchean allies, while at the same time teaching Vietnam a military lesson similar to that which it had inflicted on India in the Sino-Indian War of 1962.

Course of War

China invaded Vietnam with an initial force of 75,000 (17 Feb. 1979), eventually committing 200,000 men to the campaign. They were opposed by 50,000 Vietnamese regulars and 50,000 militia. The initial assault carried the Chinese army a short distance into northern Vietnam, where it captured and destroyed the provincial capitals of Langson, Cam Duong and Lao Kay. The Vietnamese army, hoever, put up a strong resistance and China proposed negotiations (1 March) and began to withdraw (5 March).

Political result

After the completion of the Chinese withdrawal (16 March), unsuccessful negotiations for a settlement took place. Fighting continued sporadically, with China often bombarding the border area with up to 10,000 shells a day.

Remarks

The Chinese army (known as the People's Liberation Army), although the largest in the world, had been weakened by domestic upheavals, while

Vietnam possessed a combat-hardened military. The war was effectively a defeat for China, which was unable to dent the Vietnamese military seriously, or even to force Vietnam to redeploy forces from the Kampuchean theater. Some financial stress was inflicted on Vietnam, however, by the destruction of its northern provinces and its need to increase defenses in this area.

10 Middle Eastern Wars

First Arab-Israeli War 1948–9

Belligerents: Israel
                     Egypt, Transjordan, Syria, Lebanon, Iraq

Cause

Palestine formed part of the Ottoman Empire until the end of the First World War, when it was assigned as a League of Nations mandate to Britain (formally effective Sept. 1923). The original purpose was to establish a Jewish homeland, which Britain had supported in the Balfour Declaration (2 Nov. 1917). This plan aroused opposition from the local Arab population, the Palestinians. Britain, mindful that the Balfour Declaration had also promised protection for the rights of non-Jewish communities in Palestine, followed an ambivalent policy in the face of growing Arab-Jewish friction. During the period of the mandate the Jewish population increased from 56,000 to 650,000. After the Second World War pressure mounted for an independent Jewish state, partly in reaction to the holocaust of the European Jews during the war. Britain, however, had begun to back away from the concept of the Balfour Declaration, a 1939 White Paper having resulted in Jewish immigration to Palestine being severely restricted. These regulations remained in force during and after the holocaust. This resulted in a campaign of growing violence on the part of the Jewish settlers, which made Palestine ungovernable and finally forced the British to opt for surrendering the mandate and referring the problem to the United Nations (2 April 1947).

The United Nations responded by establishing a Special Committee on Palestine (UNSCOP) to deal with the matter. UNSCOP recommended partition into Arab and Jewish states, with Jerusalem as an international city under the United Nations. This plan was adopted by the UN General Assembly (29 Nov. 1947) but was rejected by the Arabs. Communal fighting erupted as the British withdrawal was in progress. The surrounding Arab states (including Iraq) agreed on joint military action to prevent the creation of an independent Jewish state (25 April 1948), but took no steps

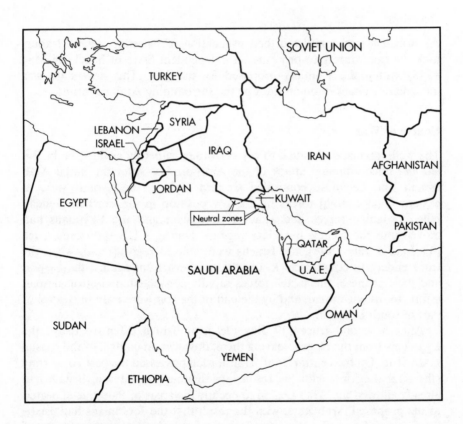

13 Modern Middle East

towards military coordination until the summer. This was due in great measure to the crossed political purposes of the Arab states. These conflicting goals were also shown by the creation in Syria of an Arab Liberation Army (ALA) consisting mostly of Arabs from Palestine. The aim of this force was not only to oppose the creation of Israel but also to block the aspirations of the ruler of Transjordan, Abdullah, to a Transjordanian/ Palestinian kingdom.

Occasion

As British forces completed their evacuation of Palestine, Jewish leaders took the opportunity to proclaim an independent State of Israel (14 May 1948) within the frontiers proposed by the UN. This new state was immediately attacked on all sides by the surrounding Arab countries.

Course of War

The well-commanded Israeli forces performed superbly against the badly-led and uncoordinated attack of the Arab armies. After the initial Arab assault, the Lebanese controlled western Galilee, the Syrians were in eastern Galilee, Iraqi forces held a key position in the northern Judean hills, Jordanian forces had attacked Jerusalem and the Egyptians had moved into the Negev and Gaza regions. During a UN-sponsored truce (11 June–9 July 1948), the Israelis were able to regroup and, when the truce ended, to counterattack. On the northern front against the Syrians and the Lebanese, the Israeli forces rapidly consolidated control, despite efforts to dislodge them, and by the end of the war were even in control of part of south Lebanon.

After a second truce (17 July–Oct.), an Israeli offensive drove the Egyptians from the Negev, leaving them, however, in control of the coastal Gaza Strip. On the central front, Transjordan possessed the best Arab army (the Arab Legion), with the result that fighting was intense. Britain had already allowed the Arab Legion to occupy the areas of Palestine allocated to the proposed Arab state, with the result that the Jordanians had established control over the West Bank of the Jordan and over the old city of Jerusalem (east Jerusalem), while the Israelis held the western part of the city.

A ceasefire agreed with Egypt effectively ended the war (7 Jan. 1949). Arab casualties are unknown, but Israel suffered 6,000 dead (including 2,000 civilians), which remains the highest total ever suffered by Israel in a war.

Political result

Armistices were concluded under United Nations auspices with Egypt (24 Feb. 1949), Lebanon (23 March), Transjordan (3 April) and Syria (20

July). Iraq refused an armistice but agreed to a truce (18 July). Israel was left in control of all the areas allotted to it by the UN, together with western Galilee and part of Jerusalem. Under the armistice terms, Egypt and Transjordan (now renamed Jordan) divided the areas of the Palestine mandate not occupied by Israel. Egypt took the Gaza Strip and Jordan the West Bank. Jordan subsequently officially annexed its part of Arab Palestine (24 April 1950).

Remarks

This Arab defeat was a contributory factor in the overthrow of the Egyptian monarchy by officers who had served in the war, and the formation of a radical government (1952). In Syria the defeat led to political instability, involving three coups during 1949 alone. At least 700,000 (and possibly almost 1 million) Palestinian Arabs fled as refugees to neighboring Arab states. This in turn led to anti-Jewish pressures in Arab countries, causing about an equal number of Jews to flee to Israel.

In general the war marked the end of centuries of imperial control of the Middle East, first by the Ottomans and then by the British and French. The removal of external controls unleashed a complex series of forces which have left the Middle East one of the most volatile areas in the world, subject to inter-Arab as well as Arab-Israeli tensions.

Suez War (Second Arab-Israeli War) 1956

Belligerents: **France, Great Britain, Israel**
                    Egypt

Cause

The Middle East continued to be the center of a complex web of conflicts after the First Arab-Israeli War of 1948–9. The Egyptian monarchy had been overthrown in 1952 and Colonel Nasser became president in 1954. Nasser's government embarked on a campaign of escalating confrontation with Israel. Palestinian *fedayeen* ('self-sacrificing') units were formed to carry out attacks within Israel. Egypt also blocked Israeli shipping from passing through the Suez Canal, or out of the Gulf of Aqaba at Sharm el-Sheikh, to the Red Sea (Sept. 1955). Nasser began to build up the Egyptian army with arms purchased from Soviet-controlled Czechoslovakia (1955), a move which also worried the Western powers. France had poor relations with Egypt, because of the latter's support for the insurgents in Algeria fighting for independence from French rule. Britain likewise had poor relations with Egypt, which generally opposed British influence and pro-British régimes in the region.

Occasion

In accordance with a 1954 Anglo-Egyptian treaty, Britain withdrew its last forces from the Suez Canal (13 June 1956). This was soon (26 July) followed by Nasser's decision to nationalize the Suez Canal (jointly owned by Britain and France) in order to raise the funds to build a vast hydro-electric complex at Aswan. Britain, France and Israel therefore considered joint action against their common enemy. The result was Anglo-French-Israeli collusion in the secret Sèvres Protocol (24 Oct.). Under this plan Israel would attack Egypt, advancing to the canal, and Britain and France would then demand that the belligerents should each withdraw from the canal area, to ensure its protection. For the purposes of enforcement, an Anglo-French force would intervene to take control of the canal under the 1954 Anglo-Egyptian treaty, which allowed intervention if the security of the canal was threatened. Israel duly initiated the scheme by attacking Egypt (29 Oct.).

Course of War

Israeli forces were extremely successful, quickly reaching the Suez Canal (2 Nov.) and taking Sharm el-Sheikh (5 Nov.), thereby reopening the Gulf of Aqaba. In accordance with the collusion scheme, an Anglo-French ultimatum had been given (30 Oct.), but it was not until 5 November that an Anglo-French force landed, by airdrop, near the canal. This was followed by an amphibious landing (6 Nov.). Meanwhile, both the United States and the Soviet Union, in a rare act of concurrence, demanded a ceasefire through the UN (2 Nov.). In the face of such international pressure, particularly that from the United States, the British and French agreed to desist and a ceasefire was agreed (midnight, 6 Nov.). Casualties included at least 1,600 Egyptian, 189 Israeli and 26 Anglo-French dead. In addition, over 6,000 Egyptians were taken prisoner by Israel, which also captured most of the Egyptians' tanks and heavy weapons.

Political result

A United Nations Emergency Force (UNEF) was dispatched to separate the belligerents in the Sinai (15 Nov.). The Anglo-French force was soon evacuated (Dec. 1956) and Israeli forces withdrew from Egypt (Jan. 1957) and from the Gaza Strip (March 1957). Although Israeli forces withdrew, the Gulf of Aqaba was opened and the United States guaranteed that it would remain so. The Suez Canal was cleared by a UN salvage fleet and reopened (March 1957).

Remarks

A more rapid Anglo-French response might have won the day. The delay in actually landing forces allowed international opinion to mount against them. The Soviet Union took the opportunity caused by this distraction to crush the liberal Hungarian government, which was attempting to break from the Soviet bloc. In the Middle East, British and French prestige was badly damaged by their humiliating withdrawal. Only Israel gained, by reopening its sea-lanes and removing the *fedayeen* threat. The British prime minister, Anthony Eden, who had supported the intervention, resigned (9 Jan. 1957).

Six Day War (Third Arab-Israeli War) 1967

Belligerents: **Israel**
                    Egypt, Jordan, Syria

Cause

The long-running Arab-Israeli tensions again began to mount during 1966–7. A coup in Syria had brought the radical wing of the Ba'ath party to power (23 Feb. 1966). Determined to demonstrate its ability to be tough with Israel, the new government initiated bombardment of Israeli settlements from the vantage of Syrian bases in the Golan Heights. An Egyptian-Syrian alliance directed against Israel was also concluded (Nov. 1966). An inaccurate Soviet report to Egypt (13 May 1967) that Israel was massing troops on the Syrian border caused President Nasser to reinforce Egyptian positions on the Israeli border (14 May). Nasser then ordered the withdrawal of the United Nations Emergency Force (UNEF) which separated Israel and Egypt (18 May) and reimposed an Egyptian blockade on the Gulf of Aqaba from the Egyptian base at Sharm el-Sheikh, thereby blocking Israel's access to the Red Sea (23 May). Jordan concluded a mutual security pact with Egypt (30 May) and many other Arab states promised their support. War was inevitable under these conditions.

Occasion

Israel, seeing war as inevitable, decided on a pre-emptive strike, launching its attack on 5 June 1967.

Course of War

In a remarkable six-day campaign Israel defeated all of its adversaries. The Egyptian, Syrian and Jordanian airforces were destroyed, mostly on the ground, leaving Israel with complete air superiority. Within four days the Israelis reached the Suez Canal (9 June). Israel also defeated the Jordanian forces, who were under Egyptian command, and seized the West Bank of the Jordan and east Jerusalem. In the last two days of the war Israel focused on Syria, taking the Golan Heights, with some Israeli units advancing to within 40 miles of the Syrian capital, Damascus (10 June). Iraq and Saudi Arabia contributed token forces to the Arab side. The war ended with a UN-sponsored ceasefire. Israeli deaths in the war were 705; the combined Arab death toll was between 20,000 and 25,000.

Political result

The Arab states refused to negotiate with Israel, which they had never recognized. This left Israel in occupation of the Sinai, the West Bank and the Golan Heights. The Suez Canal, blocked by the Egyptians during the fighting, remained closed, causing a serious fall in revenues.

Remarks

Egypt followed this defeat with a 'war of attrition' against Israel (1968–70). This was ended by an American-negotiated ceasefire (8 Aug. 1970) and the death of President Nasser of Egypt (28 Sept. 1970).

October War (Fourth Arab-Israeli War) 1973

Belligerents: **Egypt, Syria**
                     Israel

Cause

The war of attrition which followed the Six Day War was ended by a ceasefire (8 Aug. 1970). The Egyptians then moved their lines forward so as to be able to cover any crossing of the Suez Canal, while the Israelis constructed a defensive line, the Bar-Lev Line, across the Sinai. President Sadat of Egypt concluded that in order to obtain a satisfactory negotiated settlement with Israel, Egypt would first need to achieve passable military success. It was hoped that Israel would then be persuaded to negotiate a settlement which would lead to a return of the occupied Egyptian territories.

Occasion

President Sadat of Egypt and President Assad of Syria met in Cairo (12 Sept. 1973) and agreed on a date for the commencement of war. This was followed by Egyptian and Syrian maneuvers and troop concentrations which were considered routine by Israel: Sadat had announced Egypt's intention to attack so frequently that these latest actions were dismissed. The Egyptian attack was launched on Yom Kippur (6 Oct.), the Jewish day of atonement.

Course of War

Egyptian forces achieved total tactical surprise. The Egyptian army crossed the Suez Canal, while Syrian forces moved across the Golan Heights. The war saw one of the largest tank battles in history, in which the Egyptians, after establishing themselves across the canal, launched an offensive, deploying 2,000 tanks, which was repulsed by the Israelis (14 Oct.). Israel now counterattacked with a thrust across the Suez Canal, establishing a bridgehead on the African side and moving to encircle the Egyptian army. This forced the Egyptians to request a ceasefire, which was arranged by the American secretary of state, Henry Kissinger. In the north the Syrians were also initially successful, but were soon halted by the Israelis (8–9 Oct.) and then driven back by an Israeli counteroffensive (10–12 Oct.). The Arab allies were assisted in the war by token units from Iraq, Jordan, Morocco and Saudi Arabia. A ceasefire, after one failed attempt (22 Oct.), finally came into effect on 24 October.

Political result

Henry Kissinger negotiated disengagement agreements between Israel and Egypt (17 Jan. 1974 and 4 Sept. 1975) and between Israel and Syria (31 May 1974). The first of these enabled Egypt to reopen the Suez Canal (5 June 1974). The Camp David Accords (17 Sept. 1978), an Egyptian-Israeli agreement negotiated by the American President Jimmy Carter at the presidential retreat at Camp David, was followed by a peace treaty signed at Washington (26 March 1979). The settlement arranged for a phased restoration of the pre-1967 Israeli-Egyptian frontiers, which was completed on 25 April 1982. The Gaza Strip, however, remained under Israeli administration. Israel was guaranteed free passage of the Suez Canal and normal diplomatic relations between Egypt and Israel were established for the first time (Feb. 1980). Another agreement aimed at resolving the status of the other territories occupied by Israel since 1967 was never implemented, due to the failure of Jordan, Lebanon and Syria to enter into negotiations.

Remarks

The war also involved a dangerous confrontation between the superpowers. During the hostilities the Soviet Union conducted a massive airlift of supplies to Egypt, as did the United States to Israel. As Egyptian forces began to be pushed back, the Soviet Union informed the United States that it would respond to an Egyptian request for assistance by deploying forces (23 Oct.). If this had happened, the result would have been a Soviet-Israeli war. The United States replied with a counter-threat, placing American forces on alert (25 Oct.). In the face of this response the Soviet Union backed down.

During the war the Arab oil-producing states utilized the economic weapon of embargoing or restricting the sale of oil to the United States and Western Europe, in the hope that this would cause the governments concerned to apply pressure on Israel. Although the embargo was lifted in 1974, oil prices had in the meantime risen fourfold, introducing a new age of higher energy prices with consequences for many countries far beyond the realm of the Arab-Israeli conflict. In the longer term, the greatest distress was suffered by poor developing states whose economies were devastated by higher energy costs.

President Sadat's peace settlement with Israel was not popular either in the Arab world or among some Egyptians. Two-and-a-half years after its signature, he was assassinated by Muslim fundamentalists (6 Oct. 1981).

Lebanon Conflict 1976–

Belligerents: **Israel**
                      Syria, Palestine Liberation Organization (PLO)
                      Lebanon

Cause

Lebanon dissolved into a state of civil war in early 1975. This brought about the involvement of a number of external forces in Lebanese politics, in addition to the domestic factions. The civil war in general was focused on a confrontation between the Christian and Moslem communities in the country, but within this dispute there also exists a changing kaleidoscope of factions. The Palestine Liberation Organization (PLO), which had established its main base in Beirut after being expelled from Jordan in 1970, initially remained aloof from the conflict but eventually gave its support to the left-oriented Moslem Lebanese factions, although opposing the pro-Syrian Moslem groups. As the civil war developed Syria was increasingly drawn in. The Christian Maronite community turned to Syria for help and this resulted in Syrian intervention, in part to crush the PLO (1 June 1976). Fighting continued until a ceasefire sponsored by the Arab League took effect (21 Oct. 1976), after 50 previous ceasefires had failed. The Arab Deterrent Force (ADF), an Arab League peacekeeping force of 30,000 men (mostly Syrian), was deployed (from Oct. 1976). This phase of the conflict cost about 60,000 dead.

The Palestinians, having been checked in the Beirut area, now focused their activities on the portion of Lebanon south of the Litani river, bordering Israel. The Syrians had meanwhile resolved their differences with the PLO and broken with the Christians. After a Palestinian terrorist raid into Israel (11 March 1978), Israeli forces entered southern Lebanon, seeking to crush the PLO forces there (14 March). To separate the combatants, the UN set up and deployed UNIFIL (United Nations Interim Force in Lebanon) (22 March). Israeli forces withdrew (June 1978), but transferred their positions to a pro-Israeli, Maronite Christian militia, the South Lebanon Army (SLA).

In 1981 fighting erupted between the right-wing Christian Phalangist forces and the Syrians in the area around Beirut and in the Bekaa valley. Control of the Bekaa valley by a friendly group was considered by Syria as essential to its own security. Fighting also occurred around the town of Zahle in the Bekaa valley, which had been taken by the Phalange, leading to an attack by the Syrians and Palestinians. A United States sponsored ceasefire (24 July 1981) brought about the evacuation of the town, which was then occupied by the Lebanese army.

Occasion

The preoccupation of the major powers during the Falklands War (April–June 1982) provided an opportunity for Israel to strike against the PLO bases in Lebanon. The immediate occasion was the attempted assassination of the Israeli ambassador in London by Arab terrorists (3 June).

Course of War

The three-pronged Israeli invasion (6 June 1982) was remarkably successful, taking Tyre (7 June), Sidon (8 June) and surrounding Beirut (14 June). The Israelis then settled down to a two-month siege of Beirut, heavily bombarding west Beirut, where the Palestinian forces were located. The Lebanese civil war continued in tandem with this PLO-Israeli confrontation. The evacuation of the PLO was negotiated by the United States and a former Lebanese premier, Saeb Salam. After it began (22 Aug.), amid increasing chaos, the Phalangist leader, Bashir Gemayel, was elected president of Lebanon, partly through the absence of Moslem deputies (23 Aug.). Before he could take office, however, he was assassinated, with 60 others, in a bomb explosion (14 Sept.). The following day the Israeli army occupied Beirut. The Phalangist forces took the opportunity to enter the Palestinian refugee camps at Sabra and Chatila and massacred the inhabitants (16 Sept.). The international outcry at this event forced the Israelis to withdraw to the outskirts of the city. This left the country occupied by the Syrians in the north and the Israelis in the south, while simultaneously a bloody civil war was being conducted among the Lebanese.

Political result

Negotiations began in 1983 between the Lebanese and Israeli governments for the withdrawal of Israeli forces from Lebanon. No lasting agreement was reached, but Israel did redeploy its forces south of Beirut along the Awali river. This created a power vacuum, resulting in severe fighting between Christian and Druze militias. The PLO, meanwhile, had been going through a power struggle and fighting between rival Palestinian factions occurred (May 1982–Dec. 1983). Finally the PLO chairman, Yasser Arafat, was besieged by opposing PLO forces in the Lebanese port of Tripoli until a truce was arranged which allowed the evacuation of his supporters to other Arab states. A Multi-National Force (MNF) was deployed to protect the refugees, with troops being provided by France (2,000 men), Italy (2,000), the United States (1,600) and Britain (100). Both the French and Americans suffered heavily from fanatical Moslem attacks. The MNF was withdrawn (Feb.–March 1984). The civil war, however, increased in intensity, with the Lebanese government increasingly losing power and authority to the various factional militias.

For Israel the cost of maintaining its army in Lebanon, both financially and in terms of casualties, finally forced it to announce its intention of withdrawing without first obtaining a similar pledge from Syria. A phased Israeli withdrawal was conducted (Feb.–June 1985). The pro-Israeli SLA, however, was left in control of part of southern Lebanon. Syrian forces remain in Lebanon and have continued to play a significant role in the convoluted politics of the continuing Lebanese civil war.

North Yemen-South Yemen Dispute 1979

Belligerents: **Yemen Arab Republic (YAR or North Yemen)**
People's Democratic Republic of Yemen (PDRY or South Yemen)

Cause

The two Yemens had an uneasy relationship, dating from when the PDRY, formerly the British colony of Aden, became independent (1967). There was suspicion of PDRY involvement in the assassination of the YAR president, al-Ghashmi, reportedly by a bomb in a suitcase carried by a PDRY envoy (24 June 1978). This was used as an excuse by PDRY dissidents two days later to depose President Rubai Ali, who was later executed.

Occasion

The new president of the YAR, Lieutenant-Colonel Ali Abdullah, survived an assassination attempt (Sept. 1978) and a coup attempt (Oct.), in both of which episodes PDRY involvement was suspected. Tension increased with a series of border clashes (Oct. 1978–Jan. 1979), finally erupting into open warfare (Feb. 1979).

Course of War

The YAR received support from Saudi Arabia, which went on alert and recalled its detachment from the Arab League forces in Lebanon. The United States also rushed supplies to the YAR, all paid for by Saudi Arabia. The pro-Soviet PDRY benefited from the presence of Soviet bloc advisers (1,000 Soviet, 500–700 Cuban and 100 East German). In addition, a YAR opposition group, the National Democratic Front (NDF), based in the PDRY, also assisted the PDRY effort. To show its support for Saudi Arabia, the United States sent a naval task force to the area. This crisis coincided with President Carter's mediation efforts between Egypt and Israel, resulting in the Camp David Accords, and these actions were meant to reassure America's ally, Saudi Arabia. A mediation effort by Iraq, Jordan and Syria led to an abortive ceasefire (2 March). Fighting was finally halted under an Arab League sponsored ceasefire (effective 17 March), supervised by Arab League patrols.

Political result

At a meeting of the two Yemeni heads of state in Kuwait it was agreed that the best solution was eventual unification (30 March 1979). Constitutional and unification talks went on until 1982, when a constitution was agreed for the proposed new unified Yemeni republic. Despite these talks NDF activity continued, with attacks on some YAR towns in 1982. Unification of the two states as the Republic of Yemen finally occurred in 1990.

First Gulf War (Iran-Iraq War) 1980–8

Belligerents: **Iran**
                    Iraq

Cause

The Iran-Iraq border along the Shatt al Arab waterway had long been a matter of dispute, with Iraq claiming sovereignty over the eastern bank while Iran claimed that the border was the centerline (or thalweg) of the waterway. In the Algiers Agreement (1975), Iraq agreed to accept the centerline of the deep-water channel of the Shatt al Arab as the border, in return for Iran ending its support of Kurdish rebels in Iraq. The Iranian Islamic revolution led by the Ayatollah Khomeni (1979) brought about a deterioration in relations. The now-dethroned shah of Iran had built up Iranian military power in close alignment with the West, proclaiming his intention to act as the 'policeman of the Gulf'. Under Khomeni, Iran's break with the West, and its internal revolutionary turmoil, weakened its military capabilities. This provided an opportunity for the Iraqi leader,

Saddam Hussein, to attempt to assert a more dominant role to regain control of the Shatt al Arab, possibly to take Khuzestan and to block the threat of Iranian Shiite fundamentalism.

Occasion

Tension began to rise by mid-1979, with ethnic clashes occurring in Iran's predominantly Arab Khuzestan province, bordering Iraq. This was followed by border clashes (June–Aug. 1980), the Iranian shelling of Iraqi border areas (Sept.), the Iraqi abrogation of the Algiers Agreement (17 Sept.) and finally a full-scale Iraqi invasion of Iran (22 Sept.)

Course of War

The first six weeks of the war saw the Iraqi forces advance, capturing Khorramshahr (24 Oct. 1980), before coming to a halt near Abadan, the chief Iranian oil city, and Ahwaz, the capital of Khuzestan. A stalemate ensued until May 1981, followed by an Iranian counteroffensive (May 1981–June 1982) which recaptured virtually all the lost territory, including Khorramshah (24 May 1982). During 1981–8 Iraq fought a defensive war against annual Iranian spring offensives. Iraq's response included the use of poison gas, one of the few uses of this weapon since the First World War.

Iranian policy was committed to the overthrow of the Iraqi president, Saddam Hussein, and an opposition group, the Supreme Assembly of Islamic Revolution in Iraq (SAIRI), was established at Teheran (17 Nov. 1982). Subsequent Iranian offensives gained ground in Iraqi Kurdistan, while the major Iranian victories were the capture of one of Iraq's chief oilfields, Majnoon Island (1 March 1984) and of the Fao peninsula, an important prewar oilport (10 Feb. 1986). A major Iranian offensive against the key Iraqi city of Basra, preceded by heavy bombardment and involving heavy assaults, failed to capture the city (Jan.–Feb. 1987). Another phase of the conflict was the 'war of the cities' (1985–7), focusing on civilian targets, including aerial and missile attacks on the Iranian capital, Teheran, and the Iraqi capital, Baghdad.

A different aspect of the struggle was the Tanker War, which began in 1984 with an Iraqi attack on Iranian tankers and the Iranian oil terminal at Kharg Island. This led to Iranian attacks on Kuwaiti and other tankers suspected of transporting Iraqi oil. In 1987 the United States deployed a naval force to protect Kuwaiti oil tankers in the Gulf, and Great Britain, France, Belgium, Italy and the Netherlands all sent naval vessels to assist in the protection of international shipping.

In the final phase of the war (Spring 1988), an Iranian offensive in Iraqi Kurdistan penetrated just short of the reservoir supplying Baghdad, being halted in part by the use of poison gas. A simultaneous Iraqi offensive in the south regained much lost territory, including the Fao peninsula (17–18

April 1988) and Majnoon Island (26 June 1988). In July 1988 the belligerents accepted a UN-sponsored ceasefire, which took effect on 20 August.
Casualties in the war are disputed; one figure suggests that Iran suffered
400,000–600,000 dead to Iraq's 150,000, while others suggest a combined
total of up to one million dead.

Political result

UN Security Council Resolution 598 (20 July 1987) formed the basis of
the settlement. It called for an immediate ceasefire and the withdrawal of
forces to the prewar boundaries. Iraq accepted the resolution (22 July
1987), but Iran did not do so until 18 July 1988. The implementation of
the ceasefire was overseen by UNIIMOG (United Nations Iran-Iraq
Military Observer Group). Peace talks began (25 Aug. 1975), but soon
became deadlocked over the validity of the 1975 Algiers Agreement. After
the outbreak of the Second Gulf War (Kuwait Crisis) in 1990, Iraq moved
to secure its Iranian flank by concluding a settlement (15 Aug. 1990). This
led to the return by Iraq of all Iranian territory still under its control,
together with the acceptance both of the terms of UN Security Council
Resolution 598 and of the 1975 Algiers Agreement.

Second Gulf War (Kuwait Crisis) 1990–1

Belligerents:　**Iraq**

**Kuwait, United States, Argentina, Australia, Bahrain,
Bangladesh, Belgium, Canada, Czechoslovakia,
Denmark, Egypt, France, Great Britain, Greece,
Honduras, Italy, Morocco, the Netherlands, New
Zealand, Niger, Norway, Oman, Saudi Arabia,
Senegal, Spain, Syria, Turkey, United Arab Emirates**

Cause

The origins of this war lie in a long-running territorial dispute between Iraq
and Kuwait. Modern-day Iraq under the Ottoman Empire comprised the
provinces (*vilayets*) of Basra, Baghdad and Mosul, with Kuwait lying
within Basra province. At the end of the nineteenth century Kuwait broke
away from the Ottoman Empire, and became a protectorate of Great
Britain (1899). After the collapse of the Ottoman Empire, Iraq became a
British-administered mandate of the League of Nations, becoming
independent in 1932. At the time of Iraq's independence the border
between Iraq and Kuwait was agreed by an exchange of letters, but the
validity of this agreement was subsequently disputed by Iraq. When Kuwait
became a fully sovereign state (19 June 1961) the Iraqi president, General
Kassem, laid claim to the entire country (25 June), on the basis that it had

originally formed an integral part of Basra province. In response to a fear of Iraqi military action, Great Britain, and subsequently Saudi Arabia, dispatched troops to protect Kuwait. After Kassem's overthrow (3 Feb. 1963) the new Iraqi government recognized Kuwait's sovereignty, although Iraq never fully gave up its claim to certain important areas. The most important of these were two islands, Bubiyan and Warba, which were important for controlling Iraqi access to the Persian Gulf. In 1973 Iraq occupied a Kuwaiti border post in the disputed region, but was forced to withdraw through diplomatic pressure. Iraqi attention was diverted from these claims by its war with Iran of 1980–8 during which it received substantial financial support from Kuwait. With the ending of that conflict, however, the Iraqi leader, Saddam Hussein, turned his attention to Kuwait.

Occasion

Tension between Iraq and Kuwait began to increase during the first half of 1990. Iraq accused Kuwait of stealing significant amounts of oil from the southern Rumaila oilfield on their border, of contributing to a glut of oil on the world market, which adversely affected the price of Iraqi oil exports, and of refusing to cancel repayment of the interest-free loans extended to Iraq during its war with Iran. As tension mounted, the Kuwaiti army was put on alert (18 July) while at the same time Iraq moved 30,000 men to the border. A solution seemed imminent after a resolution of the oil production dispute was achieved through OPEC (Organization of Petroleum Exporting Countries) (26–27 July). An Iraqi-Kuwaiti meeting (31 July) broke down, however, after only two hours. In the meanwhile, Iraq had continued to mass forces on the border and, despite numerous assurances that it would not do so, invaded Kuwait (2 Aug.).

Course of War

The war falls into four phases: 1) the initial Iraqi invasion (2 Aug.); 2) a period of diplomatic activity and military buildup (3 Aug. 1990–15 Jan. 1991); 3) the air war (16 Jan.–23 Feb.); and finally 4) the anti-Iraq coalition's assault and victory (24–7 Feb.). The Iraqi invasion was quick and effective, overrunning Kuwait by the end of the first day. The amir and crown prince fled to Saudia Arabia, where a government in exile was established. The Iraqi occupation authorities made a brief effort to establish a collaborationist government, known as the Provisional Free Government of Kuwait, before annexing the country (8 Aug.). The UN Security Council acted immediately to condemn Iraq's invasion, voting to impose sanctions against Iraq and to demand its evacuation of Kuwait (6. Aug.). There was concern that Iraqi forces might, in the wake of their initial victory against Kuwait, also move against Saudi Arabia, and several countries rushed troops to defend this oil-rich kingdom. The United States took the lead in deciding to send forces (7 Aug.) in an operation code-named Desert Shield. The American president, George Bush, was adamant in opposing the aggression committed by Iraq and it was under United States leadership that a broadbased anti-Iraq coalition was organized. One by-product of the recent end of the Cold War was Soviet acquiescence to the collective security actions being taken against its erstwhile Iraqi ally. The UN Security Council voted, in the face of continued Iraqi occupation of Kuwait, to authorize the use of 'all necessary means' to remove Iraq (29 Nov.). This coincided with a massive coalition, and particularly American, military buildup in the region, with ground forces being based in Saudi Arabia.

The United States Congress authorized the President to use force (12 Jan. 1991), and after the expiry of the deadline set for Iraqi withdrawal a massive air campaign was launched against Iraq (16. Jan.) in Operation Desert Storm. These attacks were launched from air and missile bases inside Saudi Arabia, and from ships in the Persian Gulf and Red Sea. The assault was soon broadened by the opening of what amounted to a second front with attacks from bases in Turkey (18. Jan.). This air campaign did much to destroy Iraq's military capability. While Iraq was only able to put up marginal opposition, it retaliated by launching Scud missiles (i.e. old Soviet-made missiles) against Israel and Saudi Arabia. By attacking Israel, Iraq hoped to broaden the conflict and rally Arab support behind Iraq against a traditional enemy. Israel, however, refused to be drawn into the conflict, and the Arab members of the coalition stood firm. Iraq did mount one small, and ultimately unsuccessful, offensive into the border area of Saudi Arabia around the town of Khafji (29 Jan.–2 Feb.).

The final phase of the war was a remarkable 100-hour campaign which rapidly enveloped the Iraqi forces in Kuwait and saw their total defeat. The commander of the coalition forces, and the individual most responsible for the successful plan of attack, was the American general, Norman Schwarz-kopf. It was preceded by a masterful plan of deception to convince Iraq that the main assault would be seaborne. Soon after the beginning of the air war Iraq's reconnaissance ability was effectively destroyed, and it continued to plan for an amphibious assault, unable to see the nature of coalition deployments. In fact, the main attack came on land. President Bush set a deadline (23 Feb.) for Iraq to withdraw from Kuwait or face a ground war. When this was not met land operations commenced (24 Feb.). Over 200,000 coalition forces operating over a 300-mile front destroyed much of the Iraqi military and liberated Kuwait. Many Iraqi officers deserted their men, and Iraqi soldiers engaged in wholesale surrenders. One factor in the coalition's success was the activity of special forces operating behind Iraqi lines in the lead-up to the attack. In addition, two days prior to the final coalition assault, over 3,000 US Marines had pene-trated 10 miles (15km) into Kuwait.

With the war's aim achieved, President Bush announced a unilateral cessation of hostilities (27 Feb.). Coalition casualties in this war were under

150 killed in action, while some estimates of Iraqi deaths went as high as 100,000.

Political result

Iraq accepted President Bush's ceasefire offer and agreed to discuss terms (28 Feb.). A meeting was held between Iraqi and coalition military leaders (3 March) which resulted in a formal ceasefire arrangement. Among other terms, Iraq renounced its annexation of Kuwait and accepted liability for the damage caused by its invasion and annexation attempt. The UN Security Council, in Resolution 687 (3 April), adopted a plan for a permanent ceasefire in the region, reaffirmed Iraq's financial responsibilities, and in order to limit Iraq's military capacity demanded the destruction of any nuclear, biological or chemical weapons. A UN peacekeeping force (UNIKOM) was established to guard the demilitarized zone to be established on the Iraq-Kuwait border. This was the first peacekeeping force in UN history to include soldiers from all five permanent Security Council members. Iraq accepted all the UN terms (6 April), needing to turn its attention to pressing domestic problems. With the defeat of Iraq, a number of unsuccessful revolts began against the rule of Saddam Hussein, in particular by the Kurds in the north, and the Shiite Moslems in the southern border area with Iran. The need to deal with the refugee problem caused by these revolts led to continuing foreign deployment in Iraq's border areas.

11 West African Colonial Wars

Ashanti Wars 1824–1900

Belligerents: **Great Britain**
                     Ashanti (Asante) Confederation

Cause

The Ashanti kingdom was formed in the seventeenth century in the region of modern Ghana, steadily expanding during the eighteenth century until it came to dominate most neighboring groups, although the Fante of the coastal region came under British domination. The Ashanti began a push to the coast from 1807, which brought them increasingly into conflict with Britain, which had trading posts and forts there. In 1821 the British government assumed direct control of these posts and forts and a new governor, Sir Charles Macarthy, began to organize the Fante to resist the Ashanti.

First Ashanti War 1824–31

Occasion

The war grew out of an incident in which an Ashanti trader verbally abused the governor to a policeman, who in turn abused the Ashanti ruler (May 1822). The policeman was later kidnapped (Nov. 1822) and killed by Ashanti (Feb. 1823). As a result, Macarthy resolved on war with the Ashanti, who in turn decided to strike first. British power was only effective on the maritime fringe of Africa, where its naval strength could assist; inland its military dominance was not so clear. An Ashanti army began the war with an invasion of Fante country (Dec. 1823).

Course of War

The Ashanti advanced on the coast in 12 columns. Macarthy's forces were poorly deployed and he unexpectedly encountered the main Ashanti army

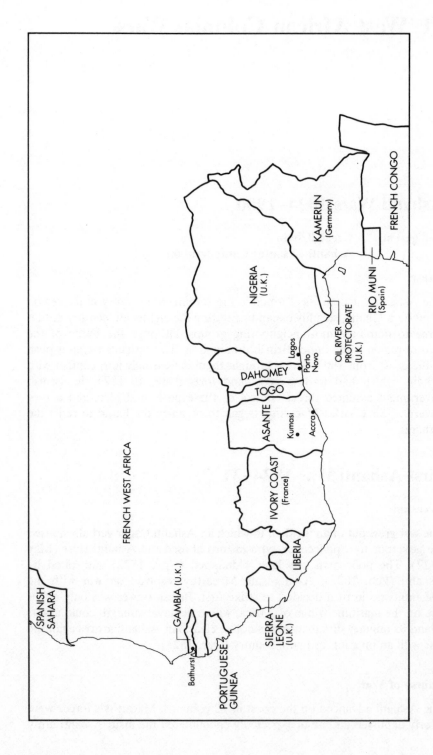

14 Colonial West Africa

of 10,000, with only 500 of his own men, at Essamko (Bonsaso). In the ensuing engagement (21 Jan. 1824) Macarthy's forces were defeated and Macarthy killed himself to avoid capture (his skull later being made into a royal drinking cup for the Ashanti ruler). The British defeat was hastened when the ordnance keeper mistakenly delivered vermicelli instead of more ammunition. Some further skirmishes followed, but no significant action took place between May 1824 and July 1826. The Ashanti force withdrew from the coast after being dissipated by dysentery and smallpox.

In January 1826 a new Ashanti army invaded the Fante territories before making a bid to take Accra, concentrating their forces at Dodowa 20 miles to the north. An allied army of local tribes defended the town together with a British force of about 60 men. Each side numbered approximately 11,000. The Battle of Dodowa (Akantamasu/Katamanso) proved to be the most important engagement in the region's history (7 Aug. 1826). The British force made effective use of rockets, which helped break the Ashanti lines. Both Britain and the Ashanti were now willing to make peace, but the Fante proved difficult, with the result that no settlement was reached until 1831.

Political result

A peace treaty was signed in the Great Hall of Cape Coast Castle (27 April 1831), by which the Ashanti were to hand over 600 ounces of gold and to surrender two members of their royal family as hostages. These securities were to be returned after six years. The Ashanti recognized the kingdoms of Denkera, Akim and Assin as independent. A border was also agreed, with the area south of the Prah river being recognized as British. From this point onwards Ashanti power began to decline.

Second Ashanti War 1873–4

Occasion

A period of peace and stability followed the First Ashanti War of 1824–31 after which tension again began to rise out of the humiliation of the peace settlement, as well as disputes concerning relations with the coastal peoples. Over the latter issue the Ashanti held the British responsible for the local tribes' actions, while Britain claimed to be no more than the protecting power. A period of skirmishing and raiding erupted (1863–72) over the British refusal of the Ashanti king's demand for the return of a fugitive chief. The Ashanti won some early victories, leading the British governor to propose an attack on the Ashanti capital at Kumasi, but this was rejected by London. In 1867 the new Ashanti king, Kofi Karikari, announced: 'My business shall be war.' Two separate issues indeed led to war.

The first concerned the transfer of the Dutch coastal fort at Elmina to Britain (1872). The Ashanti king considered himself overlord of this area, and that therefore the fort was subject to him and could not be transferred without his consent. A second issue concerned the capture by the Ashanti in 1869 of four German missionaries in neighboring Togo, who were still prisoners when the Elmina incident occurred. Hostilities began in 1873 with a full-scale attack by the Ashanti against the Fante, leading in turn to war with Britain.

Course of War

The Ashanti crossed the Prah river in force (22 Jan. 1873), defeating the Fante. London now decided on decisive action, parliament voting £800,000 for the war and Sir Garnet (later Lord) Wolseley being sent out as governor. On his arrival (Oct. 1873) Wolseley found the Ashanti about to withdraw, having been badly weakened by smallpox and fever. He decided to move on Kumasi, while the Ashanti conducted an orderly retreat. The Ashanti king, on arriving at his capital at Kumasi (22 Dec.), attempted to arrange a peace, but Wolseley was determined on outright victory. The British captured the city and burned it (4 Feb.) before leaving (6 Feb.), by now themselves suffering from illness. The British force included over 2,500 European soldiers, of whom 70 per cent were eventually on the sicklist (there being 70 deaths, mainly from disease).

Political result

By the Treaty of Fomena (13 Feb. 1874), the Ashanti agreed to pay 50,000 ounces of gold; to surrender their claims to the former Dutch possessions as well as to the kingdoms of Adansi, Akin, Assim and Denkera; to give up human sacrifice; and to promote trade. The British withdrew their forces from Ashanti territory.

Remarks

Several states previously subject to the Ashanti now turned to Britain for protection, which the Colonial Office refused, with the result that the Ashanti were given an opportunity to regroup. Many clauses of the Fomena treaty were ignored (for example, only 4,000 ounces of gold were ever paid). After the war Britain reorganized its coastal holding into the Gold Coast colony.

Third Ashanti War 1895–6

Occasion

In 1885 the European powers at the Congress of Berlin placed the Ashanti area within the British sphere of influence. In 1886 a new Ashanti king, Prempeh, emerged after a long succession crisis, imposing his rule throughout the Ashanti Confederation by 1893. British policy now moved inexorably towards either establishing a protectorate over the Ashanti, or annexation. In 1895 the Ashanti, who believed it was the British intention to annex their country, sent an embassy to London to appeal directly to the government, over the head of the Gold Coast governor. Britain, however, demanded fulfillment of the 1874 Fomena treaty, and an ultimatum was presented to the Ashanti king, giving him three weeks to comply. The king refused to answer these demands, on the basis that he was awaiting the report of his embassy, and hostilities duly commenced (31 Oct. 1895).

Course of War

British forces under Sir Francis Scott began a carefully planned advance (Dec. 1895) causing Prempeh to sue for peace. The British expeditionary force, however, had orders to take the Ashanti capital and British forces occupied Kumasi (17 Jan. 1896). Although no actual fighting occurred during the war, many British soldiers died from disease. At the end of January the British force began its return to the coast.

Political result

The Ashanti Confederation was dissolved. Prempeh was forced to perform an act of submission to the governor of the Gold Coast, by prostrating himself and kissing the governor's feet (20 Jan. 1896). He was then exiled, first to Elmina, then to Sierra Leone and finally to the Seychelles. A British resident was established at Kumasi and Ashanti became a British protectorate.

Fourth Ashanti War 1900

Occasion

In 1900 the governor of the Gold Coast, Sir Frederic Hodgson, visited Kumasi (28 March) and declared it an insult to the British crown that he was not seated on the Golden Stool. This symbol of Ashanti sovereignty had been hidden away after the Third Ashanti War of 1895–6 and the dissolution of the Ashanti Confederation; in fact, the Golden Stool was never sat on, even by the Ashanti king. Within three days all the Ashanti lands had risen in revolt at this insult.

Course of War

Governor Hodgson and the British officials were besieged at Kumasi for three months before finally escaping in June. It took until December 1900 for the British to crush the rebellion, with British casualties of around 1,000, including almost 700 deaths.

Political result

By an Order in Council (26 Sept. 1901) Britain formally annexed the Ashanti lands, which became a crown colony administered by a chief commissioner responsible to the governor of the Gold Coast.

Remarks

The Gold Coast later became the first British African colony to become independent (1957, as Ghana), with the Ashanti playing an important role in the independence movement.

Barra War 1831

Belligerents: **Great Britain**
                    Barra Kingdom

Cause

The king of Barra, Burungai Sonko, in what is today the Gambia, agreed to transfer to Britain the sovereignty over the Gambia river, together with a strip of land extending one mile inland from its right bank. In return for the loss of river dues the king was to receive an annuity. This was agreed in what became known as the Ceded Mile Treaty (June 1826). Commodore Bullen moved immediately to make effective Britain's new rights by constructing an emplacement at the river's mouth, consisting of two cannon, which became known as Fort Bullen. The Barra feared, however, that these cannon could be turned against them. A separate British military presence on James Island was abandoned in 1829 and this was one of several factors which led the Barra to believe that the Ceded Mile Treaty had now lapsed. Indeed, since the signature of the treaty the king of Barra had continued to exercise effective sovereignty over the Ceded Mile.

Occasion

Fighting began in the aftermath of an incident which occurred in the summer of 1831. Two villagers of Essau entered Fort Bullen, which suffered from lax security, and demanded drink. On being refused they opened fire before fleeing. The commander of the fort gave the alarm, which was heard in the chief settlement at Bathurst (Banjul). A detachment of 30 soldiers was sent to Barra Point the following day and, after joining with some of the garrison there, proceeded to march to Essau to demand the surrender of the two intruders. The British forces' arrival was clearly expected; instead of obtaining the surrender of the two wanted men, the British were severely mauled by fire from the well-defended village and forced to retreat. This in effect began the Barra War.

Course of War

The British settlement at Bathurst, unable to cope with this crisis, was forced to appeal for help to the British colony at Sierra Leone and the French colony at Gorée and St Louis. Reinforcements soon arrived, first a French warship (8 Sept. 1831), followed by more French forces (10 Oct.) and then by British forces (7 Nov.). With such reinforcements Barra Point was retaken (7 Nov.) and Essau attacked, albeit unsuccessfully (17 Nov.). Barra, however, was distracted by an opportunistic attack by neighboring native states, with the result that the king sued for peace. Anglo-French casualties numbered around 50 dead and 150 wounded.

Political result

The Fort Bullen Convention (5 Jan. 1832) provided for an apology by the king for the events which had occurred, and hostages were provided as tokens of his good faith. The Ceded Mile Treaty was confirmed.

First Dahomey War 1890

Belligerents: **France**
           Dahomey

Cause

French interest in the trade of the West African coast led to the establishment of a protectorate over the Kingdom of Porto Novo (1863–4, reestablished 1884). France claimed that the king of Dahomey (present-day Benin) had ceded the port of Cotonou by the Treaty of Whydah (19 April 1876). However, the transfer of actual sovereignty was disputed by Dahomey and trouble soon arose with King Gelele (Glegle), who claimed the right to collect customs duties at Cotonou as well as to raid Porto Novo. The French on their part wished to develop Cotonou as a port, planning to pay for this through the collection of import duties.

Occasion

A French mission under Jean Bayol, one of France's greatest exponents of colonial empire, travelled to Abomey, the Dahomean capital, to negotiate with Gelele over the Cotonou question (Nov.–Dec. 1889). Bayol, however, failed to reach an agreement with Gelele and returned to Cotonou. The Dahomeans had suggested during the negotiations that some of France's difficulties were due to it no longer having a king, an observation which infuriated the staunchly republican Bayol. Gelele died soon after the French mission left (28 Dec. 1889) and was succeeded by his son, Behanzin. Simultaneously, Bayol successfully requested more military support. After the arrival of reinforcements Bayol informed Behanzin of the French annexation of Cotonou.

Course of War

Bayol seriously underestimated the capacity of the Dahomeans, who fought effectively. Dahomean forces almost immediately attacked the French at Cotonou and elsewhere, capturing some French hostages (24 Feb. 1890). The French government was deeply concerned that Bayol had over-extended himself, recalled him and attempted to make peace with Behanzin. Fighting nevertheless continued and a battle fought at Atchoupa (20 April) resulted in heavy casualties. Behanzin, however, then agreed to an exchange of hostages (8 May). The onset of the rainy season prevented further military action and allowed time for Bayol's replacement, Admiral Cuverville, to arrive (June). Negotiations were reopened with Gelele, and a settlement was reached (Oct.).

Political result

By the Franco-Dahomey Agreement (3 Oct. 1890), Behanzin recognized the French protectorate over Porto Novo and their indefinite occupation of Cotonou, in return for an annual payment of 20,000 francs. In a secret clause, Behanzin agreed not to accept the protection of any power other than France.

Second Dahomey War 1892–4

Belligerents: **France**
                          Dahomey

Cause

King Behanzin of Dahomey (present-day Benin), in the aftermath of the First Dahomey War with France in 1890, moved to improve his military establishment. This included the purchase of firearms, mostly from Germany. To pay for these it was necessary to increase through raiding the number of slaves available for sale. These raids virtually depopulated some districts and led to renewed tension with France.

Occasion

Both Behanzin and King Tofa, the nominal ruler of the French coastal protectorate of Porto Novo, claimed the Wheme valley. Behanzin extended his slave-raiding into the valley, thereby bringing about a direct confrontation with France. A French boat sent to investigate the situation was attacked (27 March 1892), and the well-armed Dahomean forces made a tentative move on Porto Novo itself before withdrawing. Behanzin also asserted to the French his sovereignty not only over the Wheme valley but over Porto Novo as well. France believed its position in the region was now being seriously threatened and parliament voted credits for a war. Colonel A. A. Dodds was appointed as commander and took command at Cotonou (29 May 1892).

Course of War

Dodds attempted to negotiate with Behanazin, who made some conciliatory gestures but would not compromise on the matter of territorial sovereignty. Dodds thereupon imposed a coastal blockade (15 June) and with a force now numbering over 2,000 men moved to the offensive. The French crossed the Wheme river (2 Oct.) and advanced on the Dahomean capital of Abomey. As Dodds' troops approached Cana, Behanzin offered to make a settlement, promising to cede to France the entire coastline, to surrender his recently acquired modern weapons, to end human sacrifice and to pay an indemnity of 15 million francs. Dodds, however, decided to take Abomey, claiming that the Dahomeans had surrendered insufficient arms. The capital was burned by Behanzin before fleeing, the French taking only a ruined city (17 Nov.).

Political result

The French declared Behanzin deposed (3 Dec. 1892), the coastal areas were annexed and the remainder of the Dahomean kingdom was declared a French protectorate. The French installed Behanzin's brother Agoli-Agbo (Gucili) as the new ruler, with the title of king of Abomey (15 Jan. 1894). Behanzin, who had fled north, still commanded significant support and Dodds was forced to mount a new campaign against him (Oct. 1893). Behanzin finally surrendered (25 Jan. 1894) and was exiled to Algeria, where he died (1906). Agoli-Agbo was himself deposed and exiled by the French (1900), as they tightened their control in West Africa.

Benin War 1897

Belligerents: **Great Britain**
                     Benin

Cause

During the nineteenth century British interest grew steadily in what is now Nigeria. The first British consul was appointed in 1849 and a protectorate was established over southern Nigeria in 1885. In 1892 Overami (Oven-ramwen), the oba (king) of Benin, in southwest Nigeria, agreed to a treaty which made Benin a protectorate of Britain. By its terms the king was required to end the slave trade and human sacrifice.

Occasion

Problems arose concerning both the suppression of human sacrifice and British trading rights in Benin, leading the acting British consul-general, J. R. Phillips, to propose a visit to Benin City. Phillips insisted on proceeding without an adequate escort, despite warnings from many quarters not to do so. The court at Benin was split as to the implications of the mission, some members seeing it as a declaration of war. The British party was attacked and Phillips and eight other Europeans were killed (4 Jan. 1897). When the British authorities learned of their deaths, immediate military action was ordered.

Course of War

The logistical virtuosity of the British in this campaign was remarkable. Within 29 days a force of 1,200 men was gathered from points as far as 4,000 miles from Benin. British forces landed (10 Feb.) and marched on Benin City, which quickly fell to them (18 Feb.). British dead numbered 17. The campaign completed, the bulk of the British force quickly re-embarked (27 Feb.), thus reducing the number of deaths from disease and heatstroke which so often afflicted European campaigns in West Africa.

Political result

The king of Benin was exiled to Calabar (on the far east of the Nigerian coast) and six chiefs implicated in the deaths of the nine Europeans were executed. A Council of Chiefs, together with a British resident, took over the administration of the country (Sept. 1897). The situation in Benin remained unsettled, resistance to British rule being led by Chief Ologbosheri. A second expedition was required in 1899 finally to establish British control. Overami died in exile (1914) and was succeeded in Benin as oba by his son, who accepted British suzerainty.

Sokoto War 1903

Belligerents: **Great Britain**
                    Sokoto

Cause

During the late-nineteenth-century colonial scramble for Africa by the European powers, Britain established a protectorate over southern Nigeria and in 1900 proclaimed a separate protectorate over northern Nigeria. To support its power in this region, Britain established the West African Frontier Force (1897), which was to play a notable military role in the establishment of British authority. As Britain moved to make its control of the Nigerian region effective, it came into conflict with the independent Moslem states in the north grouped under the Sokoto Empire (Caliphate). The Sokoto Empire, encompassing a number of vassal emirates, had grown in power in the early nineteenth century through a series of religious wars (*jihads*) which established the dominance of the Fulani over the local people, who were predominantly Hausa.

Occasion

The caliph of Sokoto was antagonistic to the growth of British power in the region, which threatened the predominance of his own régime. Conflict became inevitable as Britain extended its sway over the emirates which had traditionally looked to Sokoto. The incident which led to war was the death of Captain Moloney, the British resident at Nassarawa, who was killed by the magaji of Keffi (Oct. 1902). The magaji fled for protection to Kano, whose emir refused a British demand for his surrender. Sir Frederick Lugard, the British high commissioner of the Protectorate of Northern Nigeria and the architect of British power in Nigeria, collected an army of about 1,000 men and ordered it into the emirate of Kano (Jan. 1903).

Course of War

The British force successfully captured one important walled town after another. Kano, which was surrounded by walls 40 feet thick and 30 to 50 feet high, was taken with remarkable ease (3 Feb. 1903). The emir of Kano had meantime joined the caliph of Sokoto. The British advanced on Sokoto, where they encountered a force of 4,500, including 1,500 cavalry. The Sokoto forces fought with fanatical fervor, but were defeated by the British, who took the city (15 March). The caliph, Attahiru Ahmadu, fled, but was pursued by the British. In the six-hour Battle of Burmi (27 July), the caliph and 900 of his men died.

Political result

The British installed a new caliph (21 May 1903), while all the sovereign rights of the Sokoto Empire passed to Britain. All local rulers were now appointed by the British, the importation of arms, other than flintlocks, was prohibited and slavery was abolished. The caliph of Sokoto still continues as the spiritual leader of the Fulani.

12 Southern African Colonial Wars

Zulu War 1879

Belligerents: **Great Britain**
  Zulu Kingdom

Cause

Afrikaners disenchanted with British colonial control in the Cape Colony embarked on the Great Trek (1835–7), which brought them into collision with the Zulu kingdom. The Battle of the Blood River (1838) established this river as the boundary between the new Afrikaner republic of the Transvaal and the Zulus. The border was never clearly defined, however, leading to disputes, particularly as Afrikaners began to settle east of the river in Zulu-claimed territory. The Zulu king, Cetewayo, conducted a foreign policy based on good relations with Britain and with the neighboring British colony of Natal, with which there were no border problems. The British annexation of the Transvaal (1877), however, destroyed the policy on which Cetewayo had pinned Zulu security. The British, who had previously supported the Zulus in the border dispute with the Transvaal, now altered their view and supported the Transvaal border claims, in part to win the support of the Afrikaner population. The British administrator of the Transvaal, Theophilus Shepstone, and the British high commissioner, Bartle Frere, decided to use this dispute to further British control.

Occasion

A British ultimatum was sent to Cetewayo (11 Dec. 1878) demanding that he disband his army within 30 days and accept a British resident. Cetewayo refused these demands and British forces invaded the Zulu kingdom (11 Jan. 1879).

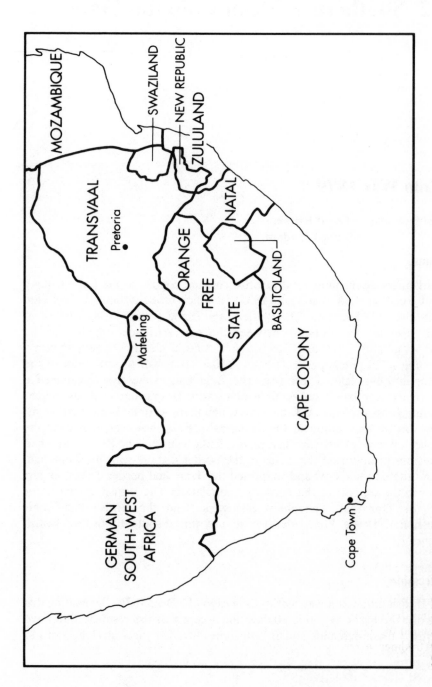

15 Colonial Southern Africa

Course of War

There were three notable actions, Isandhlwana, Rorke's Drift and Ulundi. The British under Lord Chelmsford had an army of 5,000 European and 8,200 native soldiers. The well-organized and disciplined Zulu army of 40,000 men was based on mass conscription until the age of 40, the warriors being organized into *impis* (regiments). The British army divided into three columns, intending to converge on the Zulu capital of Ulundi. At the Battle of Isandhlwana (22 Jan. 1879) the Zulu army surprised one British column and virtually annihilated it. Of 1,800 European and 1,000 native soldiers in the British column, all but 55 Europeans and 300 natives were killed. It was the greatest British military disaster since the 1853–6 Crimean War. At Rorke's Drift (22–3 Jan.) about 4,000 Zulus attacked a small British camp of about 85 able-bodied and 30 to 40 wounded men. In a heroic defence, which even won them the praise of their attackers, the small force held off the Zulu attack. This action resulted in the award of more Victoria Crosses (eight) than any other single action in British military history. Lord Chelmsford was forced to await reinforcements before again advancing, but the superiority of British arms over the Zulu army, which relied principally on *assagis* (spears), finally assured British victory. In the Battle of Ulundi (4 July 1879) the British under Chelmsford, with 6,200 men, crushed a Zulu army of 10,000. The British suffered only 15 dead to the Zulus' 1,500. The Zulu army was effectively destroyed, Ulundi was burned and Cetewayo after attempting to flee was captured and sent into exile.

Political result

The defeat at Isandhlwana shocked Britain, which decided not to annex Zululand but rather to remove it as a possible threat. Cetewayo was banished to Cape Town and the country was divided between 13 chiefs, none of whom was allowed an army, and there was to be a British resident. Relations were regulated by a Treaty on the Conditions of Appointment of Chiefs (1 Sept. 1879). This arrangement led to such disorder, as chiefs argued with other chiefs and internal rivals, that in 1882 Britain decided to allow Cetewayo to return as paramount chief. His return, however, sparked more internal unrest; Ulundi was again destroyed and Cetewayo was wounded (July 1883), dying in February 1884. Afrikaner settlers helped Cetewayo's son, Dinuzulu, become paramount chief, in return for which they took northwest Zululand, erecting it into a 'New Republic' which joined the Transvaal in 1886. Britain, in order to restore order and to block Afrikaner expansion, annexed Zululand in 1887, placing it under the governor of Natal. Dinuzulu attempted a rebellion (1888) and was exiled to St Helena until 1898.

Transvaal Revolt (First Boer War) 1880–1

Belligerents: **Great Britain**
                     Transvaal

Cause

In 1877 Great Britain annexed the Afrikaner republic of the Transvaal. Theophilus Shepstone of the British colonial government in Natal had taken advantage of a period of political demoralization in the Transvaal to enter with a small escort and to proclaim its annexation to Britain (12 April 1877).

Occasion

Afrikaner opposition to British rule was strong, but a rebellion was delayed by hopes that the possible return of a Liberal administration in London under Gladstone might restore Transvaal's independence. When it became obvious that this would not happen, revolt became inevitable. In late 1880 a wagon belonging to a farmer was attacked for failure to pay taxes, but was rescued by a local armed band. This sparked a revolt against British rule, leading to a reconvening of the Transvaal parliament, the Volksraad, which gave power to a triumvirate consisting of Piet Joubert, Paul Kruger and Marthinus Pretorius (30 Dec. 1880).

Course of War

The war consisted chiefly of two engagements, Laing's Nek and Majuba. At the Battle of Laing's Nek (28 Jan. 1881) 2,000 Afrikaners under Joubert (who had invaded Natal colony) defeated 1,400 British regulars under General Colley, the high commissioner for Southeast Africa. At the Battle of Majuba Hill (27 Feb. 1881) Colley, after a brilliant night march which placed him on Majuba Hill overlooking the Transvaal lines, was defeated. The Afrikaners under Joubert overwhelmed the British force of 550 men, killing Colley and 91 of his men, with only negligible casualties to themselves. Diplomatic contacts, already underway, now rapidly achieved a settlement.

Political result

The Convention of Pretoria (3 Aug. 1881) gave the Transvaal self-government under British suzerainty. Britain was given the right of transit for military forces through the Transvaal in time of war, a British resident was to have special powers over African natives and Britain was to control Transvaal's foreign affairs. The Convention of London (27 Feb. 1884) superseded the Pretoria convention, after Britain had found itself embroiled in crises elsewhere and had decided to improve relations with the Afrikaner republics. In the new convention, no reference was made to British suzerainty and Britain abandoned its special rights over African natives. In return, the republics could not expand to east or west, nor make treaties with other states (except each other) without British permission.

Second Boer War 1899–1902

Belligerents: **Great Britain**
Transvaal, Orange Free State

Cause

By the end of the nineteenth century the Transvaal had become the world's largest gold producer, a factor which gave it great importance in an age when the gold standard was the basis for international monetary relations. British gold magnates and key British government officials accordingly wished to gain control of the two Afrikaner republics, the Transvaal and the Orange Free State. The Jameson Raid (1896) was a bungled attempt to stage a rising by the *uitlanders* (foreigners), mostly engaged in mining in the Transvaal, which would serve as a pretext for a British intervention. The British government, however, disclaimed all responsibility for the raid. Increasing German interest in the region led Kaiser Wilhelm II to send congratulations to the Transvaal president, Kruger, on his success in defeating the raiders. The 'Kruger Telegram' helped convert a colonial incident into an international one and fanned anti-German feeling in Britain.

In 1897 Alfred Milner was sent to South Africa as high commissioner by the colonial secretary, Joseph Chamberlain. Both were ardent imperialists. Milner went with the intention of gaining control of the Afrikaner republics, by force if necessary.

Occasion

Milner used the demands of the *uitlanders* for voting rights as the excuse for British interference. He demanded that the Transvaal's Franchise Law be altered to give entitlement to vote after five, rather than 14, years' residence. Kruger was willing to compromise but Milner rejected this and broke off negotiations. Kruger, seeing the intention of Milner's policy, decided on a pre-emptive war. The Transvaal began mobilization (28 Sept. 1899), followed by the Orange Free State (2 Oct.). Kruger sent a 48-hour ultimatum to Britain, demanding arbitration of the dispute and the withdrawal of British forces from the common frontier (9 Oct.). This in fact served as a joint declaration of war, the Orange Free State joining the Transvaal in accordance with the treaty of mutual assistance they had concluded after the Jameson Raid. War therefore began on 11 October.

Course of War

While Milner was planning a war, the War Office in London was not, so that Britain began the struggle badly prepared. This allowed the Boers to enjoy some early successes. The Transvaal, with its vast wealth, had been building up its armaments for years. However, Britain was able to isolate the two-landlocked republics from external assistance through British control of the seas and a timely reaffirmation of its centuries-old treaty of alliance with Portugal, which helped stop the shipment of weapons through the neighboring Portuguese colony of Mozambique (14 Oct. 1899).

During the war Boer forces numbered up to 88,000 men (73,000 from the two republics, 13,000 sympathizers from the British-controlled colonies and 2,000 foreign volunteers), while Britain deployed almost 450,000 men (256,000 regulars, 109,000 volunteers, 53,000 South African colonists and 31,000 from the dominions). The war itself fell into three phases. The first was the Boer offensive (Oct. 1899–Feb. 1900), which saw a string of Boer successes, including the sieges of Mafeking, Ladysmith and Kimberley, together with a notable victory in the Battle of Colenso (15 Dec. 1899). At Colenso, 18,000 British soldiers were defeated by 6,000 Boers, with casualties of 5 per cent of the force, one of the highest rates since the Indian Mutiny of 1857–8. The second phase (Feb.–Sept. 1900) saw Britain turn the tide with the use of overwhelming force. A British offensive succeeded in relieving the besieged towns, invading the republics and occupying their capitals. Kruger fled into exile (11 Sept. 1900). The annexation of the Orange Free State was proclaimed (28 May 1900), followed by that of the Transvaal (25 Oct. 1900). Britain had presumed victory too soon, however, as the Boers turned to guerrilla warfare, which dominated the third and final phase of the war (Nov. 1900–May 1902). In response, Britain adopted a campaign of rounding up civilians, burning farms, constructing blockhouses and deploying flying columns. Under such harsh treatment the Boer resistance began to wane and negotiations were opened which ended the war. The Second Boer War cost Britain 22,000 dead and £200 million.

Political result

By the Vereeniging Agreement (31 May 1902), the two Afrikaner republics lost their independence and became British crown colonies; Dutch became a subsidiary language to English, although self-government was promised at some future date.

Remarks

The British army's appalling generalship led to a diminished international reputation, while the policy of rounding up the families of Afrikaner guerrilla soldiers into 'concentration camps', in which 20,000 women and children died of disease, caused an international outcry. Britain's dangerous diplomatic isolation during the war caused it to reassess its traditional policy of no peacetime alliances with other powers. This led to a shift in diplomatic strategy which resulted in the Anglo-Japanese Alliance (1902) and the Anglo-French Entente (1904). In South Africa the attempt to suppress the local Dutch dialect, Afrikaans, led rather to a flowering of it as a literary language in reaction. The Liberal government in London, which replaced the Conservatives in 1905, embarked on a policy of reconciliation in South Africa. In 1906 self-government was introduced, and the Union of South Africa linking the four colonies was established in 1910. South Africa remained loyal to Britain through the two World Wars, with many former Boer leaders serving the British cause.

13 Struggle for the Horn of Africa

Anglo-Ethiopian War 1867–8

Belligerents: **Ethiopia**
                    Great Britain

Cause

Under the Emperor Theodore, the consolidator of the modern Ethiopian state, Ethiopia (also known as Abyssinia) began an era of recovery and development after a long period of political chaos. The building of the Suez Canal (1869) raised the strategic importance of the Red Sea region, causing the European Great Powers to become increasingly interested in the Horn of Africa.

Occasion

The direct cause of hostilities was Theodore's belief that he had been slighted by Britain. In October 1862 he had sent a letter via the British consul, C. D. Cameron, to Queen Victoria, which the Foreign Office failed to answer. In January 1864, in anger at the failure of Britain to respond, Theodore arrested Cameron and his staff, having already detained several other British subjects and missionaries. The Foreign Office now made an unsuccessful attempt to remedy the situation, but this only led to the arrest of the new emissaries. Britain accordingly decided on military action (July 1867). Meanwhile, Theodore's increasingly capricious rule was undermining his power within the country.

Course of War

In January 1868 General Napier landed with an expedition of 36,000 men at Annesley Bay (Gulf of Zuk). In a masterful advance Napier led his expedition 400 miles across rugged and little-known terrain to Theodore's stronghold at Magdala. The emperor's army, which at one time had numbered 100,000, was now rapidly dwindling through desertion.

Theodore abandoned and burnt his capital at Debra-Tabor and marched with his remaining followers to Magdala to meet Napier, showing remarkable engineering skill on the way. An Ethiopian army of 3,000 attacked Napier's force near Magdala, which succeeded in withdrawing in good order (10 April). The following day Theodore sued for peace. Napier's terms were the release of the prisoners and that Theodore submit to Queen Victoria. Theodore released the prisoners but could not accept the act of submission. Napier then stormed and captured Magdala (13 April), with almost no casualties, to find that Theodore had committed suicide.

Political result

By May 1868 British forces had left Ethiopia. After Theodore's death Ethiopia was once again convulsed by civil war (1868-72) until the ruler of Tigre Province emerged as the new emperor, John IV. Ethiopian weakness led to Egyptian attempts to seize key districts, which resulted in the Egyptian-Ethiopian war of 1875-6.

Egyptian-Ethiopian War 1875-6

Belligerents: **Ethiopia**
                    Egypt

Cause

Egypt under the Khedive Ismail took advantage of Ethiopia's difficulties after the Anglo-Ethiopian War of 1867-8 to acquire key territory at Ethiopia's expense. Egypt seized the key ports of Berbera, Zeyla, Suakkim and Massawa (Mesewa), thereby cutting Ethiopia off from the sea by February 1875. On the advice of the Swiss-born governor of Massawa, Werner Munzinger, Egypt in 1872 annexed the northern Ethiopian provinces of Bogus and Hamasan. Ismail decided to continue this expansionist policy into the northern Ethiopian plateau with the intention of creating a Greater Egypt which would control the area from the Nile to the Indian Ocean.

Occasion

In 1875 Egyptian forces conquered Harar and expeditions were prepared to conquer the remainder of Ethiopia.

Course of War

The Egyptians mounted a three-pronged invasion of Ethiopia. The war began with an invasion of Harar province by an Egyptian army of 1,200 men operating from Zeyla (11 Oct. 1875). Munzinger meanwhile marched on Awsa, where his force of 400 men was surprised and defeated, and Munzinger killed. The largest Egyptian force, numbering 2,500–3,000 well-equipped men armed with Remingtons, advanced from Massawa into Tigre Province, where at the Battle of Gundet (13 Nov. 1875) Emperor John's army virtually annihilated the Egyptian army, commanded by the Danish-born S. A. Arendrup. Another Egyptian force under Ratib Pasha, with a staff consisting mostly of Americans and Europeans, was defeated the following year at the Battle of Gura (25 March 1876), ending Egyptian ambitions against Ethiopia.

Political result

The peace settlement took seven years to achieve, with Emperor John patiently waiting out Egyptian procrastination. At one stage he smuggled out a mediation request to the European powers, through the Egyptian blockade, in the shoe of an Ethiopian courier. It was only when Egypt was faced with revolt at home, the Mahdist uprising in the Sudan and the British seizure of Alexandria, that a serious effort was made at settlement. The Treaty of Adowa, or Hewitt Treaty (3 June 1884), was negotiated by the British Admiral Hewitt. It gave the Ethiopians free transit of goods through Massawa and returned Bogus Province to Ethiopian rule. Future differences were to be submitted to British arbitration.

Remarks

The defeat by the Ethiopians marked the end of Ismail's dreams of expansion and contributed to his downfall (1879). The financial overextension of the Egyptian government in the pursuit of this policy led to financial collapse, the intervention of the European states and the effective end of Egyptian independence. The Ethiopians had fought fiercely, seeing the attack as a threat to their land as well as a struggle between Christian and Moslem. The Italian seizure of Massawa in the aftermath of the settlement led to the First Italo-Ethiopian War of 1887–9.

First Italo-Ethiopian War 1887–9

Belligerents: **Italy**
                     Ethiopia

Cause

Italy's involvement in the Horn of Africa was part of a general rush by the European powers for some presence in this region after the opening of the Suez Canal (1869). In that year the Italian Rubattino Co. purchased from local sultans the port of Assab near the southern end of the Red Sea. In 1879 an Italian commissioner was appointed and a small Italian force landed, with both the Ottoman Empire and Egypt protesting against the Italian occupation. In 1882 the area formally became an Italian territory.

Occasion

The bankrupt Egyptian government abandoned Massawa (Mesewa) in 1884, although the British-arranged Treaty of Adowa which had ended the 1875–6 Egyptian-Ethiopian War guaranteed Ethiopia free transit of goods through Massawa, while ignoring its future disposition. The British, fearing regional instability, encouraged the Italians to seize the port, which they did (Feb. 1885). The Italians ignored the guarantees of the peace treaty and levied duties on goods passing through the port, simultaneously moving to control the hinterland. This led to direct confrontation with Ethiopia.

Course of War

The main action of the war was the Dogali (Tedale) massacre, in which an Ethiopian army of 7,000 led by the local governor attacked an Italian detachment of 500 (26 Jan. 1887), leaving 400 Italians dead. An Italian expeditionary force sent to redress the situation reached Massawa on 8 November 1887. In March 1888 Emperor John of Ethiopia led a large army to confront the Italians but did not attack for fear of provoking an all-out war. John withdrew his army (2 April), being at the time primarily concerned with the threat posed by the Mahdist forces in the Sudan. In May the Italian army returned home. At the Battle of Mettemma, John defeated the Mahdist army but was himself killed (9 March 1889). In the succession crisis which followed, Menelik II, a member of the old Solo-monid dynasty, emerged as emperor. During this period of internal upheaval the Italians were able to seize Keren and Asmara. Italian possessions were now reorganized into the colony of Eritrea (1 Jan. 1890).

Political result

The Treaty of Uccialli (2 May 1889) was a treaty of friendship and commerce concluded between Italy and Menelik II. Article 17 bound Ethiopia to use the Italian government in its dealings with foreign governments. The Italians interpreted this as giving them a protectorate over Ethiopia, which was accepted by most European powers. Menelik, however, rejected this interpretation and denounced the treaty (Feb. 1893), bringing about the Second Italo-Ethiopian War of 1895–6.

Remarks

Italy's intervention came in the aftermath of the Congress of Berlin (1885), at which the European powers partitioned most of Africa. Italy's intervention was wholly in accord with these ideas.

Second Italo-Ethiopian War 1895–6

Belligerents: **Italy**
                     Ethiopia

Cause

Italy's attempts to establish a protectorate over Ethiopia, which it claimed on the basis of the 1889 Treaty of Uccialli, were successfully thwarted by Emperor Menelik II. After attempting negotiations to resolve the problem, Menelik finally informed the Italians (27 Feb. 1893) that, in accordance with the provision allowing its termination on one year's notification, he was ending the treaty as of 1 May 1884. Having failed using diplomatic methods, the Italian government of Francesco Crispi now opted for military action.

Occasion

In December 1894 an incident occurred on the border of Italian Eritrea and the Ethiopian province of Tigre, leading to an indecisive battle (12–14 Jan. 1895). This was followed by the Italian annexation and partial occupation of Tigre (March–April 1895). Menelik busily made meticulous preparations for war and after the end of the rainy season he issued a general call to arms (Sept. 1895). Attempts to negotiate a settlement were, however, continued until February 1896.

Course of War

The chief engagement of the war occurred at Adowa, where the Italian General Baratieri held a fortified position which was besieged by Menelik's army. Baratieri, running low on supplies, came out to engage the Ethiopians, and the result was a devasting defeat for the Italian army (1 March 1896). Out of a force of 20,000, the Italians suffered 7,000 dead and 1,500 wounded, with 3,000 captured. Of Menelik's army of 90,000, 4,000–6,000 were killed and 8,000 wounded. The Italians were completely routed and left behind all their artillery. Ethiopian tactics were well-coordinated, whereas the Italians allowed their four brigades to fight separately.

Political result

By the Treaty of Addis Ababa (26 Oct. 1896), Italy recognized Ethiopian independence and the Treaty of Uccialli was entirely abrogated.

Remarks

This defeat was a humiliation for Italy and led to the downfall of Crispi's government. European powers now took Ethiopa seriously as a state and there was a general rush to the newly-built capital at Addis Ababa to gain influence. The French were particularly successful in this and constructed the Addis Ababa-Djibouti railway (completed 1918), which gave Ethiopia access to a port other than the Italian one at Massawa.

Sudanese War 1896–9

Belligerents: **Great Britain, Egypt**
                    Mahdist State (Sudan)

Cause

The northern Sudan had been conquered by the great Egyptian ruler, Mehemet Ali, in 1820–2, and over the following decades Egyptian rule was extended southwards. In 1883 a rebellion against the cruel and extortionate rule of the Egyptians was led by a religious leader, the Mahdi, which by 1885 had succeeded in freeing Sudan of Egyptian control. One famous event of the revolt was the siege of Khartoum by the Mahdist forces which resulted in the death of the British General Gordon (1885), who had been sent south in an attempt to restore orderly government. The period 1885–98 is known in Sudanese history as the Mahdia, although the Mahdi had died in 1885 and was succeeded by Khalifa (lieutenant) Abdullah.

Occasion

Egypt and Britain (which had occupied and taken effective control of Egypt in 1882), initially acquiesced in the loss of the Sudan. As French colonial expansion continued, however, there arose the possibility that the headwaters of the Nile might fall into French hands. In November 1894 the French government authorized an expedition under Captain Marchand to the Upper Nile; in March 1896 the British government decided to avenge Gordon's death while simultaneously gaining control of the Nile.

Course of War

The Anglo-Egyptian expedition was placed under General Kitchener, who was the *sirdar* (commander-in-chief) of the Egyptian army. Kitchener moved down the Nile in a carefully planned campaign, accompanied by a flotilla of gunboats and building a railway to provide logistical support. The advance began with the capture of the northern province of Dongola (Sept. 1896). Having extended the railway across the Nubian desert to the Nile river town of Abu Hamed (which fell 7 Aug. 1897), Kitchener defeated a Mahdist army in the Battle of Attbara (8 April 1898), which left 3,000 Sudanese dead as against an Anglo-Egyptian loss of 81.

The crucial engagement of the war was the Battle of Omdurman (2 Sept. 1899), before the khalifa's capital. Here an Anglo-Egyptian army of 26,000 confronted the khalifa's army of 40,000 and defeated it. The battle is notable as a point of transition in modern warfare. It included the last full-scale British cavalry charge (by the 21st Lancers and including the young Winston Churchill) and also showed the effectiveness of machine guns, of which the British used 20 with great deadliness. At Omdurman 11,000 Sudanese died in comparison with an Anglo-Egyptian loss of 49 killed. The khalifa fled and subsequently died in battle (Nov. 1899).

Immediately after Omdurman, Kitchener marched south to Fashoda to prevent the French expedition under Captain Marchand laying claim to the southern Sudan. This incident, which involved no bloodshed, almost brought Britain and France to war before the problem was resolved diplomatically.

Political result

In the Anglo-Egyptian Condominium Agreement (19 Jan. 1899), Britain, having established control of the Sudan by right of conquest, and Egypt, claiming to have regained its rebellious provinces, agreed to exercise joint sovereignty, with the governor-general being nominated by Britain. The first incumbent was General Kitchener. By an Anglo-French Declaration (March 1899), Britain and France defined their spheres of influence, making this an addition to the Niger Convention of 1898.

Third Italo-Ethiopian War (Abyssinian Crisis) 1935–6

Belligerents: **Italy**
Ethiopia

Cause

Ethiopia (also known as Abyssinia), a member of the League of Nations, was in the 1930s one of the two remaining independent states in Africa, bounded on two sides by the Italian colonies of Eritrea and Italian Somaliland. The Italian dictator, Mussolini, revived Italian ambitions in the region, which had lain dormant since the Italian defeat at Adowa in 1896 during the Second Italo-Ethiopian War.

Occasion

The crisis began with the Wal-Wal incident (Dec. 1934) on the border with Italian Somaliland, which led to Italian demands for an apology and extensive compensation. Ethiopia responded by requesting League of Nations arbitration, to which Italy agreed. Mussolini, however, was intent on war and Italian forces proceeded to invade Ethiopia without a declaration of war (3 Oct. 1935).

Course of War

The League acted promptly in declaring Italy the aggressor (7 Oct.), and in voting for sanctions on arms, credits and raw materials (18 Nov.). Oil and coal, however, were not included in the embargo, although both were critical to Italy. Britain and France were ambivalent, for while opposing such aggression they wanted Italian cooperation in the Stresa Front (April 1935) which was aimed at restraining Hitler's Germany. This led to the abortive Hoare-Laval Pact (Dec. 1935), negotiated by the British foreign secretary and the French premier, which proposed giving Italy effective control of Ethiopia while retaining a nominally independent Ethiopian government. The plan failed when it was leaked to the press and public indignation led to the resignations of Hoare and Laval.

The military campaign itself in Ethiopia was particularly brutal. The initial Italian advance was across the Mereb river, forming the border between Eritrea and Ethiopia. Adowa, the site of Italy's humiliating defeat in 1896, soon fell (5 Oct. 1935). The Italian commander, de Bono, nevertheless moved cautiously, remembering earlier disasters. Mussolini, however, wanted greater speed and replaced him with Badoglio (Nov.). The Ethiopians pulled back in an attempt to force the Italians to overextend their lines, which they did, and the Ethiopians then launched their 'Christmas Offensive'. The Italians were pushed back and defeated in battle at the Dembequene Pass. Desperate not to repeat their previous failure in Ethiopia, the Italians turned to the use of heavy aerial bombardment of military and civilian targets, as well as poison gas (in violation of the 1928 Geneva Convention). Employing such weapons, the Italians resumed the offensive with one of the largest armies ever used in a colonial war – 70,000 men – though they continued to meet determined resistance. In the Battle of Amba Aradam (19 Feb. 1936) the Ethiopians were heavily defeated. This was followed by another Italian victory in the Battle of Tembien (29 Feb. 1936). The war ended with the fall of the Ethiopian capital, Addis Ababa (5 May 1936).

Political result

King Victor Emmanuel of Italy was proclaimed emperor of Ethiopia (9 May) and Italian territory in the region was reorganized as Italian East Africa. Emperor Hailie Selassie went into exile, making a dramatic speech to the League on his country's plight (30 June 1936). On 15 July the League abandoned sanctions against Italy.

Remarks

This was one of the crises prior to the Second World War which revealed the ineffectiveness of the League of Nations in maintaining international security. Britain's and France's half-hearted support of sanctions alienated Mussolini, who moved closer to Hitler. This eventually resulted in the Rome–Berlin Axis (Oct. 1936). Hitler took the opportunity of general international distraction to remilitarize the Rhineland in contravention of the Versailles Treaty of 1919. Ethiopia regained its independence during the Second World War, with Hailie Selassie returning to Addis Ababa on its liberation (1941). Italy surrendered all claim to Ethiopia in the Paris Peace Treaty (10 Feb. 1947).

14 Somalian Wars

Ethiopia-Somalia Dispute 1964

Belligerents: **Ethiopia**
                  Somalia

Cause

Somalia was formed by a union of the colonies of British and Italian Somaliland, becoming independent in 1960. One of the aspirations of the new state was the creation of a Greater Somalia, through uniting the Somali people inhabiting portions of bordering states. This has brought it into conflict, either diplomatically or militarily, with its neighbors. One of the areas it hoped to extend its sovereignty over was the southeast Ethiopian desert province of Ogaden, inhabited primarily by nomadic Somalis, which had been conquered by Ethiopia in the nineteenth century. Somalia on independence refused to recognize the border with Ethiopia.

Occasion

Somalia had already alleged Ethiopian repression of Somali nomads in the Ogaden (Sept. 1961) and accused the Ethiopian government of complicity in a plot to kill the Somali president (Sept. 1962), when it began to receive substantial Soviet military aid. Somalia's aim was the creation of a powerful army of 20,000 men. Amid this increasing tension, border skirmishing erupted into warfare.

Course of War

Fighting broke out along the Ethiopian-Somali 900-mile border on 16 January 1964. The Somalis were aided by an insurrectionist force in the Ogaden which had begun fighting during 1963, and which established a 'liberation government'. An OAU-sponsored ceasefire was ineffective (16 Feb.), as skirmishing continued, but it was finally implemented on 1 April.

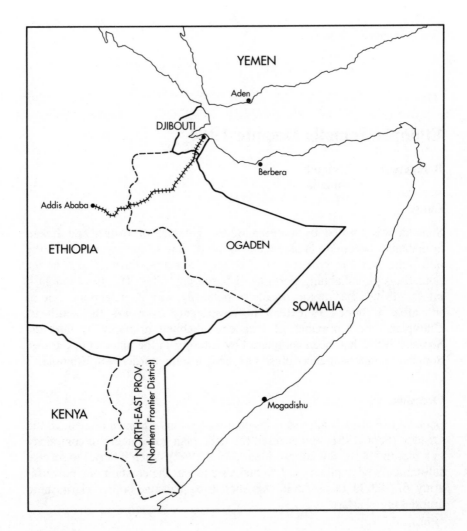

16 Somalia

Political result

The prewar situation was restored.

Kenya-Somalia Dispute (Shifta War) 1963–7

Belligerents: **Kenya**
                    Somalia

Cause

One of the areas Somalia hoped to unite to it was the Northern Frontier District (NFD) of the British colony of Kenya. The NFD had a population of around 400,000, of whom about half were Somalis.

Occasion

On the eve of Kenya's independence, a British commission inspected the NFD and reported that the largest group there wished for union with Somalia (Dec. 1962). Hoping to avoid bad relations with the Kenyan government when it became independent, Britain attempted a compromise by which the NFD would not be allowed to secede but instead would become a separate province of Kenya (8 March 1963). In response, Somalia broke off diplomatic relations with Britain (12 March). The matter was still unresolved on Kenyan independence (12 Dec. 1963). The British decision sparked a guerrilla war by Somali nationalists in the NFD, popularly known in Kenya as *shifta* (bandits).

Course of War

The guerrilla war lasted four years, although the Somali government denied any involvement. The Voice of Somalia radio broadcasts, however, were an important factor in promoting Somali nationalism. The OAU was unhappy with Somalia's challenge to established frontiers, fearing the precedent might wreck the fragile stability of Africa's borders. It was through the efforts of the OAU that a settlement was reached.

Political result

The Arusha Agreement (8 Oct. 1967), negotiated under the auspices of the OAU and with the mediation of President Kaunda of Zambia, effect-ively ended the war. Fighting was to stop, normal relations were to be resumed and propaganda ended. Full Kenyan-Somali, as well as Anglo-Somali, diplomatic relations were restored (Jan. 1968). Somalia, however, continued to maintain its claims to the NFD. In 1984 a rapprochement between Kenya and Somalia led to alleged Somalian cooperation in suppressing the *shifta*.

Ogaden War (Ethiopia-Somalia War) 1977–8

Belligerents: Ethiopia
                    Somalia

Cause

In 1973 oil was discovered in Ethiopia's Ogaden desert. In the following year, with Ethiopia in a state of disarray following the overthrow of Emperor Haile Selassie, Somalia again escalated its attempt to gain the Ogaden which had previously resulted in the Ethiopia-Somalia Dispute of 1964. Somalian support was provided for the WSLF (Western Somalia Liberation Front), founded in 1974 and operating in Ogaden.

Occasion

A major rebellion staged by the WSLF in January 1977 coincided with a renewed crisis in Ethiopia, where in February Colonel Mengistu seized power. Simultaneously, the ongoing conflict in the Ethiopian province of Eritrea was becoming critical. The 3,000–4,000-strong WSLF rapidly routed the isolated Ethiopian forces, who fell back to a line near the strategically important Addis Ababa-Djibouti railway. Despite this the WSLF succeeded in cutting the line (July 1977), whereupon Somalia moved to consolidate these gains, its forces openly entering Ogaden.

Course of War

Somalia was able to mount its invasion with the benefit of military aid provided by its ally, the Soviet Union. There were 1,000 Soviet advisers in Somalia and 2,400 Somalis had trained in the Soviet Union. However, the Soviet Union was also now supplying the new, left-oriented Ethiopian government of Mengistu. In November Somali anger at this dual Soviet role led to the abrogation of its treaty with the Soviet Union, the expulsion of Soviet advisers and the termination of Soviet use of the important naval base at Berbera. Soviet aid now flowed into Ethiopia along with 11,000–16,000 Cuban soldiers and 1,500 Soviet advisers. With the help of this backing the Ethiopians proceeded to push back the Somalis, and in the climactic battle of Diredawa-Jigiga (2–5 March 1978) the Somali forces were defeated. Somali President Siad Barre then requested a ceasefire (8 March), simultaneously withdrawing his army from Ethiopia. Over one and a half million refugees fled to Somalia in the wake of this defeat. Some insignificant WSLF activity continued, but by 1985 the movement was effectively defunct. Subsequently, the Ethiopians gave support to two opposition groups within Somalia, even seizing two towns 30 km inside Somalia for them (1982). However, neither movement was strong enough to take advantage of this.

Political result

Both countries agreed (4 April 1988) to restore diplomatic relations, to withdraw their forces to a common border and to exchange prisoners of war. Somalia also regained the two towns seized in 1982.

Remarks

The Ogaden conflict took place on two levels. On one level it was part of a decades-long conflict between Ethiopians and Somalis for control of the Ogaden. There is no reason to believe that the problem has been permanently settled. On another level, the war was seen as part of growing Soviet influence on the Horn of Africa, with a twist being added by the seeming Soviet shift in sides partway through the conflict. Soviet involvement inevitably led to the United States becoming concerned, and in 1980 a US-Somali military cooperation agreement was concluded which gave Somalia military aid and provided for American use of the naval and air facilities at Mogadishu and Berbera. After 21 years in power, President Siad Barre was overthrown by rebel forces and obliged to flee the country (Jan. 1991). The Ethiopian regime of President Mengistu was overthrown in a rebellion four months later (May 1991).

15 Maghreb Wars

Bizerta Crisis (Franco-Tunisian Dispute) 1961

Belligerents: France
                      Tunisia

Cause

Tunisia became independent from France in 1956, although France retained several military bases, including the key naval base of Bizerta (Banzart), the northernmost town in Tunisia. It was the seizure of Bizerta by France in 1881 that had led to French control of the country. France in the 1950s and early 1960s was embroiled in the Algerian revolt, and in support of the Algerian cause Tunisia expelled all French forces (1957). After the French bombing of the Tunisian border town of Sakhiet (8 Feb. 1958), which was being used by Algerian rebels, Tunisia demanded the evacuation of Bizerta. In June 1958 General de Gaulle returned to power in France and agreed to evacuate all French bases in Tunisia except Bizerta, which was to be subject to further negotiations, and some outposts in the Sahara. Franco-Tunisian relations then briefly improved.

Occasion

France expanded its facilities at Bizerta during 1961, although public pressure in Tunisia continued to push for French withdrawal. President Bourguiba of Tunisia officially requested France to leave (5 July 1961), simultaneously renewing a 1959 demand for part of French Algeria bordering southern Tunisia. These demands were reinforced with a blockade of Bizerta (announced 17 July), whereupon France dispatched paratroopers to reinforce the garrison (19 July) and fighting followed.

Course of War

Fighting took place (19–22 July) in the Bizerta district. The French succeeded in taking the Tunis-Bizerta road and railway, together with much of Bizerta itself. The main body of the Tunisian army was meanwhile busy in the south of the country, attempting to assume control of areas still controlled by France. A UN-sponsored ceasefire ended hostilities, which had caused the deaths of 1,300 Tunisians, mostly civilians, and 21 French soldiers.

Political result

An agreement was signed (21 Sept. 1961) which led to the phased withdrawal of French forces from Bizerta, commencing on 1 October 1961 and completed in June 1962. France, however, was allowed to retain rights at the airbase. Full control over the Bizerta base was handed over to Tunisia in late 1963.

War of the Sands (Morocco-Algeria Dispute) 1963

Belligerents: **Algeria**
                    Morocco

Cause

The Algerian-Moroccan border had been determined by the former colonial power, France, to the satisfaction of neither state. The Moroccan king, Hassan II, wished to create a Greater Morocco and this led to a series of border clashes and regional wars. Morocco particularly wanted to establish its control over the western Algerian region around Tindouf, an area rich in iron ore, oil and natural gas. When Algeria became independent (1962), King Hassan attempted to seize the existing Algerian border posts, but was defeated. President Ben Bella of Algeria also requested a border rectification, which Morocco ignored. Relations between the two states deteriorated, with Hassan considering the radical Algerian régime a threat to the Moroccan monarchy.

Occasion

Algeria extended its control over Tindouf (Oct. 1962), with the loss of some life in incidents with pro-Moroccans. A visit by Hassan to Algiers (March 1963) briefly improved relations, but in July a plot against the king was uncovered, in which Algerian involvement was suspected, and the border issue was revived.

Course of War

The War of the Sands lasted only three weeks, with neither side possessing sufficient equipment or logistical support for a lengthy campaign. Fighting broke out on 13 October 1963 and Moroccan forces advanced to near Tindouf before being halted. The radical Egyptian government of President Nasser rushed supplies and men to Algeria which proved critical in allowing it to halt the Moroccan advance. Fighting ended with a truce sponsored by the newly-created OAU at a conference at Bamako (cease-fire 2 Nov. 1963).

Political result

The Bamako Agreement (30 Oct. 1963) was reached under the mediation of the Ethiopian emperor, Hailie Selassie. A ceasefire was agreed, and an OAU-sponsored force from Ethiopia and Mali was to occupy the disputed district. The final frontier was left for an OAU arbitration commission. The Treaty of Ifrane (15 June 1969) restored good relations between Algeria and Morocco. By the Rabat Agreements (15 June 1972), Morocco finally accepted the French-demarcated frontier, which placed Tindouf inside Algeria.

Remarks

This was the first war between two recently independent Arab states and was a prelude to the post-1975 Saharan War.

Saharan War 1975–

Belligerents: **Morocco, Mauritania, (France)**
                           Algeria, POLISARIO

Cause

In 1975, in the face of growing anti-colonial sentiment, Spain indicated a willingness to leave its phosphate-rich colony of Spanish (Western) Sahara. This area was claimed by the neighboring states of Morocco and Mauritania, while an independence movement, POLISARIO (Popular Front for the Liberation of Saguia el Hamra and Rio de Oro), founded in 1972, enjoyed Algerian support. A United Nations mission to the colony reported that a majority of the inhabitants favored independence (15 Oct. 1975), and the following day the International Court of Justice supported the concept of self-determination.

Spain was affected at this point by a political crisis with the collapse (17 Oct.) and death (20 Nov.) of its dictator, Franco. Concerned about domestic problems, the Spanish government sought a rapid solution to the Saharan crisis and began negotiations with Morocco (21 Oct.). King Hassan of Morocco immediately applied pressure to Spain by organizing the Green March of 350,000 unarmed Moroccans into the colony; they penetrated only six miles before being halted, but Morocco had made its point. Spain agreed to abandon its colony to Morocco and Mauritania, in return for a guarantee of Spanish economic interests. Hassan then recalled the marchers (9 Nov.). The tripartite Madrid Agreement (14 Nov.) bound Spain to leave the colony by the end of February 1976. Moroccan forces moved to fill the vacuum left by Spain, occupying the capital, El Aaiún (11 Dec.). Morocco and Mauritania subsequently divided the country between themselves, with Morocco getting most of the mineral resources.

Occasion

In response to the Madrid Agreement, POLISARIO proclaimed the Saharawi Arab Democratic Republic (SADR), with a government-in-exile based in Algeria (27 Feb. 1976). This action led Morocco to break off relations with Algeria (7 March).

Course of War

POLISARIO waged an active war against Morocco and Mauritania, frequently bringing the fighting into their prewar territory. In June 1976 POLISARIO succeeded in launching a dramatic attack against the Mauritanian capital, Nouakchott, 900 miles distant. France became involved in late 1977, carrying out aerial attacks on POLISARIO camps in support of Mauritania and Morocco. The war, however, took a heavy economic toll, which contributed to a coup in Mauritania (10 July 1978). By the Algiers Agreement (5 Aug. 1979), the new Mauritanian government made peace with POLISARIO and surrendered its claims in Western Sahara. Mauritania subsequently severed relations with Morocco and allowed POLISARIO to operate from its territory, while King Hassan claimed the reversion of the former Mauritanian area.

The war now intensified, being carried at times into Morocco proper. This led Morocco to develop a strong defensive strategy, involving a heavy defensive perimeter around the 'useful triangle' which contained most of the mineral deposits and the southern port of Dakhla (completed 1982). The largest battle of the war was at Guelta Zemmour (13 Oct. 1981), where 3,000 POLISARIO soldiers with tanks defeated 200 Moroccans. POLISARIO's introduction of Soviet-made SAM-6 missiles led to a dramatic increase in United States aid for Morocco. Desultory fighting continued until May 1988, when Algeria dramatically abandoned POLISARIO and resumed relations with Morocco.

Political result

As a result of the resumption of relations between Algeria and Morocco, all sides accepted a UN-sponsored ceasefire (Aug. 1988) to be supervised by a UN peacekeeping force. A referendum was to determine the territory's future. Fighting, however, continued sporadically, and as at mid-1991 no agreement has been reached on how or when the referendum should be held.

Remarks

In February 1982 the OAU seated the SADR, causing a split in which many members (including Morocco) walked out and threatening the future of the organization. By 1990 some 70 countries had recognized the SADR. The war cost Morocco more than the revenues from its mining, causing it to have one of the world's largest international debts.

16 Post-Independence African Wars

South Africa-Angola War 1975–91

Belligerents: **Angola, Cuba**
                        South Africa, UNITA

Cause

Angola received its independence from Portugal in 1975 after a lengthy armed struggle. This had not only resulted in a civil war but had also embroiled Angola in regional and East-West competition. During the independence struggle three anti-Portuguese groups had emerged: the (Marxist) MPLA (People's Movement for the Liberation of Angola), the FNLA (National Front for the Liberation of Angola) and UNITA (National Union for the Total Independence of Angola). Both South Africa and Rhodesia (now Zimbabwe) had provided support for the Portuguese, in order to prevent a black, and possibly radical, government coming to power in Angola. The Portuguese forces had performed well and had successfully contained the insurrection.

Occasion

After the revolution of 1974, Portugal decided to grant independence to its colonies. Independence day for Angola was set for 11 November 1975. Immediately all three Angolan resistance groups began fighting among themselves for power. This civil war soon acquired an international dimension as foreign powers provided assistance to the differing factions. The MPLA was supported by the Soviet bloc, the FNLA and UNITA by China, the United States, South Africa and other Western powers. Cuba sent troops to support the MPLA, while a South African force entered Angola in support of UNITA (23 Oct. 1975). The question of which external power intervened first is still a matter of debate.

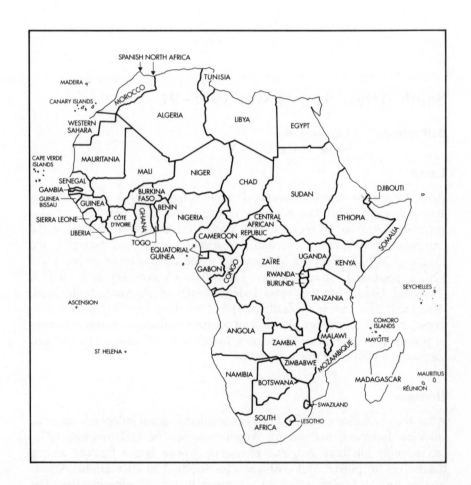

17 Modern Africa

Course of War

The MPLA defeated its opponents with the help of Cuban soldiers and Soviet assistance. South African support for UNITA probably influenced several countries opposed to South Africa's domestic racial policies to recognize the MPLA as the legitimate government of Angola. China ended its support for the FNLA shortly after independence. In the United States congressional restraints prevented aid to anti-MPLA forces equalling that being provided by the Soviet bloc, which further enhanced the MPLA's military position. This combination of diplomatic and military factors finally forced the South Africans to withdraw their forces (Jan. 1976). The UNITA headquarters at Huambo, as well as the last FNLA base, soon fell to the MPLA (11 Feb. 1976).

There followed a period of MPLA rule over most of Angola, although UNITA retained control of a corner of southeast Angola, where it enjoyed the protection of the South African airforce. The FNLA now effectively collapsed. Significant fighting in Angola resumed, however, as a result of Angolan-South African antagonism. The Angolan MPLA government supported SWAPO (South West African People's Organization) in its fight for independence from the South African administration of Namibia (formerly South West Africa), which had originally been assigned to South Africa as a League of Nations mandate at the end of the First World War. Since 1978 South Africa had occasionally conducted raids inside Angola against SWAPO bases. In addition, Angola also provided sanctuary for members of the South African ANC (African National Congress), which was attempting to remove the white minority government of South Africa. During 1981, in Operation Protea, a South African force penetrated up to 120 km into Angola. The government's preoccupation with this crisis allowed a resurgence in UNITA activity. UNITA and South African forces increasingly cooperated against the MPLA forces.

The Namibian crisis, however, began to diminish after a 1978 promise by South Africa to grant Namibia independence, which was first formalized by an international agreement in 1981 but not finally achieved until 1990. In 1985 the American Congress allowed the renewal of aid to UNITA. In 1987 the MPLA launched a large offensive against UNITA, aimed at its headquarters at Jamba. South Africa intervened in support of UNITA and in the Battle of the Lomba River (Sept. 1987) the MPLA forces were defeated. UNITA counterattacked and laid siege to the last remaining MPLA base in southern Angola, Cuito Cuanavale. With the help of Cuban reinforcements, the town withstood the UNITA siege and bombardment. In March 1988 South Africa withdrew most of its forces from Angola. A Cuban advance to the southern border brought about a number of serious clashes with the South Africans, until a ceasefire was agreed (Aug. 1988). The new post-1985 Soviet leadership under Mikhail Gorbachev did not find the Angolan involvement cost-effective; it is estimated that Soviet support for Angola was costing it over $1,000 million a year.

Political result

In the Geneva Agreement (5 Aug. 1988) between Angola, Cuba and South Africa a plan was adopted for ending the conflict, resulting in a ceasefire being signed by South Africa and Angola at Ruacana. This linked the withdrawal of Cuban forces from Angola to the South African withdrawal from Namibia. Plans for Namibian independence were to proceed, with the UN-supervised election of a Namibian constituent assembly. A UN force (UNTAG) was to be sent to Namibia to ensure order and South Africa was allowed to retain 1,500 men in two southern bases. South African forces were duly withdrawn from Angola by the end of August 1988. This plan was further elaborated by the New York Agreements (22 Dec. 1988), involving Angola, Cuba and South Africa. These laid down a timetable for Namibian independence and for the withdrawal of Cuban forces, estimated at 50,000, under the supervision of a UN force (UNAVEM), between April 1989 and July 1991. The first contingent of Cuban troops left in January 1989. Namibia achieved full independence on 21 March 1990.

The Estoril Peace Accord (31 May 1991) between the MPLA-dominated Angolan government and UNITA formally ended the civil war. The settlement, mediated by Portugal, arranged for the country's first multi-party elections to be held in 1992. A political military commission comprising members from the two opposing Angolan groups as well as from Portugal, the Soviet Union and the United States would supervise the ceasefire and prepare for elections. UNAVEM was retained as an observer force for this agreement, becoming known as UNAVEM-2.

Chad-Libya War 1978-87

Belligerents: **Chad, (France)**
                     Libya

Cause

Chad, which became independent of France in 1960, is divided between the predominantly Islamic and Arabic north, and the basically Christian or non-Moslem and black South. Differences between these populations led to extended domestic conflict, which allowed Libya to seize the Aozou strip in northern Chad in June 1973. Libya's leader, Colonel Qadaffi, justified this action on the basis of a 1935 Franco-Italian protocol, subsequently disavowed by France in 1938, and a 1943 treaty between Vichy France and Italy, which then ruled Libya. The area is reputedly rich in uranium and manganese and the desire to control it led to extended Libyan involvement in the tangled web of the Chadean civil war.

Occasion

In 1975 the new Chadean leader, General Malloum, asked the French to withdraw their troops, which had retained a residual presence since independence. The following year Colonel Qadaffi began providing support for the Arab-dominated opposition movement, FROLINAT (National Liberation Front). Qadaffi's claim to the Aozou Strip divided FROLINAT. One group, under Goukouni Oueddi, acquiesced in the claim while another faction under Hissène Habré opposed it. The Libyan threat was defeated by renewed French intervention. A ceasefire in the civil war was arranged in 1978, and an interim government, the GUNT (Gouvernement d'union nationale de transition) was established, with Goukouni Oueddi as president.

Course of War

The Libyans, seeing in Chadean unity a threat to their claims, invaded northern Chad (April 1978) but were pushed back by the Chadeans with French help. In 1980 President Goukouni signed a friendship treaty with Libya, allowing Libyan intervention if the internal security of Chad was threatened. In October 1980 Libyan forces did intervene to suppress the rebel forces led by Habré, who fled to Cameroon. In January 1981 Goukouni signed an agreement with Libya for the eventual merger of the two countries. Following this, 6,000 Libyan troops were dispatched to Chad, a development deeply unpopular with many Chadeans, as well as with Western powers concerned about Qadaffi's power. The French, working through the OAU and with United States support, brought about the reluctant evacuation of the Libyans (Oct. 1981). As the Libyans withdrew, Habré's forces again renewed their attacks, and in June 1982 captured the capital, N'Djaména. Habré now formed a government, while Goukouni fled, establishing an exile Government of National Salvation with Libyan support.

In March 1983 Habré complained to the United Nations about Libya's continued occupation of the Aozou Strip. In the face of Libya's support for Goukouni's forces, which were concentrated in the north, Habré appealed for help, receiving aid from France, the United States and Zaïre. As Goukouni's forces advanced south under Libyan air cover, the United States dispatched airplanes to nearby Sudanese airfields. In August 1983, as the situation deteriorated further, President Mitterrand of France decided on direct French intervention, code-named Operation Manta. A French force of about 3,000 established a no-go area, the *zone rouge*, between the warring armies. In September 1984 an agreement was reached for the withdrawal of foreign forces, but while the French withdrew the Libyans remained. In February 1986 Libyan forces crossed the 16th parallel, which had divided the opposing groups, hoping that the French parliamentary elections then being held would distract French attention. Habré's forces, however, fought very well, French forces were rapidly deployed in Operation Sparrowhawk, and the United States provided $10 million. President Mitterrand declared the conflict an international one (Nov. 1986). With heavy Franco-American support, Habré's forces began a successful northern drive, defeating the Libyans, taking the town of Aozou (8 Aug. 1987) and regaining control of the Aozou Strip. The last action of the war was the first Chadean raid into Libya, in which 1,700 Libyans were killed and aircraft and tanks were destroyed (5 Sept.).

Political result

A truce was arranged by the OAU (11 Sept. 1987), and Qadaffi declared that he considered the war at an end (26 May 1988). Libya, however, continues to maintain its claim to the Aozou Strip. President Habré was overthrown by opposition forces in December 1990.

Tanzania-Uganda Dispute 1978–9

Belligerents: **Tanzania**
                     Uganda

Cause

After independence from Britain the three east African states of Kenya, Tanzania and Uganda formed the East African Community to further economic cooperation. By 1977 the community had collapsed amidst mutual recriminations. In Uganda Idi Amin had seized power in a bloody coup in 1971, with the former president, Milton Obote, taking refuge in Tanzania. There followed a series of border skirmishes between the two states during August 1971.

Occasion

Against the backdrop of growing domestic unrest and declining support for his increasingly brutal and erratic regime, Amin decided to divert attention with an invasion of Tanzania. During May 1978 he began to mass his forces; after a tentative probe of Tanzania (9 Oct.), a full-scale invasion was launched on 30 October.

Course of War

Ugandan forces never penetrated more than 20 miles into Tanzanian territory and by the end of November Tanzanian forces had driven the Ugandan army back across the border. In January 1979 Tanzania carried the war into Uganda, determined to overthrow Amin. The Tanzanian army, numbering 20,000, was supported by 1,200 Ugandan refugees who were part of the UNLF (Uganda National Liberation Front), and there was hope of a general revolt against Amin. His forces soon collapsed, although the Libyan régime of Colonel Qadaffi provided Amin with 1,500 men. These poorly-trained militiamen were annihilated when the capital, Kampala, fell (April 1979).

Political result

Tanzanian forces crushed the pro-Amin forces and a short-lived civilian régime was established under President Godfrey Binaisa, but this was over-thrown by a military coup (March 1980). In October 1980 Amin loyalists staged an abortive invasion from the Sudan and Zaïre, but were quickly routed by the Tanzanians, who had retained a garrison of 10,000 men. Milton Obote returned to become president (Dec. 1980), with Tanzanian support, and in June 1981 Tanzania finally withdrew its forces. Uganda, however, remained in turmoil and Obote was again overthrown (27 July 1985), taking refuge once more in Tanzania.

Christmas War (Burkina Faso-Mali War) 1985

Belligerents: **Burkina Faso**
                   Mali

Cause

Part of the border between Burkina Faso (known as Upper Volta until 1984) and Mali had been in dispute since their independence from France in 1960. The disputed district, known as the Agacher Strip and measuring about 90 miles by 12, was important as it possessed the only fresh water supplies in the region. Negotiations (1961–74) failed to achieve a solution and were followed by border skirmishes (Dec. 1974 and June 1975). In 1983 the two states agreed to submit the dispute to the International Court of Justice (ICJ). By September 1985 much progress had been achieved by the border commissions of both states, over 1000 km of frontier demar-cation having been agreed. Political relations, however, suddenly worsened.

Occasion

A deterioration in relations became evident when Burkina Faso expelled the secretary-general of the Economic Community of West African States (ECOWAS), who was a Malian, for making critical remarks about the policies of Burkina's president, Captain Thomas Sankara (Aug. 1985). This was followed by the dispatch of Burkina military units to some villages in the disputed district, ostensibly to conduct a census (10–20 Dec. 1985). Mali responded militarily to this action and war began on Christmas Day.

Course of War

In a five-day war (25–30 Dec.), the fighting stretched along most of the common frontier, spilling beyond the disputed area of the Agacher Strip and including air attacks. It appears that Mali enjoyed French support and Burkina Faso Libyan support. A ceasefire was finally arranged through the efforts of President Houphouët-Boigny of the Ivory Coast (Côte d'Ivoire). The war caused about 60–100 casualties.

Political result

A public reconciliation between President Sankara of Burkina Faso and President Mousa Traore of Mali took place at Yamoussoukro in the Ivory Coast (17–18 Jan. 1986). The belligerents agreed to accept the decision of the ICJ as to the demarcation of the border. The ICJ ruling (22 Dec. 1986) divided the disputed district roughly equally between Burkina Faso and Mali. President Sankara was later overthrown and killed in a coup (15 Oct. 1987).

17 South American Wars

Argentine-Brazilian War 1825–8

Belligerents: **Argentina**
                      Brazil

Cause

Uruguay had long been an area of Spanish-Portuguese rivalry during the colonial era, forming a disputed region between the Spanish in Argentina and the Portuguese in Brazil. The struggle for control here continued into the early years of independence in the nineteenth century. In 1680 the Portuguese established the town of Novo Colonia do Sacramento on the Rio de la Plata opposite the Argentine capital of Buenos Aires. The Spanish established Montevideo (now the capital of Uruguay) in 1726 as a garrison and proceeded to push back the Portuguese. In 1776 Uruguay was incorporated into the Spanish colony of Argentina. Buenos Aires became independent from Spain in 1810 and several years of upheaval followed. José Artigas, now considered Uruguay's national hero, wanted Uruguay to become an autonomous part of Argentina, but he was crushed by powerful conservative forces from Buenos Aires afraid of his ideas on reform. In 1816 Portuguese-Brazilian forces invaded Uruguay, taking Montevideo in 1817 and incorporating it in the Brazilian Empire as the province of Banda Oriental.

Occasion

During the period of Brazilian domination, opponents of the new régime fled to Buenos Aires where they organized a liberation movement. In April 1825 a group of these expatriates, 'the 33 immortals', invaded Uruguay with the aim of incorporating it in Argentina. The Argentine government accepted this request for annexation. In response, Brazil declared war on Argentina (1 Dec. 1825).

VENEZUELA

GUYANA (British Guiana)
SURINAM (Dutch Guiana)
FRENCH GUIANA

Bogotá

COLOMBIA

Quito

ECUADOR

Guayaquil

PERU

ACRE (to Brazil 1903)

BRAZIL

Lima

Callao

Chincha Is.

Ayacucho

La Paz

(to Chile 1883) TACNA

BOLIVIA

CHACO (to Paraguay 1938)

ARICA
(to Chile 1883–1929,
to Peru 1929)

to Brazil 1870

TARAPACA
(to Chile 1883)

Concepcion

Rio de Janeiro

PARAGUAY

ATACAMA
(to Chile 1884)

Antofagasta

Asuncion

to Argentina 1874

URUGUAY

Valparaiso

Buenos Aires

Santiago

Montevideo

CHILE

ARGENTINA

FALKLAND
ISLANDS

Course of War

Argentina reacted by electing a national executive, with Bernardo Rivadavia as president. A strong centralist, he led the Unitarian Party in opposition to the Federalists. He produced a new unitary constitution, which was rejected by virtually all the other Argentine provinces except Buenos Aires. Most of the other provinces were not interested in this conflict and as a result Buenos Aires was left to fight the war on its own. The Brazilian navy attempted a blockade of Buenos Aires, but in an engagement at Juncal (9 Feb. 1827) the Brazilian squadron was defeated and all its vessels captured. The Brazilian army was defeated at the Battle of Ituzaingó (20 Feb. 1827), known to the Brazilians as the Battle of Paso del Rosario. British policy, which was opposed to one state controlling both sides of the Rio de la Plata, intervened when an Argentine victory seemed likely and forced a settlement.

Political result

By the Convention of Rio de Janeiro (27 Aug. 1828), Brazil and Argentina recognized the establishment of Uruguayan independence, which became the smallest independent state in South America. Rivadavia resigned as Argentine president in protest at the failure to gain Uruguay. A peace treaty between Argentina and Brazil was not finally concluded until the Treaty of Parna (7 March 1856), which reaffirmed the terms of the 1828 convention.

Peru-Gran Colombia War 1828-9

Belligerents: Peru
                    Gran Colombia

Cause

Peru became independent of Spain in 1821, and in the following year Ecuador likewise achieved independence and became part of the new state of Gran (Greater) Colombia. A dispute arose between Peru and Gran Colombia over the sovereignty of the border provinces of Jaén and Maynas. During the Spanish period they had at various times been ruled by the viceroyalty of Nueva Granada (which formed the basis for Gran Colombia) and by the viceroyalty of Peru. Both provinces had joined with Peru in 1821, but in 1822 Gran Colombia claimed that the provinces should belong to it.

Occasion

The dispute culminated with a Gran Colombian ultimatum to Peru (Feb.

1828) to relinquish the provinces within six months. The Peruvians responded by voting for war preparations. At the end of the six-month period Gran Colombia duly declared war on Peru.

Course of War

Peru's forces were led by its president, de la Mar, while the president of Gran Colombia, Simon Bolívar, delegated command to Marshal Sucre. During the first phase of the war the Peruvian navy quickly gained command of the seas and occupied Guayaquil (19 Jan. 1829), one of the most important harbors on the west coast of South America. The Peruvian army of 7,500 faced a Gran Colombian force of 4,600, but Sucre, rather than engaging de la Mar, began to retreat northward, forcing the Peruvians to follow him. At the narrow pass at Tarqui, Sucre's forces turned and under General Flores defeated de la Mar (27 Feb.). After an abortive effort at a peace settlement, de la Mar decided to continue the war, but was deposed by one of his generals, Gamarra. The new Peruvian leader wished to end the war with Gran Colombia, evacuating Guayaquil (20 July) as a prelude to concluding a peace.

Political result

By the Treaty of Guayaquil, sometimes called the Larrea-Gual treaty (22 Sept. 1829), both sides recognized their boundaries as being those of the old viceroyalties. A boundary commission was to be appointed to fix the frontier. Subsequent efforts to define the frontier failed, however, leading to further conflict.

Remarks

This border dispute has been the cause of two further wars, the Ecuador-Peru Wars of 1941 and 1981.

War of the Peruvian-Bolivian Confederation 1836–40

Belligerents: **Peruvian-Bolivian Confederation**
                     Argentina, Chile

Cause

In the years following independence (in 1821) Peruvian political life was dominated by the 'marshals of Ayacucho', the generals who had defeated the Spaniards. These included Santa Cruz, Gamarra, Obregoso and

Castilla. In 1833, on the election of Obregoso as president, troops loyal to the outgoing president, Gamarra, staged an unsuccessful revolt. In 1835 another revolt broke out under Felipe Salaverry and Peru dissolved into a civil war between Obregoso, Gamarra and Salaverry. Obregoso turned for help to the president of Bolivia, Santa Cruz, who had previously been the Peruvian minister to Chile and was an advocate of a Bolivian-Peruvian union. Santa Cruz defeated Gamarra, went on to defeat and kill Salaverry (Feb. 1836), and established a Peruvian-Bolivian Confederation with himself as protector (28 Oct. 1836). Santa Cruz, who claimed Inca descent, dreamt of reviving the Inca Empire.

Occasion

Chile and Argentina feared the creation of such a large northern state, both politically and economically, and this led Chile to intervene on behalf of Gamarra. Two Chilean naval vessels captured three Peruvian-Bolivian ships, almost the entire navy of the Confederation, in Callao harbor. Chile, having achieved naval supremacy, now sent an ultimatum demanding the dissolution of the confederation. This was rejected and Chile declared war (26 Dec. 1836), an action followed by Argentina (9 May 1837).

Course of War

Santa Cruz defeated the initial Chilean landing of 3,500 men, capturing the entire invading force. The Chilean commander, Admiral Blanco Encalada, agreed to the humiliating peace Treaty of Paucarpata (17 Nov. 1837), which was subsequently repudiated by his government. Santa Cruz also successfully defeated an Argentine invasion (1838). Chile mounted a new invasion of 6,000 soldiers (July 1838) under General Bulnes, a force which included a large number of Peruvian opponents of the confederation, among them Gamarra and Castilla. At the Battle of Yungay (20 Jan. 1839), the Chileans defeated Santa Cruz's army and he was forced to flee. The confederation was dissolved, with Peru and Bolivia again becoming separate states. Chilean forces were finally withdrawn from Peru in October 1840.

Political result

A Preliminary Peace Convention was signed at Lima (19 April 1840). This attempted to resolve the crisis which had begun in 1835, stipulating that any further disputes arising out of this period were to be referred to the arbitration of the president of New Granada (Colombia). Gamarra became president of Peru (24 Feb. 1839), but was killed during the Peruvian-Bolivian War of 1841. In Bolivia the supporters of Santa Cruz overthrew the provisional president, Velasco, and installed General Ballivián, who remained in power until 1847. The removal of Velasco led Peru to invade Bolivia in the 1841 war between the two countries.

Peruvian-Bolivian War 1841–2

Belligerents: **Peru**
Bolivia

Cause

This was a sequel to the events of the War of the Peruvian-Bolivian Confederation of 1836–9. In 1841 the Bolivian president, Velasco, was overthrown and for a period there were three competing governments in Bolivia.

Occasion

President Gamarra of Peru invaded Bolivia to prevent a return to power of the former president, Santa Cruz, and in the hope of annexing Bolivia to Peru. This invasion rallied most Bolivians around General Ballivián, who had been installed as provisional president by the supporters of Santa Cruz.

Course of War

Gamarra's well-trained force of 6,000 Peruvians took the Bolivian capital of La Paz. Ballivián's 3,800 troops, however, reinforced by cavalry provided by his erstwhile rival, Velasco, succeeded in defeating a Peruvian army of 5,200 in the brutal Battle of Ingavi (18 Nov. 1841), which lasted only 50 minutes and in which Gamarra was killed. A Bolivian attempt to drive home their victory with an invasion of Peru was thwarted by Chile.

Political result

The peace Treaty of Puno (7 June 1842) was mediated by Chile and arranged for a mutual renunciation of financial claims arising out of the war. Gamarra's death was followed by another period of domestic turmoil in Peru until a stable government was established in 1844 under Ramón Castilla, who dominated the country until his death in 1868 (president 1845–51 and 1855–62).

Remarks

This was the last attempt to achieve Simon Bolívar's dream of a Federation of the Andes.

First Ecuador-Colombia War 1862

Belligerents: **Ecuador**
Colombia

Cause

In 1830 Gran (Greater) Colombia dissolved into the states of Venezuela, New Granada (Colombia) and Ecuador. Within Colombia a civil war was fought (1860–2) over the issue of whether it should be a centralized or a decentralized state. The protagonists in this struggle were the conservative government forces led by President Mariano Ospina and the liberal forces led by former President Mosquera.

Occasion

Many of Mosquera's followers had taken refuge across the border in Ecuador, from where they continued to raid Colombia. When the conservative forces pursued the liberals into Ecuador, they were stopped at the frontier by an Ecuadorean officer. In the ensuing altercation the officer was wounded by the Colombians. President García Moreno of Ecuador moved immediately to redress this insult, gathered an army of mostly untrained, conscripted men and marched against Colombia.

Course of War

In the only engagement of the war, the Battle of Tulcán (31 July 1862), the Colombian leader, Arboleda, succeeded with a force of 3,500 men in getting behind the 800-man Ecuadorean army and cutting their supply and communication lines. The Ecuadorean army was defeated and García Moreno and his minister of war, Daniel Salvador, were captured.

Political result

The Ecuadoreans were released in return for recognition of Arboleda's 'Granadine Confederation'. By a secret clause, which was never fulfilled, Ecuador agreed to pay Arboleda $20,000 and supply him with arms. Arboleda, however, was assassinated soon afterwards (12 Nov. 1862) in the civil war raging in Colombia.

Second Ecuador-Colombia War 1862–4

Belligerents: **Ecuador**
                    Colombia

Cause

The Colombian civil war, which had raged for over two years, came to an end in 1862 when the conservative Colombian leader, Ospina, was defeated by the army of the liberal leader, Mosquera. A new federalist constitution was adopted and the country's name was altered to the United States of Colombia (1863). Mosquera hoped to restore the old state of Gran (Greater) Colombia and this led him to intervene first in the Venezuelan civil war and then in Ecuador.

Occasion

In 1862 President García Moreno of Ecuador, in pursuit of a pro-clerical policy, concluded a concordat with the Papacy. Mosquera, an anti-clerical, gave support to anti-clerical groups within Ecuador in the vain hope of gaining their support for his plans for a new Gran Colombia. He issued a declaration at Popayan, calling on his countrymen to support Moreno's opponents. García Moreno decided to use Mosquera's actions as an excuse for war, hoping that this would rally support for the concordat, which the Ecuadorean Congress was refusing to ratify, as well as spreading abroad his own conservative vision.

Course of War

President García Moreno's father-in-law, General Flores, led an Ecuadorean army of 7,000 men against Colombia. A hoped-for simultaneous revolt by Colombian conservatives in support of the conservative Ecuadorean forces failed to occur. At the Battle of Cuaspud (6 Dec. 1862), a Colombian army of 4,000 under Mosquera routed a 6,000-strong force under Flores. The Colombians killed 1,500 Ecuadoreans and captured a further 2,000, together with all their artillery, small arms and ammunition, as well as all the Ecuadorean musicians. Flores and 100 men escaped in a headlong flight, not halting until they were five days from Cuaspud.

Political result

In the Treaty of Pinzaquí (30 Dec. 1864), Mosquera offered a generous peace to Ecuador, allowing a restoration of the prewar status quo and not demanding, as had been expected, the incorporation of Ecuador into a Greater Colombia. Neither did he demand an indemnity or reparations.

Remarks

Two disastrous wars with Colombia, together with Mosquera's generosity, did much to undermine García Moreno's régime. Although he managed to cling to power, his brutality became infamous throughout Latin America. He was assassinated in 1875.

Peruvian-Spanish War 1864–6

Belligerents: **Spain**
                    Peru, Bolivia, Chile, Ecuador

Cause

Spain had never recognized Peru's independence (achieved in 1821), and when France became involved in a war with Mexico in 1861, Spain attempted to re-establish some of its former colonial influence in the New World. The former colony of Santo Domingo (Dominican Republic) was reabsorbed and a large fleet was sent to the west coast of South America. Fears of Spanish ambitions were aroused among many Latin American states as a result.

Occasion

The Spanish fleet was clearly looking for a pretext to interfere in South American affairs. In the case of Peru, tension arose over former colonial debts and the treatment of immigrants (large numbers of Spaniards, particularly Basques, had continued to emigrate from Spain). In a demonstration of force, the Spanish navy seized the guano-rich Chincha Islands off the coast of Peru (14 April 1864). President Pézet of Peru was anxious to compromise and in the Treaty of Callao (27 Jan. 1865) agreed to pay a large indemnity to Spain in return for the evacuation of the islands, which were a major economic asset to Peru. Popular outrage at these terms led to a military coup which brought Colonel Prado to power. The Spaniards had, meanwhile, in accordance with the treaty, evacuated the islands and sailed to the Chilean port of Valparaiso. Here they accused the Chilean authorities of fomenting anti-Spanish feeling in Peru.

Course of War

The new Peruvian government under Prado organized a broad anti-Spanish alliance and with this support declared war on Spain (14 Jan. 1866). Chile, Ecuador and Bolivia also joined in the war against Spain. Many Latin American states felt that Spain's actions threatened their independence and a series of defensive alliances was therefore concluded.

A Chilean-Peruvian alliance (5 Dec. 1865) was later joined by Bolivia (11 April 1866). A more general Treaty of Alliance was concluded between Bolivia, Chile, Colombia, Ecuador, Peru, El Salvador and Venezuela (10 July 1865). A Treaty of Alliance was also agreed between Chile, Ecuador and Peru (30 Jan. 1866).

The two main actions of this war were the Spanish bombardments of the Chilean port of Valparaiso (31 March 1866) and of the Peruvian port of Callao (2 May 1866). Chilean forces did manage to capture one Spanish ship, causing the Spanish admiral to commit suicide at this disgrace. During the bombardment of Callao, the Peruvians inflicted severe damage on the Spanish fleet, which then returned to Europe. Spain now ceased active warfare, although it was only through United States mediation that an armistice was finally reached between Spain and the Latin American allies of Peru, Chile, Bolivia and Ecuador (11 April 1871).

Political result

The Treaty of Paris (14 Aug. 1879) settled the dispute between Peru and Spain and normal relations were re-established. Spain restored relations with Bolivia by the Treaty of Paris (21 Aug. 1879), with Chile by the Treaty of Lima (12 June 1883) and with Ecuador by the Treaty of Madrid (28 Jan. 1885).

Remarks

The war helped spur Chile to develop its naval strength, which it was to use with great effectiveness against Bolivia and Peru in the War of the Pacific of 1879-84.

War of the Triple Alliance (López War) 1864-70

Belligerents: **Paraguay**
                     Argentina, Brazil, Uruguay

Cause

Paraguay had remained in comparative isolation after achieving independence from Spain (1811), mostly due to troubled relations with Argentina, which continued to view it as a member of the Argentine Confederation. It was not until 1853 that Paraguay received general international recognition. In 1862 Francisco López succeeded his father as president; his megalomaniac ambition would quickly bring his country to the verge of annihilation. Influenced by a tour of the allied positions in the Crimean War of 1853-6 he focused his energies, and the national wealth, on building up Paraguayan military power. López created the largest army in South

America – 60,000 well-trained and armed men – and constructed one of the greatest fortresses – Humaitá, 'the Sebastopol of the Americas', mounting 380 cannon – near the confluence of the Paraná and Paraguay rivers. He envisaged a powerful place for his country in the affairs of the Rio de la Plata region and this brought him into conflict with his two powerful neighbors, Argentina and Brazil.

Occasion

In 1864 Argentina and Brazil intervened in Uruguay in support of the *Colorados* (liberals) against the *Blancos* (conservatives). López apparently feared that these states planned to take control of Uruguay and eventually Paraguay. Acting to support Uruguayan independence, López invaded the Brazilian state of Matto Grosso (26 Dec. 1864). A request to the Argentine government to allow the Paraguayan army transit rights through Argentina was denied, but López sent his army across it regardless. Paraguay formally declared war on Brazil (5 March 1865) and on Argentina (18 March). Uruguay, dominated by its powerful neighbors, joined Argentina and Brazil in a Triple Alliance explicitly aimed against López (1 May 1865).

Course of War

The Paraguayan forces enjoyed some early successes, cutting off Matto Grosso from the rest of Brazil. The Paraguayan invading force, however, was surrounded and captured (18 Sept. 1865) and the allied forces invaded Paraguay (April 1866). The Brazilian navy had already achieved control of the Paraguay river after the Battle of Riacuelo (June 1865), but the allies were halted at Humaitá. The allies were subsequently weakened by the departure of their land commander, President Bartolomé Mitre of Argentina, who returned home to deal with domestic problems, as well as by the assassination of the Uruguayan president, Venancio Flores. López defeated his enemies at the Battle of Curupaytí (22 Sept. 1866), inflicting 9,000 casualties on the allied army but only losing under 100 Paraguayan dead and wounded. The war, however, remained a stalemate, with both sides weakened by disease.

During 1867 a Brazilian offensive drove López north, leaving Humaitá besieged. It finally surrendered to the allies after having sustained a 13-month siege which cost 100,000 lives (2 Aug. 1867). López now fell back on his capital at Asunción, following a scorched earth policy as he went. At the Battle of Ypacarí (25 Dec. 1867), the allies broke through the Paraguayan defenses below Asunción, which was captured and sacked by the Brazilians (31 Dec.). Pursued by the allies, López fled northward but was finally trapped and killed by the Brazilians in the Battle of Aquidaban (1 March 1870). A Brazilian army of occupation remained in the shattered country until 1876.

Political result

Brazil and Argentina took the opportunity to settle outstanding border disputes with Paraguay to their advantage, taking about 55,000 square miles of territory. Argentine-Brazilian rivalry, however, forestalled Brazilian aspirations of annexing Paraguay. A preliminary peace treaty was agreed at Asunción (20 June 1870), where Brazil and Argentina promised not to interfere in the reorganization of Paraguay. By the Treaty of Asunción (9 Jan. 1872), peace was formally concluded between Brazil and Paraguay, their border being adjusted by a separate treaty signed the same day. A definitive Argentine-Paraguayan peace was concluded by the Treaty of Buenos Aires (3 Feb. 1876), the disputed territory between the Pilcomayo and Verde rivers being left to arbitration. The arbitral award was made by President Hayes of the United States (12 Nov. 1878), who found in favor of Paraguay.

Remarks

Paraguay had undergone a remarkable total mobilization, its people fighting with incredible bravery and tenacity in a struggle seen by them as a war of national existence and in which they suffered a staggering number of casualties. Of the prewar population of 525,000, only about 28,000 men, 106,000 women and 86,000 children survived. Allied casualties numbered nearly 100,000. In Brazil the cost of the war helped to weaken the monarchy, contributing to its eventual overthrow in 1889.

War of the Pacific 1879–84

Belligerents: Chile
                     Bolivia, Peru

Cause

An 1866 Bolivian-Chilean treaty agreed a frontier running along the 24th parallel, with Chile enjoying a half share in the customs, full mining and export rights and full trading rights between the 23rd and 24th parallels. In 1870 Chile purchased from Bolivia for $10,000 the right for an Anglo-Chilean company to mine nitrate north of the 24th parallel. Discontent began to grow in Bolivia at the wealth being earned by the Chileans, while in Peru discontent was growing over Chile's hold on the mineral-rich (nitrates and guano) southern Peruvian province of Tarapacá. In 1873 a secret Bolivian-Peruvian agreement of mutual defense against any future aggression was concluded, an understanding clearly aimed at Chile.

Occasion

The Bolivian authorities seized the property of the Chilean Nitrate Co. at the port of Antofagasta, then part of the Bolivian province of Atacama. Chile responded by blockading Bolivian ports, ostensibly to protect Chilean property. This was followed by the occupation of Antofagasta (14 Feb. 1879). As a result of this action Bolivia declared war on Chile (1 March). Peru attempted mediation, but Chile refused this offer, as it was aware of the secret Bolivian-Peruvian treaty. Chile hoped to gain the Peruvian province of Tarapacá and, using the purely defensive Bolivian-Peruvian treaty as an excuse, declared war on Peru (5 April 1879).

Course of war

Chilean naval supremacy was established at the Battle of Cape Angamos (8 Oct. 1879) and was a key factor in the war, allowing Chile to land troops at will and giving it control of the entire Bolivian coast. During the first year of the war Chile gained control of the Bolivian seaboard, took control of Tarapacá and annihilated the Peruvian navy. In 1880 Chile, through a seaborne invasion, took the Tacna Arica area of Peru, defeating the Bolivians in the Battle of Campo de la Alianza (26 May 1880) and the Peruvians at Arica (7 June). Bolivia from this point on was effectively eliminated from the conflict. During 1881 the Chileans defeated the Peruvians at Chorillos (13 Jan.), and the survivors of this battle at Miraflores (15 Jan.). These Chilean victories resulted in revolutions in both Bolivia and Peru, which brought the war to a close, although a Chilean army remained in occupation of the Peruvian capital, Lima, and the coast until 1884.

Political result

The Chileans formed a friendly administration in Peru under General Iglesias, with whom they concluded the Treaty of Ancón (20 Oct. 1883). By its terms Peru lost Tarapacá, while Chile was allowed to occupy Tacna and Arica for ten years, with final sovereignty to be decided by plebiscite. It was specified, however, that no Chilean territory formerly belonging to Peru could be ceded to a third party (e.g. Bolivia) without Peru's consent. After the Chilean forces evacuated Peru in 1884, the Peruvian forces of the interior refused to recognize Iglesias, who resigned in 1885. The Tacna-Arica plebiscite never took place, because of procedural arguments, and the dispute soured Chilean-Peruvian relations for many years. The problem in fact lingered on into the twentieth century, leading to the Tacna-Arica Dispute of 1921–9. A settlement was finally reached in 1929 under the Treaty of Ancón, through United States mediation, by which Chile received Arica and Peru regained Tacna.

A settlement with Bolivia proved harder to achieve. A Bolivian-Chilean truce was signed (4 April 1884) which left Chile in control of Atacama province. A subsequent treaty led to Bolivia ceding half of its coast to Chile, including the port of Cobija. A full peace treaty, however, was not reached until the Treaty of Santiago (20 Oct. 1904). In this, Chile agreed to build a railway from Arica to La Paz and Bolivia finally surrendered the Atacama desert and coastal littoral to Chile. This had the effect of making Bolivia a landlocked state.

Remarks

Bolivia continued to look for access to the sea, but was defeated in all directions. Its attempt to take control of the Gran Chaco from Paraguay led to the Chaco War of 1932–5.

War of Acre 1902

Belligerents: **Brazil**
                     Bolivia

Cause

The district of Acre in northeast Bolivia, bordering on Brazil, had attracted little attention before the late nineteenth century. An 1876 Bolivian-Brazilian treaty, which was never implemented, had left open the question of their boundary in this area. The growth of the wild rubber industry, after the discovery of the process for vulcanizing rubber, made the area potentially lucrative.

Occasion

Brazilians, who were already heavily engaged in the rubber boom, began to move into Acre to exploit its rubber resources. The Bolivian government, unable to exercise control over distant Acre, granted an American-based syndicate exploitation rights, together with full administrative control of the area. The Bolivians also established a customs post at Puerto Alonso to prove their rights and to control the Brazilians' export of rubber. This brought about a confrontation with Brazil.

Course of War

A Brazilian-inspired rebellion broke out in Acre under the leadership of a Brazilian, Placido de Castro (Aug. 1902). He soon captured the Bolivian customs post and took control of the entire province. Brazil threatened direct intervention if Bolivia attempted to assert its sovereignty. This forced the Bolivians to give in and the exploitation concession granted to the American syndicate was revoked.

Political result

By the Treaty of Petropolis (17 Nov. 1903), Bolivia ceded the disputed district, totalling 73,000 square miles, to Brazil in return for a small payment and a Brazilian promise to construct a railway from Madeira to Mamoré. Bolivia, in compensation, was to receive a small slice of territory which would give it access to the Madeira river, together with a pledge of perpetual free navigation. Bolivia hoped this might provide it with its desired access to the sea. Brazil was also to pay Bolivia £2,000,000. Peru, which also claimed part of the Acre area, finally abandoned its claims in the Treaty of Rio de Janeiro (8 Sept. 1909).

Chaco War 1932–5

Belligerents: **Bolivia**
                 Paraguay

Cause

The war arose over a territorial dispute concerning the sovereignty of the Chaco Boreal, that is, the Chaco region north of the Pilcomayo river. In the colonial period it had been administered at various times as part of Paraguay and of Bolivia. After independence, neither state had been much concerned about exercising control over an inhospitable district with few natural resources. This changed, however, with Paraguay's loss of territory in the López War of 1864–70 and Bolivia's loss of its seacoast in the War of the Pacific of 1879–84. Bolivia hoped to gain a port on the Paraguay river, which is navigable to reasonable-sized ships, through taking control of the Chaco. From 1906 on, Bolivia began constructing small forts along the Pilcomayo river and eventually Paraguay, to strengthen its claim through occupation, established a settlement of Canadian Mennonites in the district (1926). Skirmishing between the rivals began in 1927 and war was just averted the following year, when Paraguayan forces destroyed a Bolivian outpost, Vanguardia, by the fortuitous intervention of the Pan American Conference on Conciliation and Arbitration then meeting at Washington.

Occasion

The Bolivians had built up their military, trained by the German General Hans Kundt, in preparation for a war, which finally broke out when the Bolivians captured Fort López (Pitiantuta) (15 June 1932).

Course of War

The Bolivian soldiers, who were used to higher altitudes, suffered greatly in the jungle conditions of the Chaco. The Paraguayans, as in the López War, fought tenaciously, expanding their army from 3,000 to 60,000. By mid-July 1932 the Paraguayans had recaptured Fort López. The architect of Paraguayan victory was General Estigarribia, who fought a brilliant war of maneuver. By 1935 Paraguayan forces had established control of the Chaco and a truce was concluded (14 June). The war cost 100,000 lives.

Political result

By the Treaty of Buenos Aires (21 July 1938), Paraguay received three quarters of the Chaco, while Bolivia was guaranteed access to the Atlantic via the Paraguay river. The cost of fighting the war reduced Paraguay's already weak currency by five sixths. Despite its victory, dissatisfaction both with the failure to fight on to total victory and with domestic conditions, exacerbated by financial problems, led to a military coup in Paraguay (1936) and inaugurated a period of political instability.

First Ecuador-Peru War (Zarumilla-Marañón War) 1941

Belligerents: **Ecuador**
                           Peru

Cause

The causes of this war lay in the same territorial dispute which had brought about the Peru-Gran Colombia War of 1828-9, Ecuador having succeeded to the claims of Gran Colombia. Despite occasional efforts at mediation to agree to a frontier, the most recent in 1936-8, no solution had been found. Peru had held most of the disputed area since independence in 1821, but the potential resources of the Amazonian valley made this a desirable area to control.

Occasion

Border skirmishes began to occur when Ecuadorean units moved beyond the de facto frontier to new outposts. A clash between an Ecuadorean patrol and the Peruvian Civil Guard (5 July 1941) ignited the mounting tensions between the two countries.

Course of War

The Peruvians fielded an army of 15,000 men, against an ill-prepared and poorly equipped Ecuadorean army of 4,000. The Peruvians throughout had total command of the air and effective command of the seas, the Ecuadoreans keeping their one battleship out of the war zone. The most important engagement was the Battle of Zarumilla, which broke the Ecuadorean resolve to fight (25 July). The United States, preoccupied with the Second World War, was anxious to avoid conflict in Latin America and so, together with Argentina and Brazil, sponsored a ceasefire to come into effect on 31 July, to be followed by negotiations. In the final hours before the armistice the Peruvians launched a *blitzkrieg* assault on Ecuador, seizing strategic points and overrunning the southernmost Ecuadorean province of El Oro. This war saw the Peruvians make the first use of airborne troops in the New World.

Political result

The Protocol of Rio de Janeiro (29 Jan. 1942) was negotiated between Ecuador and Peru by Brazil, Argentina, Chile and the United States. By its terms Ecuador recognized Peruvian sovereignty over the disputed districts, which Peru had in fact long controlled. Ecuador renounced its claims over 80,000 square miles already actually under Peruvian control and was forced to surrender a further 5,000 square miles. This denied Ecuador any chance of access to the Amazon, leading to the slogan in Ecuador that 'Ecuador has been, is and will be an Amazonian nation'. In 1960 Ecuador, over a technicality, denounced the Rio Protocol and a further war on this question was fought in 1981.

Remarks

Ecuador had been ill-prepared for war, largely through the effects of intense political instability (the period 1925–41 had seen 23 governments). As a result, no serious attention had been given to military quality and as a consequence the army suffered from poor officers and poorly equipped soldiers. Indeed, during the war Peruvian forces never encountered more than weak detachments from the Ecuadorean army, most of which remained on garrison duty.

Second Ecuador–Peru War 1981

Belligerents: Ecuador
                     Peru

Cause

The roots of this brief war lay in Ecuadorean aspirations to gain control of part of the Amazonian valley. Ecuadorean claims here had been the cause of two previous wars: the Peru–Gran Colombia War of 1828–9 and the Ecuador–Peru War of 1941. After the last war Ecuador, in the Rio Protocol (1942), had renounced its claims and agreed to a demarcation of the frontier with Peru. A small mapping error, however, provided Ecuador with an excuse to challenge the settlement. This left an 80-mile stretch of border in dispute. In 1960 Ecuador declared the Rio Protocol void, an action considered invalid by the four guarantors of the protocol, Argentina, Brazil, Chile and the United States.

Occasion

Hostilities occurred in the remote Cordillera del Condor mountains in 1981 when Ecuador accused a Peruvian military helicopter of having violated its airspace and firing on an Ecuadorean border post (23 Jan. 1981). Peru accused the Ecuadoreans of having seized three unoccupied border posts. Within five days the incident had escalated into war.

Course of War

Peruvian forces attacked Ecuadorean troops in the disputed region (28 Jan. 1981) and succeeded in driving them out by the time a ceasefire was arranged by the four guarantor powers of the Rio Protocol (2 Feb.). Under the ceasefire both sides withdrew their forces to points 15 km each side of the disputed frontier. Casualties were one Peruvian and eight Ecuadoreans killed.

Political result

No solution has yet been found to one of Latin America's longest and most intractable border disputes. Ecuador continues to hope for sovereign access to the Amazonian river system via the Marañón, a tributary of the Amazon.

Falklands War 1982

Belligerents: **Argentina**
              Great Britain

Cause

Great Britain and Argentina have had a long-running territorial dispute over the sovereignty of the Falkland Islands (Las Malvinas), lying 300 miles east of the Argentine coast. The first recorded landing was made in 1690 by British sailors, who named them the Falkland Islands. Subsequently a settlement was established in 1764 by the French, whose rights were later (1766) transferred to Spain, by whom the islands were known as Las Malvinas. A brief British settlement was also made. Eventually both settlements were withdrawn and the islands again left uninhabited. In 1820 the newly independent government in Buenos Aires claimed sovereignty over the islands, but their officials were subsequently expelled by both the United States and Great Britain. British sovereignty over the islands was proclaimed in 1833, after which Britain remained in effective control and a British settlement was established. Argentina, however, never renounced its claim, which remained an issue in Anglo-Argentinian relations.

Occasion

The military government in Argentina under General Galtieri desired a triumph to help restore its flagging popularity and it was thought that a dramatic victory in the long-running Falklands issue would do this. The Argentine government therefore increased pressure on Britain to withdraw from the islands. There had been indications that the British government might be prepared to make some arrangement, and it was probably believed that Britain would be unwilling, or unable, to fight a distant war over 1,800 people and 400,000 sheep. The war finally erupted over the illegal landing of a group of Argentinian scrap-metal merchants on South Georgia, a dependency of the Falkland Islands colony (19 March 1982). This was followed by a full-scale Argentine military landing on the Falklands (2 April). The Argentine government stated that its aim was to establish sovereignty over the Falklands, South Georgia and the South Sandwich Islands.

Course of War

The Argentinian invading force rapidly overwhelmed the Royal Marine garrisons on the Falklands and South Georgia and the British governor was deported. Britain responded to the crisis by dispatching a large naval task force, which arrived in late April after an 8,000-mile journey. During this lull in the hostilities efforts at a diplomatic solution proved unavailing. A 200-mile Total Exclusion Zone (TEZ) was declared by Britain around the Falklands. A controversial incident occurred (2 May) with the sinking of the Argentine battlecruiser *General Belgrano* while it was outside the TEZ. Several British ships were subsequently sunk or damaged by Argentine missiles. British forces soon recaptured South Georgia (25 April), following this with a series of successful landings on the Falklands (21 May) which rapidly overwhelmed the Argentine garrison of 12,000. Argentine forces on the islands surrendered unconditionally as of midnight on 14/15 June. The British also captured (19 June) a small Argentine outpost in the South Sandwich Islands which had been there since 1976. British casualties included 254 killed; Argentine deaths were approximately three times that.

Political result

No solution to the problem has yet been reached. As a result of its defeat, the Argentine military-led government of General Galtieri fell from power immediately. The new government accepted the de facto end of hostilities, resulting in the release of 12,000 Argentine prisoners of war by Britain, but refused to make a declaration of an end of hostilities. Anglo-Argentine relations improved after the restoration of civilian government in Argentina (10 Dec. 1983) and full diplomatic relations were re-established in February 1990.

18 North and Central American Wars

Mexican-American War 1846-8

Belligerents: **Mexico**
                    United States

Cause

In 1835 inhabitants of the northern Mexican territory of Texas, who had mostly come from the United States, revolted. During this rebellion (the War of Texan Independence), President Santa Anna personally led the Mexican armies. After besieging and taking the Alamo (23 Feb.–6 March 1836), Santa Anna's army of 1,600 was defeated by a Texan force of 740 under Sam Houston at the Battle of San Jacinto (21 April 1836). Santa Anna was captured and agreed to recognize the independence of the Republic of Texas (14 May 1836), an action subsequently repudiated by the Mexican government. Mexico, as a result, continued to claim sovereignty over Texas, although it exercised no control over it.

Occasion

At its own request, Texas was annexed to the United States (1 March 1845). The border between Texas and Mexico was in dispute, however, with Mexico claiming the Nueces river and the United States the Rio Grande river as the boundary. An American army moved into the disputed zone (March 1846). Inevitably, the forces of both states came into conflict, the first action occurring on 25 April. The United States formally declared war on Mexico on 13 May 1846.

Course of War

The American campaign was initially hampered by political bickering between the government in Washington and the general in the field, Zachary Taylor. Taylor was finally superseded by General Scott, but while these delays occurred the Mexican president, Santa Anna, made a dramatic

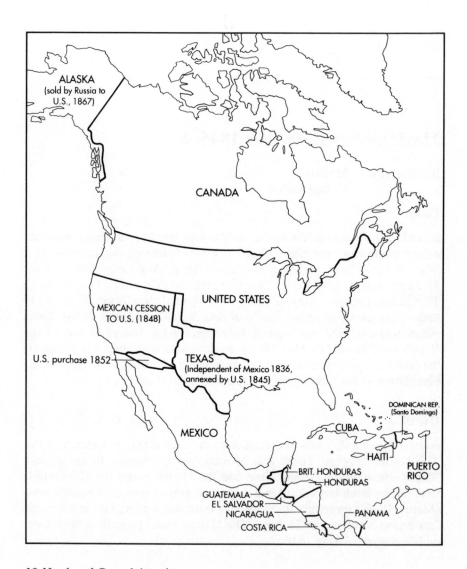

ALASKA
(sold by Russia to U.S., 1867)

CANADA

UNITED STATES

MEXICAN CESSION TO U.S. (1848)

U.S. purchase 1852

TEXAS
(Independent of Mexico 1836, annexed by U.S. 1845)

MEXICO

CUBA

HAITI

DOMINICAN REP. (Santo Domingo)

PUERTO RICO

BRIT. HONDURAS
HONDURAS
GUATEMALA
EL SALVADOR
NICARAGUA
COSTA RICA
PANAMA

19 North and Central America

winter march across the desert to attack the Americans. In the Battle of Buena Vista (known to the Mexicans as the Battle of La Angostura) (22–3 Feb. 1847), some 18,000 Mexicans attacked an American army of 4,500 under Taylor. The Americans, however, occupied the heights and could not be dislodged, forcing Santa Anna to retire. Scott's force captured the chief Mexican port of Veracruz (27 March), before proceeding to march inland on Mexico City. In the Battle of Chapultec (13 Sept.) the Americans captured the last key hill outside Mexico City. This engagement saw a heroic defence by Mexican Military College cadets. The following day Mexico City fell, but peace negotiations dragged on until February 1848.

Political result

The Texas revolution and the American war cost Mexico half its territory. The Treaty of Guadalupe-Hidalgo (2 Feb. 1848) established the Rio Grande as the Mexican-American border, while Mexico ceded the area now comprising the southwest of the United States (including California and New Mexico). The United States, however, agreed to pay Mexico $15 million in compensation for this loss. American forces had evacuated Mexico by early August 1848.

Remarks

General Taylor's popularity as a war hero led to his election as president (Nov. 1848).

Mexican-French War 1861–7

Belligerents: France
 Mexico

Cause

Civil war (the War of Reform) raged in Mexico from 1857 to 1860, when the Liberals under Benito Juárez defeated the Conservatives. The war caused a suspension in foreign debt payments (July 1861) and by the Convention of London (Oct. 1861) Britain, France and Spain agreed on a military expedition to ensure payment. A British-French-Spanish force landed at the Mexican port of Veracruz (17 Dec. 1861). Emperor Napoleon III of France hoped to use this opportunity, with the United States embroiled in a civil war of its own (1861–5), to establish French dominance in Mexico.

Occasion

The British and Spanish forces withdrew in disapproval of Napoleon III's scheming, while the French forces moved on their own towards Mexico City.

Course of War

The French advance was halted at the Battle of Puebla (Cinco de Mayo) (5 May 1862). Napoleon was forced to send 30,000 reinforcements (Sept. 1862) and in a new offensive the French took Mexico City (7 June 1863). The French established a puppet state, the Empire of Mexico, with an Austrian archduke, Maximilian, as emperor. Juárez's government, however, continued to lead resistance to this régime. With the end of the American Civil War, the United States, which had continued to recognize Juárez, threatened to intervene, deploying an army of 50,000 on the border. In the face of this threat Napoleon withdrew his army (March 1867). Maximilian refused to leave, however, and after a brief resistance was captured and executed by the Mexicans (19 June 1867).

Political result

The Mexican republic was fully restored under Juárez, who remained in office until his death (1872). The Mexican adventure led to poor relations between Napoleon III and the United States, which welcomed his defeat and overthrow in the Franco-Prussian War of 1870–1.

Spanish-American War 1898

Belligerents: **United States**
                     Spain

Cause

The cause of this war was the liberation movement in the Spanish colony of Cuba, which enjoyed widespread popular support in the United States. Rebellion broke out in Cuba in 1895 and the Spanish government responded by dispatching General Weyler, who moved to cut off the rebels' support by rounding up the civilians into camps, where many died from disease caused by poor sanitation. Weyler was recalled in 1897, but this in turn led to protests by Spanish loyalists. In the resulting political turmoil, the United States sent the USS *Maine* to Havana to assist in protecting Americans there.

Occasion

The United States battleship *Maine* sank in a mysterious explosion while at anchor in Havana harbor (15 Feb. 1898). American public opinion blamed Spain, which protested its innocence, and the loss of the *Maine* proved the final catalyst propelling American entry into the Cuban conflict. The American president, William McKinley, attempted to avoid war by sending relatively mild demands to Spain, calling for a six-month armistice with the Cuban rebels and an end to the internment camps. The Spanish government, however, feared revolution at home if it appeared too weak and so only agreed in part. As a result, the United States declared war on Spain, with the clearly stated intention of bringing about Cuba's independence (11 April 1898). The Teller Amendment to the declaration bound the United States not to annex Cuba.

Course of War

The military and naval campaigns resulted in an overwhelming American victory. The American army at the outbreak of war consisted of only 28,000 regulars and 115,000 militia. This number was soon swelled by 125,000 volunteers. The war was not limited to Cuba, as some American officials saw the opportunity of seizing Spain's Pacific colonial empire in the Philippines. In the Battle of Manila Bay (1 May), the United States Asiatic squadron, in a one-hour engagement fought at 2,000 yards, annihilated the Spanish squadron. Spanish casualties were 167 dead, while the Americans suffered no deaths. In the Caribbean at the Battle of Santiago Bay (3 July), the United States navy destroyed the entire Spanish fleet, incurring no damage to its own ships. The Battle of San Juan Hill in Cuba (1 July) was the chief land engagement. Here the Americans took control of the heights above Santiago in a battle best known for the charge of the Rough Riders, involving the future president Theodore Roosevelt. Although the American forces suffered severely from disease, Santiago fell to them (17 July). The Americans also successfully occupied the island of Puerto Rico. An armistice was agreed on 12 August 1898, together with a protocol embodying the basic peace terms.

Political result

By the Treaty of Paris (10 Dec. 1898), Spain surrendered its sovereignty over Cuba and ceded to the United States the Philippines, Puerto Rico and the Pacific Island of Guam in return for $20 million. Spain subsequently sold its remaining Pacific possessions, the Caroline and Mariana islands, to Germany (12 Feb. 1899). In the Philippines an insurrection broke out in favor of independence, involving the United States in a lengthy campaign there. The acquisition of a colonial empire aroused much opposition within the United States. The defeat of the Spaniards and the expansion of America's role did, however, mark the arrival of the United States as a great power.

Honduran-Nicaraguan War 1907

Belligerents: **Honduras**
                          Nicaragua

Cause

The Nicaraguan president, José Santos Zelaya, hoped to reunite the Central American republics, which had once formed the Central American Federation in the early nineteenth century.

Occasion

In a revolution in 1903 the liberal Honduran government, which was friendly to Zelaya, was overthrown by the conservative forces led by Manuel Bonilla. In 1906 Honduran rebels, led by Miguel Dávila and supported by Zelaya, unsuccessfully attempted to overthrow Bonilla. Honduran forces pursued the rebels into Nicaragua, leading Zelaya to demand reparations. When this demand was refused, Zelaya invaded Honduras.

Course of War

The Nicaraguan army defeated a Honduran army, supported by forces from El Salvador, in the Battle of Namasigue (18 March 1907). This battle saw the first use of machine guns in Central American warfare, which contributed to the fact that the ratio of casualties to the duration of fighting was the highest in history. The Nicaraguans went on to occupy the Honduran capital of Tegucigalpa (27 March), while Bonilla retreated to Amapala in the Gulf of Fonesca. Zelaya's forces captured this town (12 April) and Bonilla fled into exile aboard an American warship. Nicaraguan forces then began to withdraw from Tegucigalpa (17 April) and had evacuated the country by the end of June 1907. During the war the United States navy patrolled the coast to prevent the shelling of towns with large foreign populations.

Political result

The Nicaraguans installed a new government in Honduras and Bonilla fled to the United States. Civil war soon erupted between the new government and the supporters of Bonilla (1909–11). In Nicaragua Zelaya's adventurist policy led to rising discontent and he was forced to resign (16 Dec. 1909), with civil war ensuing (1909–12). Regional order was finally restored in the country by American military intervention (1912). By the Treaty of Amapala (23 April 1907), Nicaragua and El Salvador agreed that future disputes would be arbitrated by the presidents of Mexico and the United States.

El Salvador-Honduras War (Football War) 1969

Belligerents: **El Salvador**
Honduras

Cause

El Salvador, with seven times the population density of neighboring Honduras, had come to rely on the emigration of people to relieve population and economic pressures. In 1969, however, Honduras began to place restrictions on Salvadorean arrivals, refusing to renew the 1967 Bilateral Treaty on Immigration (Jan. 1969) and repatriating Salvadorean immigrants. This inevitably caused an increase in tension between the two countries, inflamed by the press.

Occasion

Further moves against Salvadorean immigrants in Honduras coincided with qualifying matches between the two countries for a place in the 1970 World Cup football (soccer) finals. Outbreaks of violence occurred at the first match in the Honduran capital of Tegucigalpa (8 June 1969), which the home side won narrowly. Much greater violence occurred at the return match in San Salvador (15 June), which El Salvador won easily. This was followed by a break in diplomatic relations (26 June), and finally by Salvadorean military action.

Course of War

The actual fighting lasted only four days. The Salvadorean forces initiated action on 14 July, the army engaging Honduran border forces, the airforce attacking Honduran installations and the navy shelling Honduran islands in the Gulf of Fonesca. The stronger Honduran airforce helped to tip the balance and the belligerents accepted an OAS peace plan (19 July), El Salvador agreeing to withdraw its forces from Honduran territory (30 July). This brief war cost approximately 2,000 lives, mostly Hondurans.

Political result

The Treaty of Lima (30 Oct. 1980) led to the reopening of the border, the resumption of normal diplomatic relations and the demarcation of two thirds of the Honduras-El Salvador border, with agreement on the remainder to be accomplished within five years. This five-year deadline was not met and by mutual consent the matter was referred for adjudication to the International Court of Justice (May 1986). Although El Salvador's military performed reasonably well in the fighting, the basic population problem was only aggravated, as any possibility of good relations with Honduras had now been destroyed and around 100,000 expatriates had to be reabsorbed.

Appendix A

First World War: Entry of countries into hostilities and declarations of war

Entry of countries into hostilities

Central powers

28 July 1914	Austria-Hungary
1 Aug. 1914	Germany
29 Oct. 1914	Ottoman Empire
11 Oct. 1915	Bulgaria

Allied and associated powers

28 July 1914	Serbia
1 Aug. 1914	Russia
2 Aug. 1914	Luxembourg
3 Aug. 1914	France
4 Aug. 1914	Belgium
4 Aug. 1914	Great Britain
9 Aug. 1914	Montenegro
23 Aug. 1914	Japan
25 May 1915	Italy
1 June 1915	San Marino
31 Aug. 1915	Romania
9 March 1916	Portugal
24 Nov. 1916	Greece (provisional government)
27 June 1917	Greece (royal government)
6 April 1917	United States
7 April 1917	Cuba
22 July 1917	Siam (Thailand)
4 Aug. 1917	Liberia
14 Aug. 1917	China
26 Oct. 1917	Brazil
10 Nov. 1917	Panama
22 April 1917	Guatemala
6 May 1918	Nicaragua
24 May 1918	Costa Rica
15 July 1918	Haiti
19 July 1918	Honduras

Declarations of War

Austria-Hungary

on Serbia	28 July 1914
on Russia	6 Aug. 1914
on Belgium	28 Aug. 1914
on Portugal	15 March 1916

Brazil

on Germany	26 Oct. 1917

Bulgaria

on Serbia	14 Oct. 1915
on Romania	1 Sept. 1916

China

on Germany	14 March 1917
on Austria-Hungary	14 Aug. 1917

Costa Rica

on Germany	23 May 1918

Cuba

on Germany	7 April 1917

France

on Austria-Hungary	12 Aug. 1914
on Ottoman Empire	5 Nov. 1914
on Bulgaria	16 Oct. 1915

Germany

on Russia	1 Aug. 1914
on France	3 Aug. 1914
on Belgium	4 Aug. 1914
on Portugal	9 March 1916
on Romania	28 Aug. 1916

Great Britain

on Germany	4 Aug. 1914
on Austria-Hungary	12 Aug. 1914
on Ottoman Empire	5 Nov. 1914
on Bulgaria	15 Oct. 1915

Entry of countries into hostilities (contd)

Greece
on Austria-Hungary,
  Bulgaria,
  Germany and
  Ottoman Empire 27 June 1917

Guatemala
on Germany   23 April 1918

Haiti
on Germany   12 July 1918

Honduras
on Germany   19 July 1918

Italy
on Austria-Hungary 23 May 1915
on Ottoman Empire   21 Aug. 1915
on Bulgaria   19 Oct. 1915
on Germany   28 Aug. 1916

Japan
on Germany   23 Aug. 1914
on Austria-Hungary 25 Aug. 1914

Liberia
on Germany   4 Aug. 1917

Montenegro
on Austria-Hungary 5 Aug. 1914
on Germany   8 Aug. 1914
on Bulgaria   15 Oct. 1915

Declarations of War (contd)

Nicaragua
on Austria-Hungary
  and Germany   8 May 1918

Ottoman Empire
on Romania   30 Aug. 1917

Panama
on Germany   7 April 1917
on Austria-Hungary 10 Dec. 1917

Portugal[1]

Romania[2]
on Austria-Hungary 27 Aug. 1916

Russia
on Ottoman Empire   2 Nov. 1914
on Bulgaria   19 Oct. 1915

San Marino
on Austria-Hungary 3 June 1915

Serbia
on Germany   6 Aug. 1914
on Ottoman Empire   2 Nov. 1914

Siam (Thailand)
on Austria-Hungary
  and Germany   22 July 1917

United States
on Germany   6 April 1917
on Austria-Hungary 7 Dec. 1917

NOTES

1 Committed itself to military actions against Germany 23 Nov. 1914. Seized German ships in its harbors Feb. 1916. Germany and subsequently Austria-Hungary then declared war on Portugal.
2 Romania surrendered 7 May 1918 by Treaty of Bucharest. It re-entered war on 10 Nov. 1918.

Appendix B

Second World War: Entry of countries into hostilities and declarations of war

Entry of countries into hostilities

Axis

1 Sept. 1939	Germany
11 June 1940	Italy
10 April 1941	Hungary
24 April 1941	Bulgaria
22 June 1941	Romania
25 June 1941	Finland
7 Dec. 1941	Japan
8 Dec. 1941	Manchukuo
12 Dec. 1941	Slovakia
14 Dec. 1941	Croatia
17 Dec. 1941	Albania (under Italian occupation)
25 Jan. 1942	Thailand
9 Jan. 1943	China (Nanking government)

Axis states which subsequently declared war against the Axis:

13 Oct. 1943	Italy
24 Aug. 1944	Romania
8 Sept. 1944	Bulgaria
15 Sept. 1944	Finland
22 Sept. 1944	San Marino
20 Jan. 1945	Hungary

Allies (United Nations)

1 Sept. 1939	Poland
3 Sept. 1939	Great Britain
3 Sept. 1939	France
3 Sept. 1939	Australia
3 Sept. 1939	New Zealand
6 Sept. 1939	South Africa
10 Sept. 1939	Canada
9 April 1940	Denmark
9 April 1940	Norway
10 May 1940	Belgium
10 May 1940	Luxembourg
10 May 1940	Netherlands
28 Oct. 1940	Greece
6 April 1941	Yugoslavia
22 June 1941	Soviet Union[3]
7 Dec. 1941	United States
7 Dec. 1941	Panama
8 Dec. 1941	Costa Rica
8 Dec. 1941	Dominican Republic
8 Dec. 1941	El Salvador
8 Dec. 1941	Haiti
8 Dec. 1941	Honduras
8 Dec. 1941	Nicaragua
9 Dec. 1941	Czechoslovakia[4]
9 Dec. 1941	China
9 Dec. 1941	Cuba
9 Dec. 1941	Guatemala
22 May 1942	Mexico
22 Aug. 1942	Brazil
1 Dec. 1942	Ethiopia[5]
17 Jan. 1943	Iraq
9 Sept. 1943	Iran
26 Nov. 1943	Colombia
4 Dec. 1943	Bolivia
26 Jan. 1944	Liberia
9 Feb. 1945	Ecuador
9 Feb. 1945	Paraguay
12 Feb. 1945	Peru
14 Feb. 1945	Chile
16 Feb. 1945	Venezuela
22 Feb. 1945	Uruguay
23 Feb. 1945	Turkey
25 Feb. 1945	Egypt
26 Feb. 1945	Syria
27 Feb. 1945	Lebanon
1 March 1945	Saudi Arabia
27 March 1945	Argentina
9 Aug. 1945	Mongolia

Declarations of war

Albania (under Italian occupation)
on British Empire   June 1940
on United States   17 Dec. 1941

Argentina
on Germany and Japan   27 March 1945

Australia
on Germany   3 Sept. 1939
on Italy   11 June 1940
on Finland, Hungary
   and Romania   8 Dec. 1941
on Japan   [6]9 Dec. 1941
on Bulgaria   [7]14 Jan. 1942
on Thailand   2 March 1942

Belgium
attacked by Germany   10 May 1940

Belgium (government-in-exile)
on Italy   21 Nov. 1940
on Japan   20 Dec. 1941

Bolivia
on Germany, Italy
   and Japan   [8]6 April 1943

Brazil
on Germany and Italy   22 Aug. 1942
on Japan   6 June 1945

Bulgaria
on Greece and
   Yugoslavia   24 April 1941
on Soviet Union   22 June 1941
on Great Britain
   and United States   13 Dec. 1941
declares neutrality   26 Aug. 1944
on Germany   8 Sept. 1944

Burma (under Japanese occupation)
on Great Britain and
   United States   1 Aug. 1943

Canada
on Germany   10 Sept. 1939
on Italy   11 June 1940
on Finland, Hungary
   and Romania   7 Dec. 1941
on Japan   [9]8 Dec. 1941

Chile
on Germany and
   Japan   14 Feb. 1945

China
on Germany, Italy
   and Japan   8 Dec. 1941

China (Japanese-controlled government at Nanking)
on Great Britain
   and United States   9 Jan. 1943

Colombia
on Germany   26 Nov. 1943

Costa Rica
on Japan   8 Dec. 1941
on Germany and Italy   11 Dec. 1941

Croatia (under Axis occupation)
on Great Britain   13 Dec. 1941
   and United States

Cuba
on Japan   9 Dec. 1941
on Germany and Italy   12 Dec. 1941

Czechoslovakia (government-in-exile)
on Japan   9 Dec. 1941
on Germany   [10]16 Dec. 1941
on Hungary   [11]16 Dec. 1941
on all countries at
   war with Allies   16 Dec. 1941

Denmark
attacked by Germany   9 April 1940

Dominican Republic
on Japan   8 Dec. 1941
on Germany and Italy   11 Dec. 1941

Egypt
on Germany and
   Japan   25 Feb. 1945

Ecuador
on Germany and
   Japan[12]   9 Feb. 1945

El Salvador
on Japan   8 Dec. 1941
on Germany and Italy   12 Dec. 1941

Ethiopia
on Germany, Italy
   and Japan   1 Dec. 1942

Finland
on Soviet Union   25 June 1941
on Great Britain   6 Dec. 1941
on Germany   [13]4 March 1945

France
on Germany   3 Sept. 1939
on Italy   11 June 1940

France (Free French National Council, in exile)
on Japan   8 Dec. 1941

Germany
invades Poland   [14]1 Sept. 1939
invades Denmark
  and Norway   9 April 1940
invades Belgium,
  Netherlands
  and Luxembourg   10 May 1940
invades Yugoslavia
  and Greece   [15]6 April 1941
invades Soviet Union   22 June 1941
on United States   11 Dec. 1941

Great Britain
on Germany   3 Sept. 1939
on Italy   11 June 1940
on Finland, Hungary
  and Romania   [16]6 Dec. 1941
on Bulgaria   28 Dec. 1941
on Thailand   25 Jan. 1942

Greece
attacked by Italy   28 Oct. 1940
attacked by Germany   6 April 1941

Guatemala
on Japan   9 Dec. 1941
on Germany and Italy   11 Dec. 1941

Haiti
on Japan   8 Dec. 1941
on Germany and Italy   12 Dec. 1941
on Bulgaria, Hungary
  and Romania   24 Dec. 1941

Honduras
on Japan   8 Dec. 1941
on Germany and Italy   13 Dec. 1941

Hungary
on Soviet Union   27 June 1941
on United States   13 Dec. 1941
on Romania   7 Sept. 1944
on Germany   28 Dec. 1944
armistice with Allies   21 Jan. 1945

Iran
on Germany   9 Sept. 1943
on Japan   [17]1 March 1945

Iraq
on Germany, Italy
  and Japan   17 Jan. 1943

Italy
invades Greece   [18]28 Oct. 1940
on France and Great
  Britain   [19]10 June 1940
on Yugoslavia   6 April 1941
on Soviet Union   22 June 1941
on United States   11 Dec. 1941
on Cuba and Guatemala   13 Dec. 1941
unconditional surrender
  to Allies   8 Sept. 1943
on Germany   13 Oct. 1943
on Japan   14 July 1945

Japan
on Australia, Canada,
  Great Britain, New
  Zealand, South
  Africa and United
  States   7 Dec. 1941
on Netherlands   11 Jan. 1942

Lebanon
on Germany and
  Japan   27 Feb. 1945

Liberia
on Germany and
  Japan   26 Jan. 1944

Luxembourg
attacked by
  Germany   10 May 1940

Luxembourg (government-in-exile)
on Italy   11 June 1940
on Japan   8 Dec. 1941

Manchukuo
on Great Britain
  and United States   8 Dec. 1941

Mexico
on Germany, Italy
  and Japan   22 May 1942

Mongolia
on Japan   9 Aug. 1945

Netherlands
attacked by Germany   10 May 1940

Netherlands (government-in-exile)
on Japan   8 Dec. 1941
on Italy   22 Dec. 1941

New Zealand
on Germany   3 Sept. 1939
on Italy   11 June 1940
on Finland, Hungary
  and Romania   7 Dec. 1941
on Japan   [20]9 Dec. 1941
on Bulgaria   29 Dec. 1941
on Thailand   25 Jan. 1942

Nicaragua
on Japan   8 Dec. 1941
on Germany and Italy   11 Dec. 1941
on Bulgaria, Hungary
  and Romania   19 Dec. 1941

Norway
attacked by Germany   9 April 1940
on Japan   [21]6 July 1945

Panama
on Japan   7 Dec. 1941
on Germany and Italy   12 Dec. 1941

Paraguay
on Germany and
  Japan   9 Feb. 1945

Peru
on Germany and
  Japan   12 Feb. 1945

Poland
attacked by Germany   1 Sept. 1939
attacked by Soviet
  Union   17 Sept. 1939

Poland (government-in-exile)
on Japan   12 Dec. 1941

Romania
on Soviet Union   22 June 1941
on Great Britain   6 Dec. 1941
on United States   12 Dec. 1941
on Nicaragua   19 Dec. 1941
on Haiti   24 Dec. 1941
armistice with Allies   23 Aug. 1944
on Germany   25 Aug. 1944
on Hungary   7 Sept. 1944
on Japan   7 March 1945

San Marino
on Great Britain   Sept. 1940
on Germany   24 Sept. 1944

Saudi Arabia
on Germany and
  Japan   1 March 1945

Slovakia (under German occupation)
on Great Britain
  and United States   12 Dec. 1941

South Africa
on Germany   6 Sept. 1939
on Italy   11 June 1940
on Finland, Hungary
  and Romania   9 Dec. 1941
on Japan   9 Dec. 1941
on Bulgaria   [22]2 Jan. 1942
on Thailand   25 Jan. 1942

Soviet Union
attacked by Germany   22 June 1941
on Bulgaria   5 Sept. 1944
on Japan   8 Aug. 1945

Syria
on Germany and
  Japan   26 Feb. 1945

Thailand
on Great Britain
  and United States   25 Jan. 1942

Turkey
on Germany and
  Japan   [23]23 Feb. 1945

United States
on Japan   8 Dec. 1941
on Germany and Italy   11 Dec. 1941
on Thailand   5 Feb. 1942
on Bulgaria, Hungary
  and Romania   18 July 1942

Uruguay
on Germany and
  Japan   22 Feb. 1945

Venezuela
on Germany and
  Japan   16 Feb. 1945

Yugoslavia
attacked by Germany   6 April 1941

Yugoslavia (government-in-exile)
on Japan   [24]13 Jan. 1942

NOTES

3 The Soviet Union had previously attacked Poland on 17 Sept. 1939, in league with Germany.

4 Czechoslovakia was occupied by Germany, Hungary and Poland in March 1939. The Czechoslovak government-in-exile issued this formal declaration.

5 Ethiopia was occupied by Italy in 1936 in the Third Italo-Ethiopian War. It was liberated in 1941.

6 Retrospective from 8 Dec. 1941.

7 Retrospective from 6 Jan. 1942.

8 Bolivia declared a state of war by cabinet decree on 7 April 1943. This was approved by Congress on 26 Nov. 1943 and announced on 4 Dec. 1943.

9 Retrospective from 7 Dec. 1941.

10 Retrospective to 15 March 1939.

11 Retrospective to 23 March 1939.

12 Retrospective to 7 Dec. 1941.

13 Retrospective to 15 Sept. 1944.

14 No Declaration of War was issued.

15 No Declaration of War was issued.

16 With effect from 7 Dec. 1941.

17 Retrospective to 30 April 1945.

18 No Declaration of War was issued.

19 With effect from 11 June 1940.

20 Retrospective to 8 Dec. 1941.

21 Retrospective to 7 Dec. 1941.

22 Retrospective to 13 Dec. 1941.

23 With effect from 1 March 1945.

24 Retrospective to 7 Dec. 1941.

Appendix C
Post-Second World War Peace Treaties

TREATIES of PARIS, 10 February 1947
with: Italy
by: Great Britain, Soviet Union, United States, China, France, Australia, Belgium, Byelorussia, Brazil, Canada, Czechoslovakia, Ethiopia, Greece, India, the Netherlands, New Zealand, Poland, South Africa, Ukraine, Yugoslavia.

with: Bulgaria
by: Great Britain, Soviet Union, United States, Australia, Byelorussia, Czechoslovakia, Greece, India, New Zealand, South Africa, Ukraine, Yugoslavia.

with: Finland
by: Great Britain, Soviet Union, Australia, Byelorussia, Canada, Czechoslovakia, India, New Zealand, South Africa, Ukraine.

with: Hungary
by: Great Britain, Soviet Union, United States, Australia, Byelorussia, Canada, Czechoslovakia, India, New Zealand, South Africa, Ukraine, Yugoslavia.

with: Romania
by: Great Britain, Soviet Union, United States, Australia, Byelorussia, Canada, Czechoslovakia, India, New Zealand, South Africa, Ukraine

JAPANESE PEACE TREATY, 8 September 1951, signed at San Francisco.
Concluded by: France, Great Britain, United States, Argentina, Australia, Belgium, Bolivia, Brazil, Cambodia, Canada, Ceylon (Sri Lanka), Chile, Colombia, Costa Rica, Cuba, Dominican Republic, Ecuador, Egypt, El Salvador, Ethiopia, Greece, Haiti, Honduras, Indonesia, Iran, Iraq, Laos, Lebanon, Liberia, Luxembourg, Mexico, the Netherlands, New Zealand, Nicaragua, Norway, Pakistan, Panama, Paraguay, Peru, Philippines, Saudi Arabia, South Africa, Syria, Turkey, Uruguay, Venezuela, Vietnam.

HELSINKI ACCORDS, 1 August 1975.
Concluded by: Austria, Belgium, Bulgaria, Canada, Cyprus, Czechoslovakia, Denmark, Federal Republic of Germany, Finland, France, German Democratic Republic, Great Britain, Greece, Hungary, Iceland, Ireland, Italy, Liechtenstein, Luxembourg, Malta, Monaco, the Netherlands, Norway, Poland, Portugal, Romania, San Marino, Soviet Union, Sweden, Switzerland, Turkey, United States, Vatican State, Yugoslavia.

TREATY ON THE FINAL SETTLEMENT ON GERMANY, 12 September 1990, signed at Moscow.
Concluded by: France, Great Britain, Soviet Union, United States, Federal Republic of Germany, German Democratic Republic.

Appendix D

United Nations Peacekeeping Operations

1947–52   UN Special Commission on the Balkans (UNSCOB)
Participants: Brazil, China, France, Great Britain, Mexico, the Netherlands, United States.

1948–   UN Truce Supervision Organisation (UNTSO). Deployed in the Middle East
Participants: Argentina, Australia, Austria, Belgium, Burma, Canada, Chile, China, Denmark, Finland, France, Ireland, Italy, the Netherlands, New Zealand, Norway, Soviet Union, Sweden, Switzerland, United States.

1949–   UN Military Observation Group in India and Pakistan (UNMOGIP)
Participants: Australia, Belgium, Canada, Chile, Denmark, Ecuador, Finland, Italy, Mexico, New Zealand, Norway, Sweden, United States, Uruguay.

1949–51   UN Commission for Indonesia (UNCI)
Participants: Australia, Belgium, China, Great Britain, United States.

1952–4   UN Military Observers of the Balkans Sub-Commission of the UN Peace Observation Commission
Participants: Colombia, France, Great Britain, Pakistan, Sweden, United States.

1956–67   UN Emergency Force (UNEF-I). Deployed on the Egypt-Israel frontier
Participants: Brazil, Canada, Colombia, Denmark, Finland, India, Indonesia, Norway, Sweden, Yugoslavia.

1958   UN Observation Group in Lebanon (UNOGIL)
Participants: Afghanistan, Argentina, Burma, Canada, Ceylon (Sri Lanka), Chile, Denmark, Ecuador, Finland, India, Indonesia, Ireland, Nepal, the Netherlands, New Zealand, Norway, Peru, Portugal, Thailand.

1960–4   UN Operation in the Congo (ONUC)
Participants: Argentina, Australia, Austria, Brazil, Burma, Canada, Ceylon (Sri Lanka), Congo, Denmark, Egypt, Ethiopia, Ghana, Guinea, India, Indonesia, Iran, Ireland, Italy, Liberia, Malaya, Fed. of Mali (Mali, Senegal), Morocco, the Netherlands, Nigeria, Norway, Pakistan, Philippines, Sierra Leone, Sudan, Sweden, Tunisia, Yugoslavia.

1962–3   UN Security Force in West New Guinea (West Irian)
          Participants: Canada, Pakistan, United States.

1963–4   UN Yemen Observation Mission (UNYOM)
          Participants: Australia, Canada, Denmark, Ghana, India, Italy, the
          Netherlands, Norway, Pakistan, Sweden, Yugoslavia.

1964–   UN Peace-Keeping Force in Cyprus (UNFICYP)
          Participants: Australia, Austria, Canada, Denmark, Finland, Great
          Britain, Ireland, New Zealand, Sweden.

1965–6   Mission of the Representative of the UN Secretary-General in the
          Dominican Republic (DOMREP)
          Participants: Brazil, Canada, Ecuador, India.

1965–6   UN India-Pakistan Observation Mission (UNIPOM)
          Participants: Australia, Belgium, Brazil, Burma, Canada, Ceylon
          (Sri Lanka), Chile, Denmark, Ethiopia, Finland, Ireland, Italy,
          Nepal, the Netherlands, New Zealand, Nigeria, Norway, Sweden,
          Venezuela.

1973–9   UN Emergency Force (UNEF-II). Deployed on the Egypt-Israel
          frontier.
          Participants: Australia, Austria, Canada, Finland, Ghana, Indonesia,
          Ireland, Nepal, Panama, Peru, Poland, Senegal, Sweden.

1974–   UN Disengagement Force (UNDOF). Deployed on the Israel-Syria
          border.
          Participants: Austria, Canada, Finland, Iran, Peru, Poland.

1978–   UN Interim Force in Lebanon (UNIFIL)
          Participants: Canada, Fiji, Finland, France, Ghana, Iran, Ireland,
          Italy, Nepal, the Netherlands, Nigeria, Norway, Senegal, Sweden.

1978–   UN Transition Assistance Group (UNTAG). Deployed in Namibia
          Participants: Australia, Austria, Bangladesh, Barbados, Belgium,
          Canada, China, Congo, Costa Rica, Czechoslovakia, Denmark,
          Egypt, Federal Republic of Germany, Fiji, Finland, France, German
          Democratic Republic, Ghana, Great Britain, Greece, Guyana,
          Hungary, India, Indonesia, Ireland, Italy, Jamaica, Japan, Kenya,
          Malaysia, the Netherlands, New Zealand, Nigeria, Norway,
          Pakistan, Panama, Peru, Poland, Portugal, Singapore, Soviet Union,
          Spain, Sudan, Sweden, Switzerland, Thailand, Togo, Trinidad and
          Tobago, Tunisia, Yugoslavia.

1988–   UN Good Offices Mission in Afghanistan and Pakistan
          (UNGOMAP)
          Participants: Austria, Canada, Denmark, Fiji, Finland, Ghana,
          Ireland, Nepal, Poland, Sweden.

1988–   UN Iran-Iraq Military Observer Group (UNIIMOG)
          Participants: Argentina, Australia, Bangladesh, Canada, Denmark,
          Finland, Ghana, Hungary, India, Indonesia, Ireland, Italy, Kenya,
          Malaysia, New Zealand, Nigeria, Norway, Poland, Senegal, Sweden,
          Turkey, Uruguay, Yugoslavia, Zambia.

1989–   UN Angola Verification Mission (UNAVEM)
          Participants: Algeria, Argentina, Brazil, Congo, Czechoslovakia,

India, Jordan, Norway, Spain, Yugoslavia.

1989–   UN Observer Group in Central America (ONUCA)
         Participants: Argentina, Brazil, Canada, Colombia, Ecuador, India,
         Ireland, Spain, Sweden, Venezuela.

1991–   UN Iraq-Kuwait Observation Mission (UNIKOM)
         Participants: Argentina, Austria, Bangladesh, Canada, Chile, China,
         Denmark, Fiji, Finland, France, Ghana, Great Britain, Greece,
         Hungary, India, Indonesia, Ireland, Italy, Kenya, Malaysia, Soviet
         Union, Thailand, Turkey, United States, Uruguay, Venezuela.

Proposed UN Mission for the Referendum in Western Sahara (MINURSO)

Appendix E
Major arms control agreements

1922   *Washington Naval Convention (Five Power Treaty).* Set a ratio of capital ships between the United States, Great Britain, Japan, France and Italy of 5:5:3:1.67:1.67. These ships were to have a maximum displacement of 35,000 tons. A ten-year ban on the construction of capital ships was agreed.

1925   *Geneva Protocol.* Prohibited the use of poison gas and bacteriological weapons. Several states reserved the right of retaliation.

1930   *London Naval Treaty.* Regulated submarine warfare, limited tonnage and gun-caliber of submarines. Limitation of aircraft carriers had been agreed in 1922. Washington Naval Convention of 1922 extended. An 'escalator clause' agreed, to allow increases if one signatory so demanded. To last until 1936. Signed by Great Britain, France, Italy, Japan and United States.

1935   *Anglo-German Naval Treaty.* Agreement limiting the German surface navy to 35 per cent and German submarines to 45 per cent of the Royal Navy.

1936   *London Naval Treaty.* Anglo-American agreement limiting size of battleships to 35,000 tons with 14-inch guns, and extending the naval building holiday on heavy cruisers and battleships.

1963   *Antarctic Treaty.* Prohibition of military activity, nuclear explosions, and the disposal of radioactive waste in Antarctica.

1963   *Test Ban Treaty.* Banned nuclear weapons tests in the atmosphere, outer space, and under water.

1967   *Outer Space Treaty.* Banned military activity on celestial bodies and the deployment of nuclear weapons in outer space.

1967   *Treaty of Tlatelolco.* Latin America declared a nuclear weapon free zone.

1968   *Non-Proliferation Treaty.* Attempt to prevent the spread of nuclear weapons.

1971   *Seabed Treaty.* Prohibition of nuclear weapons on the seabed.

1971   *Agreement on the Prevention of Accidental Nuclear War.* A United States-Soviet Union agreement which was expanded in 1973 through a further agreement on confidence building measures.

1972   *Biological Weapons Convention.* Ban on the development, production and stockpiling of bacteriological and toxic weapons.

1972   *SALT I Interim Agreement* (Strategic Arms Limitation Talks). United States-Soviet Union agreement on the limitation of offensive strategic nuclear weapons.

1972   *Anti-Ballistic Missile (ABM) Treaty.* United States-Soviet Union agreement on limiting the deployment of ABM systems.

1974   *Threshold Test Ban Treaty.* United States-Soviet Union agreement for limiting underground nuclear tests to 150 kilotons. Finally ratified in 1990.

1975   *Final Act of the Conference on Security and Cooperation in Europe (CSCE or the Helsinki Accords).* Provided for 21 days' advance notice of military maneuvers of over 25,000 soldiers.

1976   *Peaceful Nuclear Explosions Treaty.* United States–Soviet Union agreement limiting underground nuclear explosions to peaceful purposes. Finally ratified in 1990.

1976   *Agreement on the Prevention of Accidental Nuclear War.* Franco-Soviet agreement similar to the previous United States-Soviet agreement (1971).

1977   *Enmod Convention.* Banned the use of environmental modification techniques for military or hostile purposes.

1978   *Agreement on the Prevention of Accidental Nuclear War.* Anglo-Soviet agreement similar to previous United States-Soviet (1971) and Franco-Soviet (1976) agreements.

1979   *SALT II Agreement.* United States-Soviet Union agreement establishing a ceiling on strategic nuclear delivery vehicles and limiting some ground-launched nuclear missile systems. Unratified.

1980   *Convention on the Physical Protection of Nuclear Material.* Established a standard measure of physical protection for the interstate transport of nuclear material.

1981   *Weaponry Convention.* Restricted the use of inhumane conventional weapons.

1985   *Treaty of Raratonga.* Established a nuclear-weapons-free zone in the south Pacific.

1986   *Stockholm Document.* Extended the CSCE Final Act (1975). Advance notice for all maneuvers of over 13,000 soldiers; those of over 17,000 soldiers to be subject to inspection.

1987   *INF Treaty.* United States-Soviet Union agreement for eliminating intermediate range ground-launched missiles.

1987   *Agreement on Nuclear Risk Reduction Centers.* A United States-Soviet Union agreement for establishing two such centers for improved communication and information exchange in Washington and Moscow.

1988   *Ballistic Missile Test Notification Agreement.* A United States-Soviet Union agreement for prior notification of tests.

1989   *Prevention of Dangerous Military Activities Agreement.* A United States-Soviet Union agreement for preventing military incidents by establishing procedures for maintaining communication and resolving incidents involving entry into national territory.

1990   *Treaty on Conventional Armed Forces (CFE).* Concluded by members of NATO and the Warsaw Pact, setting limits on non-nuclear weapons deployed in Europe. Each grouping was to be limited to 20,000 main battle tanks, 30,000 other armored combat vehicles, 20,000 pieces of artillery, 6,800 combat aircraft and 2,000 attack helicopters.

1991   *Strategic Arms Reduction Treaty (START).* A United States-Soviet Union treaty to reduce to equal levels strategic offensive arms, to be implemented in three phases over seven years.

Further reading

General

Patrick Brogan, *World Conflicts: Why and Where They are Happening* (1989).
Alan J. Day (ed.), *Border and Territorial Disputes*, 2nd ed. (1987).
R. Ernest Dupuy and Trevor N. Dupuy, *The Encyclopedia of Military History from 3500 B.C. to the Present* (1986).
Tom Hartman, *A World Atlas of Military History, 1945–1984* (1984).
David Munro and Alan J. Day, *A World Record of Major Conflict Areas* (1990).

Post-Napoleonic Revolutionary Wars

Jonathan Helmreich, *Belgium and Europe: A Study in Small Power Diplomacy* (1976).
E. Kossman, *The Low Countries, 1780–1940* (1978).

Wars of German Unification

General

Gordon Craig, *The Politics of the Prussian Army, 1640–1945* (1955).
Otto Pflanze, *Bismarck and the Development of Germany: The Period of Unification, 1815–71* (1963).
Gerhard Ritter, *The Sword and the Sceptre: The Problem of Militarism in Germany*, 4 vols (1969).

Schleswig-Holstein Wars

W. Carr, *Schleswig-Holstein, 1815–1864* (1963).
K. A. P. Sandiford, *Great Britain and the Schleswig-Holstein Question, 1848–64* (1975).
Lawrence D. Steefel, *The Schleswig-Holstein Question* (1932).

Seven Weeks' War

Gordon Craig, *The Battle of Königgrätz* (1965).
Robert I. Geisberg, *The Treaty of Frankfort: A Study in Diplomatic History* (1960).

Franco-Prussian War

Michael Howard, *The Franco-Prussian War* (1967).
Alistair Horne, *The Fall of Paris: The Siege and the Commune, 1870–71* (1968).
Robert Tombs, *The War Against Paris 1871* (1981).

Wars of Italian Unification

G. Berkley, *Italy in the Making, 1815 to 1846* (1968).
Dennis Mack Smith (ed.), *The Making of Italy, 1796–1870* (1968).

The Decline of the Ottoman Empire

General

William Miller, *The Ottoman Empire and its Successors, 1801–1927* (1934).
Charles Jelavich and Barbara Jelavich, *The Balkans* (1965).
Charles Jelavich and Barbara Jelavich, *The Establishment of the Balkan National States, 1804–1920* (1977).
J. A. R. Marriott, *The Eastern Question: An Historical Study in European Diplomacy* (1940).

Greek War of Independence

Douglas Dakin, *The Greek Struggle for Independence, 1821–1833* (1973).
C. M. Woodhouse, *The Battle of Navarino* (1965).
Richard Clogg (ed.), *The Struggle for Greek Independence* (1973).
David Howarth, *The Greek Adventure: Lord Byron and Other Eccentrics in the War of Independence* (1976).
C. W. Crawley, *The Question of Greek Independence: A Study of British Policy in the Near East, 1821–1833* (1930).

Russo-Ottoman Wars

W. E. D. Allen and P. Muratoff, *Caucasian Battlefields: A History of the Wars on the Turco-Caucasian Border, 1828–1921* (1953).

Ottoman-Egyptian Wars

Frederick Rodkey, *The Turco-Egyptian Question in the Relations of England, France, and Russia, 1832–1841* (1972).

Crimean War

Alan Palmer, *The Banner of the Battle: The Story of the Crimean War* (1987).
David Wetzel, *The Crimean War: A Diplomatic History* (1985).
Ann Saab, *The Origins of the Crimean Alliance* (1977).
John Curtiss, *Russia's Crimean War* (1979).
John Sweetman, *War and Administration: The Significance of the Crimean War for the British Army* (1984).
Christopher Hibbert, *The Destruction of Lord Raglan: A Tragedy of the Crimean War, 1854–55* (1984).

Charles Bayley, *Mercenaries for the Crimea: The German, Swiss, and Italian Legions in British Service, 1854–56* (1977).
Alexander Kinglake, *The Invasion of the Crimea*, 9 vols (1877–88).

Montenegrin-Serbian-Ottoman War of 1876 and Russo-Ottoman War of 1877–8

Bela Kiraly and Gale Stokes (eds), *Insurrections, Wars and the Eastern Crisis in the 1870's* (1985).
William Medlicott, *The Congress of Berlin and After: A Diplomatic History of the Near East Settlement, 1878–1880* (1963).
H. M. E. Brunker, *Story of the Russo-Turkish War (in Europe), 1877–78* (1911).
J. H. Anderson, *Russo-Turkish War, 1877–78 in Europe* (1910).
Richard Shannon, *Gladstone and the Bulgarian Agitation, 1876* (1975).

Graeco-Ottoman War of 1897

George J. Marcopoulos, The selection of Prince George of Greece as high commissioner of Crete. *Balkan Studies* 10 (1969), pp. 335–50.
Theodore Tatsios, *The Megali Idea and the Greek-Turkish War of 1897: The Impact of the Cretan Problem on Greek Irredentism, 1866–1897* (1984).

Italo-Ottoman War

W. C. Askew, *Europe and Italy's Acquisition of Libya* (1942).
J. Wright, Aeroplanes and Airships in Libya, 1911–1912. *Maghreb Review* 3 (1978).

Balkan Wars

Ernst Christian Helmreich, *The Diplomacy of the Balkan Wars, 1912–1913* (1938).
Bela Kiraly and Dimitrije Djordjevic (eds), *East Central European Society and the Balkan Wars* (1986).
John D. Treadway, *The Falcon and the Eagle: Montenegro and Austria-Hungary, 1908–1914* (1983).

World Wars and Related Conflicts

First World War

Winston Churchill, *The World Crisis*, 4 vols (1923–9).
B. H. Liddell Hart, *A History of the World War, 1914–1918* (1934).
Norman Stone, *The Eastern Front, 1914–1917* (1975).
C. R. M. F. Crutwell, *A History of the Great War, 1914–1918* (1934).
J. M. Bourne, *Britain and the Great War, 1914–1918* (1989).
Alan Sharp, *The Versailles Settlement: Peacemaking in Paris, 1919* (1991).

Polish-Soviet War

Norman Davies, *White Eagle, Red Star: The Polish-Soviet War, 1919–20* (1972).

Graeco-Turkish War

Llewellyn Smith, *Ionian Vision: Greece in Asia Minor, 1919–1922* (1973).

Second World War – General

Winston Churchill, *The Second World War*, 6 vols (1948–53).
B. H. Liddell Hart, *History of the Second World War* (1973).
F. H. Hinsley, *Hitler's Strategy* (1951).
W. G. F. Jackson, *The Battle for Italy* (1967).

Winter War

Allen F. Chew, *The White Death: The Epic of the Soviet-Finnish Winter War* (1971).
Max Jakobson, *The Diplomacy of the Winter War: An Account of the Russo-Finnish War, 1939–40* (1961).
Väinö Tanner, *The Winter War: Finland Against Russia, 1939–1940* (1957).

Changkufeng Incident

Alvin Coox, *The Anatomy of a Small War: The Soviet-Japanese Struggle for Changkufeng/Khasan, 1938* (1977).

Nomonhan Incident

Alvin Coox, *Nomonhan: Japan Against Russia, 1939* (1985).

Pacific War

Ronald Spector, *Eagle Against the Sun: The American War with Japan* (1984).
Stephen Pelz, *Race to Pearl Harbor* (1974).
Gordon Prange, *At Dawn We Slept* (1981).
John Toland, *Infamy: Pearl Harbor and Its Aftermath* (1982).
Christopher Thorne, *Allies of a Kind: The United States, Britain and the War Against Japan* (1978).
Akira Iriye, *Power and Culture* (1981).

Central Asian Wars

Russo-Persian War

P. W. Avery, An Enquiry into the Outbreak of the Second Russo-Persian War, 1826–28. In C. E. Bosworth (ed.), *Iran and Islam* (1971).

Anglo-Persian War

J. B. Kelly, *Britain and the Persian Gulf, 1795–1880* (1968), Chap. XI: The Persian War, 1856–57.
James Outram, *Persian Campaign in 1857* (1860).

Anglo-Afghan Wars

Edward Ingram, *The Beginning of the Great Game in Asia, 1828–1834* (1979).
T. A. Heathcote, *The Afghan Wars, 1839–1919* (1980).
J. A. Norris, *The First Afghan War, 1838–42* (1967).
Patrick Macrory, *Signal Catastrophe* (1966).
M. E. Yapp, *Strategies of British India: Britain, Iran and Afghanistan, 1798–1850* (1980).
Brian Robson, *The Road to Kabul: The Second Afghan War, 1878–1881* (1986).
Ira Klein, Who Made the Second Afghan War? *Journal of Asian History* 8 (1974), pp. 97–121.
William Trousdale (ed.), *War in Afghanistan, 1879–80: The Personal Diary of Major General Sir Charles Metcalfe MacGregor* (1985).
G. N. Molesworth, *Afghanistan 1919: An Account of Operations in the Third Afghan War.*

Soviet-Afghan War

Mark Urban, *War in Afghanistan* (1988).

South Asian Wars

Sikh Wars

Hugh Cook, *The Sikh Wars: The British Army in the Punjab, 1845–1849* (1975).
Fauja Singh Bajwa, *Military System of the Sikh during the Period 1799–1849* (1964).

Indo-Pakistani Wars

Charles Heimsath, *A Diplomatic History of Modern India* (1971).
S. Ganguly, *The Origins of War in South Asia: Indo-Pakistani Conflicts Since 1947* (1986).
G. W. Choudhury, *The Last Days of United Pakistan* (1974).
Anthony Mascarhenas, *The Rape of Bangladesh* (1971).
Sukhwant Singh, *The Liberation of Bangladesh* (1980).
Sukhwant Singh, *Defence of the Western Border* (1981).
D. K. Palit, *The Lightning Campaign: The Indo-Pakistan War, 1971* (1972).

Sino-Indian War

Neville Maxwell, *India's China War* (1970).
George N. Patterson, *Peking Versus Delhi* (1963).
M. W. Fisher *et al.*, *Himalayan Battlegrounds: Sino-Indian Rivalry in Ladakh* (1963).
John Rowland, *A History of Sino-Indian Relations: Hostile Co-existence* (1967).

Anglo-Burmese Wars

George Bruce, *The Burma Wars, 1824–1886* (1973).
D. P. Singhal, *The Annexation of Upper Burma* (1960).

East Asian Wars

Opium Wars

Edgar Holt, *The Opium Wars in China* (1964).
Arthur Walley, *The Opium War Through Chinese Eyes* (1958).
M. Collis, *Foreign Mud* (1946).
Peter Ward Fry, *The Opium War, 1840–1842* (1975).

Franco-Indochinese Wars

Milton Osborne, *The French Presence in Cochinchina and Cambodia: Rule and Response, 1859–1905* (1969).
H. McAleavy, *Black Flags in Vietnam* (1968).

Sino-Japanese War

Hilary Conroy, *The Japanese Seizure of Korea, 1868–1910* (1960).

Boxer Rebellion

Victor Purcell, *The Boxer Uprising* (1963).
Peter Flemming, *The Siege at Peking: The Boxer Rebellion* (1959).

Russo-Japanese War

Dennis Warner and Peggy Warner, *The Tide at Sunrise: A History of the Russo-Japanese War, 1904–05* (1974).
Ian Nish, *The Origins of the Russo-Japanese War* (1985).
John Albert White, *The Diplomacy of the Russo-Japanese War* (1964).

Franco-Vietminh War

Jules Roy, *The Battle of Dien Bien Phu* (1965).
John Cady, *The Roots of French Imperialism in Indochina* (1954).

Korean War

D. Rees, *Korea: The Limited War* (1964).
James Stokesbury, *A Short History of the Korean War* (1988).
Burton Kaufman, *The Korean War: The Challenges in Crisis, Credibility, and Command* (1986).
Edgar O'Ballance, *Korea, 1950–53* (1969).
L. C. Gardner (ed.), *The Korean War* (1972).
G. D. Paige, *The Korean Decision, June 24–30, 1950* (1968).
J. L. Collins, *War in Peacetime: The History and Lessons of Korea* (1969).
Akira Iriye *et al.*, *The Origins of the Cold War in Asia* (1977).

Malaysian-Indonesian Confrontation

Harold James and Denis Sheil-Small, *The Undeclared War: The Story of the Indonesian Confrontation, 1962–1966* (1971).
J. A. C. Mackie, *The Indonesia-Malaysia Dispute, 1963–1966* (1974).

Vietnam War

Edgar O'Ballance, *The Wars in Vietnam, 1954–1980* (1981).
R. B. Smith, *An International History of the Vietnam War* (1983–).
George Herring, *America's Longest War: The United States in Vietnam, 1950–1976* (1980).
James Olson (ed.), *Dictionary of the Vietnam War* (1988).

Middle Eastern Wars

General

Chaim Herzog, *The Arab-Israeli Wars: War and Peace in the Middle East* (1982).
T. N. Dupuy, *Elusive Victory: The Arab-Israeli Wars, 1947–74* (1978).

First Arab-Israeli War

N. Lorch, *The Edge of the Sword: Israel's War of Independence, 1947–49* (1961).
Edgar O'Ballance, *The Arab-Israeli War: 1948* (1956).
Uri Bar-Joseph, *The Best of Enemies: Israel and Transjordan in the War of 1948* (1987).

Suez War (Second Arab-Israeli War)

Edgar O'Ballance, *The Sinai Campaign: 1956* (1960).
Hugh Thomas, *The Suez Affair* (1986).
A. Beauffre (trans. Richard Barry), *The Suez Expedition 1956* (1969).

Six Day War (Third Arab-Israeli War)

Edgar O'Ballance, *The Third Arab-Israeli War: 1967* (1972).
Abraham Rabinovich, *The Battle for Jerusalem: June 5–7, 1967* (1972).
Stephen Roth (ed.), *The Impact of the Six-Day War: A Twenty-Year Assessment* (1988).

October War (Fourth Arab-Israeli War)

Chaim Herzog, *The War of Atonement* (1975).
Frank Aker, *October 1973: The Arab-Israeli War* (1985).
John Bulloch, *The Making of a War: The Middle East from 1967 to 1973* (1974).
Edgar O'Ballance, *The Electronic War in the Middle East, 1968–70* (1974).

North Yemen-South Yemen Dispute

J. E. Peterson, *Conflict in the Yemens and Superpower Involvement* (1981).

First Gulf War (Iran-Iraq War)

Edgar O'Ballance, *The Gulf War* (1988).
John Bulloch and Harvey Morris, *The Gulf War: Its Origins, History and Consequences* (1989).
Ephraim Karsh (ed.), *The Iran-Iraq War: Impact and Implications* (1989).

K. H. Kaikobad, *The Shatt-al-Arab Boundary Question: A Legal Reappraisal* (1988).

West African Colonial Wars

General

John D. Hargreaves, *West Africa Partitioned* (1985).

Ashanti Wars

Alan Lloyd, *The Drums of Kumasi: The Story of the Ashanti Wars* (1964).
Henry Brackenbury, *The Ashanti War: A Narrative* (1874).
Frederick Myatt, *The Golden Stool: An Account of the Ashanti War of 1900* (1966).

Barra War

J. M. Gray, *A History of the Gambia* (1940).

Benin War

J. O. Egharevba, *A Short History of Benin* (1968).

Sokoto War

Richard Dusgate, *The Conquest of Northern Nigeria* (1985).
D. J. M. Muffett, *Concerning Brave Captains: Being a History of the British Occupation of Kano and Sokoto and the Last Stand of the Fulani Forces* (1964).
M. Perham, *Lugard: The Years of Authority, 1895–1945* (1960).
A. Haywood and F. A. S. Clarke, *The History of the Royal West African Frontier Force* (1964).
Adamu Mohammed Fika, *The Kano Civil War and British Over-rule, 1882–1940* (1978).
Michael Crowder, *The Story of Nigeria* (1973).

Southern African Colonial Wars

Zulu War

R. Furneaux, *The Zulu War, Isandhlwana and Rorke's Drift* (1963).
D. R. Morris, *The Washing of the Spears: The Rise and Fall of the Zulu Nation* (1969).
R. Coupland, *Zulu Battle Piece: Isandhlwana* (1948).
C. T. Binns, *The Last Zulu King: The Life and Death of Cetshwayo* (1963).

Transvaal Revolt (First Boer War)

O. Ransford, *The Battle of Majuba Hill: The First Boer War* (1967).
Joseph Lehman, *The First Boer War* (1972).

Second Boer War

Thomas Pakenham, *The Boer War* (1979).
J. S. Marais, *The Fall of Kruger's Republic* (1961).
Leo Amery (ed.), *The Times History of the War in South Africa*, 7 vols (1900–9).
Winston Churchill, *London to Ladysmith via Pretoria* (1900).

Struggle for the Horn of Africa

General

Sven Rubenson, *The Survival of Ethiopian Independence* (1976).

Anglo-Ethiopian War

Frederick Myatt, *The March to Magdala: The Abyssinian War of 1868* (1970).
Sven Rubenson, *King of Kings: Tewodoros of Ethiopia* (1966).

Ethiopian-Egyptian and First Italo-Ethiopian War

Zewde Gabre-Sellassie, *Yohannes IV of Ethiopia: A Political Biography* (1975).

Second Italo-Ethiopian War

Harold Marcus, *The Life and Times of Menelik II: Ethiopia 1844–1913* (1975).

Sudanese War

Winston S. Churchill, *The River War: An Account of the Reconquest of the Soudan* (1900).
P. M. Holt, *The Mahdist State in the Sudan, 1881–1898* (1970).
Ismat Hassan Zulfo (trans. Peter Clark), *The Sudanese Account of the Battle of Omdurman* (1980).

Third Italo-Ethiopian War (The Abyssinian Crisis)

Anthony Mockler, *Hailie Selassie's War* (1984).
George W. Baer, *The Coming of the Italian-Ethiopian War* (1967).
Frank Hardie, *The Abyssinian Crisis* (1974).
Angelo del Boca, *The Ethiopian War, 1935–1941* (1962).

Somalian Wars

I. M. Lewis, *A Modern History of Somalia: Nation and State in the Horn of Africa* (1980).
William Lewis, Ethiopia-Somalia (1977–1978). In Robert Harkavy and Stephanie Neuman (eds), *The Lessons of Recent Wars in the Third World* (1985).

Maghreb Wars

Bizerta Crisis

Werner Klaus Ruf, The Bizerta Crisis: A Bouguibist attempt to resolve Tunisia's border problems. *Middle East Journal* 25 (1971), pp. 201–11.

War of the Sands (Morocco-Algeria Dispute)

Karen Farsoun and Jan Paul, *War in the Sahara: 1963*, MERIP (Middle East Research & Information Project) Report 45 (1976).
Anthony S. Reyner, The case of an indeterminate boundary: Algeria-Morocco. In C. A. Fisher (ed.), *Essays in Political Geography* (1968).

Saharan War

Tony Hodges, *Western Sahara: The Roots of a Desert War* (1983).

Post-Independence African Wars
Chad-Libya War

Virginia Thompson, *Conflict in Chad* (1981).

Tanzania-Uganda Dispute

Tony Avirgan and Martha Honey, *War in Uganda: Idi Amin and His Legacy* (1982).
Larry C. Napper, The Ugandan War: some implications for crisis prevention. In Alexander George (ed.), *Managing US-Soviet Rivalry: Problems of Crisis Prevention* (1983).

South American Wars
Argentine-Brazilian War

John Lynch, The River Plate republics from independence to the Paraguayan War. In Leslie Bethell (ed.), *The Cambridge History of Latin America*, vol. 3 (1985).

War of the Peruvian-Bolivian Confederation

Lane Kimball, Andres Santa Cruz and the Peru-Bolivia Confederation. *Hispanic American Historical Review* 16 (1936), pp. 29–48.

Peruvian-Spanish War

W. C. Davis, *The Last Conquistadores: the Spanish Intervention in Peru and Chile, 1863–1866* (1950).

War of the Triple Alliance (López War)

Pelham Box, *The Origins of the Paraguayan War* (1930/1967).
Charles Kolinski, *Independence or Death! The Story of the Paraguayan War* (1965).
E. A. M. Laing, Naval operations of the Triple Alliance, 1864–70. *Mariner's Mirror* 54(3) (1968), pp. 253–79.
Jose Alfredo Fornos Penalba, Draft dodgers, war resisters and turbulent gauchos: the war of the Triple Alliance against Paraguay. *Americas* 38(4) (1982), pp. 463–79.
Harris Warren, The Paraguayan image of the war of the Triple Alliance. *Americas* 19 (1962), pp. 3–20.

Harris Warren, *Paraguay of the Triple Alliance: The Postwar Decade, 1869–1878* (1978).

War of the Pacific

William Slater, *Chile and the War of the Pacific* (1986).
V. G. Kiernan, Foreign interests in the War of the Pacific. *Hispanic American Historical Review* 35(1) (1955), pp. 14–36.
Donald Worcester, Naval Strategy in the War of the Pacific. *Journal of Inter-American Studies* 5(1) (1963), pp. 31–7.
Robert Burr, *By Reason of Force: Chile and the Balancing of Power in South America, 1830–1903* (1965).
Sir Clements Markham, *The War between Peru and Chile, 1879–1882* (1882).
William Dennis, *Tacna Arica: An Account of the Chile-Peru Boundary Dispute and of the Arbitrations of the United States* (1931).

Chaco War

William Garner, *The Chaco Dispute: A Study in Prestige Diplomacy* (1966).
A. J. English, The Chaco War. *Army Quarterly and Defence Journal* 109(3) (1979), pp. 350–8.
David Zook, *The Conduct of the Chaco War* (1960).
Pablo Max Ynsfran (ed.), *The Epic of the Chaco: Marshal Estigarribia's Memoirs of the Chaco War, 1932–1935* (1950).
Leslie Rout, *Politics of the Chaco Peace Conference, 1935–1939* (1970).

First Ecuador-Peru War

David Zook, *Zarumilla-Marañón: The Ecuador-Peru Dispute* (1964).

Falklands War

Max Hastings and Simon Jenkins, *The Battle for the Falklands* (1983).
Douglas Kinney, *National Interest and National Honor: The Diplomacy of the Falklands Crisis* (1989).

North and Central American Wars

Mexican-American War

Seymour Connor and Odie Faulk, *North America Divided: The Mexican War, 1846–1848* (1971).
Charles Dufoor, *The Mexican War: A Compact History, 1846–1848* (1968).
John Weems, *To Conquer a Peace: The War between the United States and Mexico* (1974).
K. J. Bauer, *The Mexican War, 1846–48* (1974).
Charles A. Lofgren, Force and diplomacy, 1846–1848: the view from Washington. *Military Affairs* 31 (1967), pp. 57–64.

Mexican-French War

A. J. Hanna and K. A. Hanna, *Napoleon III and Mexico: American Triumph over Monarchy* (1971).

Spanish-American War

Walter Lafeber, *The New Empire: An Interpretation of American Expansion, 1860–1898* (1963).

J. A. S. Grenville and G. B. Young, *Politics, Strategy and American Diplomacy: Studies in Foreign Policy, 1873–1917* (1966).

Robert Beisner, *Twelve Against Empire: The Anti-Imperialists, 1898–1900* (1968).

L. W. Walker, Guam's seizure by the United States in 1898. *Pacific Historical Review* 14 (1945), pp. 1–12.

Index

Aaiún, *see* El Aaiún
Abadan 134
Abbas Mirza 72
Abdul Hamid II (1842–1918) Ottoman
  sultan 30
Abdullah (1882–1951) king of Jordan
  124
Abdullah (1846–99), the Khalifa 163–4
Abdullah, Ali, president of North
  Yemen 132
Abdur Rahman (1844–1901), amir of
  Afghanistan 79
Aberdeen, Lord (1784–1860), British
  prime minister 29
ABM Treaty, *see* Anti-Ballistic Missile
  Treaty
Abomey 146–7
Abu Hamed 164
Abu Shehr, *see* Bushire
Abyssinia, *see* Ethiopia
Abyssinian Crisis *see* Italo-Ethiopian
  War, Third
Accra 141
Acre 24, 25
Acre, War of (1902) 198–9
Adansi 142
Addis Ababa 165
Addis Ababa, Treaty of (26 Oct. 1896)
  163
Addis Ababa-Djibouti railway 163, 170
Aden, *see* North Yemen-South Yemen
  Dispute
ADF *see* Arab Detterent Force
Adowa, Battle of (1 March 1896) 162
Adowa, Treaty of (Hewitt Treaty)
  (3 June 1884) 160

Adrianople (Edirne) 40–1
Adrianople, Treaty of (14 Sept. 1829)
  22, 23
Afghanistan 221; *see also*
  Anglo-Afghan Wars (1839–42,
  1878–80, 1919), Soviet-Afghan War
  (1979–89)
African National Congress (ANC) 179
Agacher Strip 183–4
Agadir Crisis (1911) 37
Agoli–Agbo (Gucili), king of Abomey
  147
Ahvaz, *see* Ahwaz
Ahwaz (Ahvaz) 134
Aiun, *see* El Aaiún
Akantamasu, *see* Dodowa
Akerman, Convention of (7 Oct. 1826)
  23
Akim 141–2
Akrotiri 35
Aksai Chin 87
ALA, *see* Arab Liberation Army
Alamo 205
Åland Islands, Battle for (7–16 Aug.
  1854) 28
Albania, 215–16; *see also* Second
  World War (1941–5)
Aleppo (Haleb, Halab) 24
Alexander (1857–93), prince of
  Bulgaria 34–5
Alexander (1893–1920), king of the
  Hellenes 52
Alexander II (1818–81), tsar of Russia
  32
Alexandria, Convention of (27 Nov.
  1840) 25

Alexandropoulis, *see* Dedeagatch
Alexsinatz (Aleksinac, Aleksinats) 31
Algeria 37, 125, 173, 222; *see also*
  Sands, War of the (1963), Saharan
  War (1975–)
Algerian-Moroccan Dispute, *see* Sands,
  War of the (1963)
Algiers Agreement (1975) 133–5
Algiers Agreement (5 Aug. 1979) 175
Ali, Rubai (1935–78), president of
  South Yemen 132
Ali Pasha (1741–1822) 20–2
Aliwal, Battle of (28 Jan. 1846) 82
Alma, Battle of (20 Sep. 1854) 28
Alsace-Lorraine 13
Amanullah Khan (1892–1960), king of
  Afghanistan 79
Amapala 210
Amapala, Treaty of (23 April 1907)
  211
Amba Aradam, Battle of (19 Feb.
  1936) 165
Amin, Hafizullah (1929–79) 80–1
Amin, Idi (b. *circa* 1925), president of
  Uganda 182–3
Amoy (Hsia–men, Xiamen) 98
An Giang 102
ANC, *see* African National Congress
Ancón, Treaty of (20 Oct. 1883) 197
Anglo-Afghan Wars: First (1839–42)
  75–6; Second (1878–80) 8–9; Third
  (1919) 79–80
Anglo-Burmese Wars: First (1823–6)
  92–4; Second (1852) 94–5; Third
  (1885) 95–6
Anglo-Egyptian Condominium
  Agreement (19 Jan. 1899) 164
Anglo-Ethiopian War (1867–8) 158–9
Anglo-French Declaration (March
  1899) 164
Anglo-French Entente (1904) 157
Anglo-German Naval Treaty (1935)
  224
Anglo-Japanese Alliance (1902) 106,
  108, 157
Anglo-Persian War (1856–7) 76–7
Angola, *see* Angolan War (1975–88)
Angolan War, *see* South Africa-Angola
  War

d'Angoulême, Duc (1775–1844) 3–4
Annam 101, 103, 104
Antarctic Treaty (1963) 224
Anti-Ballistic Missile (ABM) Treaty
  (1972) 225
Antivari (Bar) 33
Antofagasta 197
Antwerp (Antwerpen, Anvers) 4–5
Anzio, landing (22 Jan. 1944) 57
Aozou Strip 180–2
Aquidaban, Battle of (1 March 1870)
  195
Arab Deterrent Force (ADF) 130
Arab Legion 124
Arab Liberation Army (ALA) 124
Arab-Israeli Wars: First (1948–9)
  122–5, Suez War (Second) (1956)
  125–7, Six Day War (Third)
  (1967)127–8, October War (Fourth)
  (1973) 128–30
Arafat, Yasser (b. 1929) 132
Arakan 92, 94
Arboleda, Julio (1817–62) 191
Ardahan 33
Arendrup, S. A. 160
Argentina 200, 202, 215, 216, 220–3;
  see also Argentine-Brazilian War
  (1825–8), Peruvian-Bolivian
  Confederation, War of the (1836–9),
  Triple Alliance, War of the
  (1864–70), First World War (1945),
  Falklands War (1982), Gulf War,
  Second (1990–1)
Argentine-Brazilian War (1825–8)
  185–7
Arica 197–8
Armenia 72
Artigas, José (1764–1850) 185
Arunacahal Pradesh 88
Arusha Agreement (8 Oct. 1967) 169
Asante, *see* Ashanti Wars
ASEAN, *see* Association of South East
  Asian Nations
Ashanti, *see* Ashanti Wars
Ashanti Wars: First (1824–31) 139–41,
  Second (1873) 141–2, Third
  (1895–6) 143, Fourth (1900) 143–4
Asmara 161
Assab 161

Assad, Hafez al- (b. 1930) president of Syria 128

Assam 92, 94

Assin 141–2

Association of South East Asian Nations (ASEAN) 114

Asunción 195

Asunción, Treaty of (9 Jan. 1872) 196

Atacama 197–8

Atatürk, Kemal (1881–1938), president of Turkey 49, 52

Atchoupa, Battle of (20 April 1890) 146

Athens 22, 60

Attahiru Ahmadu (d. 1903), caliph of Sokoto 149

Attbara, Battle of (8 April 1898) 164

Auber, Daniel (1782–1871) 4–5

Auckland, Lord (1784–1849) 75

Australia 215–17, 220–2; *see also* First World War (1939–45), Korean War (1950–3), Malaysian-Indonesian Confrontation (1963–6), Vietnam War (1964–73), Gulf War, Second (1990–1)

Austria 3, 5, 25, 26, 28, 30, 31, 33, 37, 53, 213–14, 220–3; *see also* Neapolitan War (1821), Austro-Piedmontese War (1848–9), Austrian War with France and Piedmont (1859), Schleswig-Holstein War, Second (1863–4), Seven Weeks' War (1866), Italo-Austrian War (1866), Boxer Rebellion (1900), First World War (1914–18)

Austria-Hungary, *see* Austria

Austrian State Treaty (15 May 1955) 70

Austrian War with France and Piedmont (1859) 17–18

Austro-Piedmontese War (1848–9) 3, 14–16, 101

Ava 96

Awami League 89

Awsa 160

Ayub Khan, Muhammed (1907–74), president of Pakistan 89

Azerbaijan 72, 74

Bac-Ninh 103

Baden: *see* Seven Weeks' War (1866), Franco–Prussian War (1870–1)

Badoglio, Pietro (1871–1956) 165

Bagdad 134–5

Bagidaw, king of Burma 94

Bahrain, *see* Second Gulf War (1990–1)

Balaklava, Battle of (25 Oct. 1854) 28

Balfour Declaration (2 Nov. 1917) 122

Balkan League 38

Balkan Wars: First (1912–13) 37, Second (1913) 35, 60

Ballistic Missile Test Notification Agreement (1988) 226

Ballivián, José (1804–52), president of Bolivia 189–90

Bamako Agreement (30 Oct. 1963) 174

Bandula (c. 1780–1825) 92

Bangladesh: *see* Indo-Pakistani War, Third (1971), Gulf War, Second (1990–1)

Bangladesh War of Independence, *see* Indo-Pakistani War, Third

Banjul, *see* Bathurst

Banzart, *see* Bizerta

Bao Dai (b. 1913), emperor of Vietnam 109

Bar, *see* Antivari

Bar Lev Line 128

Baratieri, Oreste (1841–1901) 162

Barra Kingdom, *see* Barra War (1831)

Barra War (1831) 144–5

Barre, Siad 170–1

Basra 134, 135–6

Bathurst (Banjul) 145

Batum (Batumi) 33

Bavaria, *see* Franco-Prussian War (1870–1)

Bayol, Jean (1849–1905) 146

Behanzin (d. 1906), king of Dahomey 146–7

Beijing, *see* Peking

Beirut 25, 37; *see also* Lebanon Conflict

Belgium 134, 213, 215–17, 220–2; *see also* Belgo-Dutch War (1830–3), First World War (1914–18), Second

World War (1940–5), Korean War (1950–3), Gulf War, Second (1990–1)

Belgo-Dutch War (1830–3) 4–5

Belgrade (Beograd) 46, 60, 62

Ben Bella, Ahmed (b. 1916), president of Algeria 173

Bengal 92, 94; *see also* Bangladesh

Benin, *see* Benin War (1897); *see also* Dahomey

Benin City 148

Benin War (1897) 148

Beograd, *see* Belgrade

Berbera 159, 170–1

Berlin 62, 69, 70

Berlin, Congress of (1885) 143, 162

Berlin, Treaties of (Aug.–Sep. 1866) 11

Berlin, Treaty of (2 July 1850) 8

Berlin, Treaty of (13 Aug. 1866) 11

Berlin, Treaty of (17 Aug. 1866) 11

Berlin, Treaty of (13 July 1878) 33

Berlin Blockade (20 June 1948–May 1949) 69

Berlin Declaration (5 June 1945) 69

Bessarabia 28, 33, 55, 70

Bien Hoa 103

Binaisa, Godfrey (b. 1920), president of Uganda 183

Biological Weapons Convention (1972) 225

Bismarck, Otto (1815–98), chancellor of Germany 9, 10, 12

Bizerta Crisis (Franco-Tunisian Dispute) 172–3

Black Flags (Co Den) 102–3

Blanco Encalada, Manuel (1790–1876) 189

Blood River, Battle of (1838) 151

Boer War, First, *see* Transvaal Revolt

Boer War, Second (1899–1902) 155–7

Bogue Treaty (8 Oct. 1843) 98

Bogus 159–60

Bokhara 78

Boko-retto, *see* Pescadores Islands

Bolívar, Simón (1783–1830) 188, 190

Bolivia; *see* Peruvian-Bolivian War (1841), Pacific, War of the (1879–84), Acre, War of (1902),

Chaco War (1932–5), Second World War (1943–5)

Bonaparte, Louis Napoleon, *see* Napoleon III

Bonilla, Manuel (1849–1913), president of Honduras 210

Bonsaso, *see* Essamko

Bosnia-Herzegovina 33

Bouet, General (1833–87) 103

Bourguiba, Habib (b. 1903), president of Tunisia 172

Boxer Protocol (7 Sep. 1900) 107

Boxer Rebellion (1900) 106–7

Brazil; *see* Argentine-Brazilian War (1825–8), Triple Alliance, War of the (1864–70), Acre, War of (1902), First World War (1917–18), Second World War (1942–5)

Brest-Litovsk, Treaty of (3 March 1918) 45, 47

Briand, Aristide (1862–1932) 50

Brunei 113

Brusilov Offensive 45

Brussels 4–5, 57

Bubiyan 136

Bucharest 62

Bucharest, Treaty of (3 March 1886) 35

Bucharest, Treaty of (10 Aug. 1913) 41

Budapest 62

Buena Vista, Battle of (22–3 Feb. 1847) 207

Buenos Aires, Treaty of (3 Feb. 1876) 196

Buenos Aires, Treaty of (21 July 1938) 200

Bukovina 55, 70

Bulgaria 30–1, 33, 35, 213–18, 220; *see also* Serbo-Bulgarian War (1885), Balkan Wars: First (1912–13), Second (1913), First World War (1915–18), Second World War (1941–5)

Bullen, Charles 144

Bulnes, Manuel (1799–1866), president of Chile 189

Burkina Faso (Upper Volta), *see* Christmas War (1985)

Burkina Faso-Mali War, *see* Christmas War (1985)

Burma (Myanma) 216, 221–2; *see also*
Anglo-Burmese Wars: First
(1823–6), Second (1852), Third
(1885)
Burmi, Battle of (27 July 1903) 149
Burnes, Alexander (1805–41) 75–6
Burungai Sonko, king of Barra 144
Busan, *see* Pusan
Bush, George (b. 1924), US president
137–8
Bushire (Abu Shehr, Busahr) 77
Byelorussia 220
Byron, Lord (1788–1824) 21

Cachar (Kachar) 92
Cadiz, Siege of (1823) 4
Calcutta 94, 96
Callao 189, 194
Callao, Treaty of (27 Jan. 1865) 193
Cam Duong 120
Cambodia 102, 103, 109, 115–16, 220;
see also Vietnam-Kampuchea War
(1978–9)
Cameron, C. D. 158
Camp David Agreement (17 Sept.
1978) 129
Campbell, Sir Archibald 94
Campo de la Alianza, Battle of (26 May
1880) 197
Cana 147
Canada, 220–3; *see also* Korean War,
(1950–3), Gulf War, Second
(1990–1)
Canea (Khania) 35
Canning, Lord (1812–62) 77
Canton (Kwangchow, Kuang-chou,
Guangzhou) 64, 97–9
Cape Angamos, Battle of (8 Oct. 1879)
197
Cape Coast Castle, Treaty of (27 April
1831) 141
Caroline Islands 209
Carter, Jimmy (b. 1924), US president
129, 133
Castilla, Ramón (1797–1868) 189–90
Cavagnari, Sir Louis (1841–79) 78
Cavour, Camillo (1810–61), prime
minister of Italy 17
Ceded Mile Treaty (June 1826) 144

Cetewayo, Zulu king (d. 1884) 151–3
Ceylon (Sri Lanka) 220
CGDK, *see* Coalition Government of
Democratic Kampuchea
Chaco War (1932–5) 199–200
Chad, *see* Chad-Libya War (1978–87)
Chad-Libya War (1978–87) 180–2
Chamberlain, Austen (1863–1937) 50
Chamberlain, Joseph (1836–1914) 154
Chapultec, Battle of (13 Sept. 1847)
207
Charasia, Battle of (6 Oct. 1879) 78
Charles Albert (1798–1849), king of
Piedmont-Sardinia 14–17
Chatalja Line 38
Chelmsford, Lord (1827–1905) 153
Chengde, *see* Jehol
Ch'eng-te, *see* Jehol
Chenpao (Damansky Island, Zhenpao)
117
Cherniaev, M. G. (1828–89) 31
Chetniks 60
Chiang Kai-shek (Jiang Jieshi)
(1887–1975) 65
Chile, 200, 202, 215–16, 220–3; *see
also* Peruvian-Bolivian
Confederation, War of the
(1836–39), War of the Pacific
(1879–84), Second World War
(1945)
Chilean Nitrate Co. 197
Chilianwala, Battle of (13 Jan. 1849) 85
Chin Hoa, Battle of (25 Feb. 1861) 101
China 81, 90, 102, 109, 110, 119,
177–9, 213, 215–16, 220–3; *see also*
Sino-Indian War (1962), Opium
War, First (1839–42), Opium War,
Second (1856–60), Sino-French War
(1883–5), Sino-Japanese War
(1894–5), Boxer Rebellion (1900),
First World War (1917–18), Second
World War (1941–5), Korean War
(1950–3), Sino-Soviet Dispute
(1969), Sino-Vietnamese War
(1979); *see also* Nanking
Government
Chincha Islands 193
Ch'ingtao, *see* Tsingtao
Chinkiang (Zhenjiang) 98

Chittagong 92
Chongqing, *see* Chungking
Chorillos, Battle of (13 Jan. 1881) 197
Chou-shan, *see* Chusan Island
Chou En-lai (Zhou Enlai) (1898–1976) 87
Christian IX (1818–1906), king of Denmark 8–9
Christmas War (Burkina Faso-Mali War) (1985) 185–6
Chrzanowski, Wojciech (1793–1861) 16
Chuenpi, Convention (20 Jan. 1841) 98
Ch'ung-Ch'ing, *see* Chungking
Chungking (Ch'ung-Ch'ing, Chongqing) 105
Churchill, Winston (1874–1965), British prime minister 46, 56, 164
Chusan Island (Chou-shan, Zhoushan) 98
Cinco de Mayo, Battle of, *see* Puebla, Battle of (5 May 1862)
CMEA (Council for Mutual Economic Assistance) 120
Co Den, *see* Black Flags
Cobija 198
Cochin China 101–3
Colenso, Battle of (15 Dec. 1899) 156
Colley, General (1835–81) 154
Colombia, 215–16, 220–1, 223; *see also* Ecuador-Colombia War, First (1862), Ecuador-Colombia War, Second (1863), Second World War (1943–5), Korean War (1950–3)
COMECON, *see* CMEA
Conditions of Appiontment of Chiefs, Treaty on the (1 Sept. 1879) 153
Conference on Security and Cooperation in Europe, *see* Helsinki Accords
Congo 221–2
Constantine I (1868–1923), king of the Hellenes 36, 52
Constantinople (Istanbul) 23, 24, 46
Constantinople, Conference of Ambassadors at (1858) 29
Constantinople, Protocol of (28 Feb. 1877) 31–2

Constantinople, Treaty of (4 Dec. 1897) 36
Constantinople, Treaty of (29 Sept. 1913) 41
Conventional Armed Forces (CFE), Treaty on (1990) 226
Cordillera del Condor 202
Corfu 46
Corregidor 68
Costa Rica 213, 215–16, 220, 222; *see also* First World War (1918), Second World War (1941–5)
Cotonou 145–7
Council for Mutual Economic Assistance, *see* CMEA
Courbert, Amédée (1827–85) 103
Crete 24, 35–6, 40, 60
Crimean War (1853–6) 17, 27–9, 32, 77, 99, 194
Crispi, Francesco (1819–1901), prime minister of Italy 162–3
Croatia, 215–16; *see also* Second World War (1941–5)
CSCE, *see* Helsinki Accords
Cuaspud, Battle of (6 Dec. 1862) 192
Cuba 133, 170, 179–80, 208–9, 213, 215–17, 220; *see also* First World War (1917–18), Second World War (1941–5), Angolan War (1975–88)
Curupaytí, Battle of (22 Sept. 1866) 195
Curzon Line 50–1
Custozza: First Battle of (23–7 July 1848) 16, Second Battle of (24 June 1866) 19
Cuito Cuanvale 179
Cuverville, Jean de (1834–1912) 146
Cyprus 33, 220
Cyrenaica, *see* Italo-Ottoman War
Czechoslovakia 215–16, 220, 222; *see also* Second World War (1941–5), Gulf War, Second (1990–1)

Dacca, *see* Dhaka
Dahomey, *see* Dahomey Wars
Dahomey Wars: First (1890) 145–6; Second (1892–4) 146–7
Dakhla 175
Dalhousie, Lord (1812–60) 84, 95

Damansky Island, *see* Chenpao
Damascus, 24, 128
Danang (Tourane) 101
Danilo II (1826–60), prince of
  Montenegro 26, 29
Danubian Principalities *see* Romania
Danubyu, Battle of (2 April 1825) 94
Davila, Miguel (d. 1927) 210
Dawes, Charles (1865–1951) 49
Dawes Plan (1924) 49
D-Day (6 June 1944) 57
De Bono, Emilio (1866–1944) 165
de Gaulle, Charles (1890–1970) 172
de la Mar, José, president of Peru 188
Debra-Tabor 159
Dedeagatch (Alexandropoulis) 41
Deligrad 41
Dembequene Pass 165
Denkera 141, 142
Denmark, 215–17, 220–3; *see also*
  Schleswig-Holstein War, First
  (1848–9), Schleswig-Holstein War,
  Second (1863–4), Second World
  War (1940–5), Gulf War, Second
  (1990–1)
Derbent (Derbend) 72
Dewan Mulraj 84
Dhaka (Dacca) 90
Dien Bien Phu, Siege of (20 Nov.
  1953–7 May 1954) 110
Dinh Tuong 102
Dinuzulu 153
Diredawa-Jigiga, Battle of (2–5 March
  1978) 170
Djunis, Battle of (29 Oct. 1876) 31
Dobrudja 33, 40, 70
Dodds, Alfred A. (1842–1922) 147
Dodecanese Islands 37, 70
Dodowa (Akantamasu, Katamanso),
  Battle of (7 Aug. 1826) 141
Dogali (Tedale) 161
Dogger Bank Incident 108
Dominican Republic 215–16, 220; *see
  also* Second World War (1941–5)
Domkos, Battle of (17 May 1897) 36
Dongola 164
Dost Mohammed (1789–1863), amir of
  Afghanistan 75–8, 85
Dragashani, Battle of (19 June 1821) 20

Dubrovnik, *see* Ragusa
Dulcingo 33
Düppel, *see* Dybbøl
Dutch East Indies 68; *see also*
  Indonesia
Dybbøl (Düppel) 9

East Germany, *see* German Democratic
  Republic
Eastern Rumelia 33–4
ECOWAS, *see* West African Economic
  Community
Ecuador 215–16, 220–3; *see also*
  Ecuador-Colombia Wars, First
  (1862), Second (1863),
  Ecuador-Peru War (1941); Second
  World War (1945), Ecuador-Peru
  War (1981)
Ecuador-Colombia Wars: First (1862)
  191; Second (1863) 192–3
Ecuador-Peru Wars: First (1941)
  200–1; Second (1981) 201–2
Eden, Anthony (1897–1977), British
  prime minister 127
Edhem Pasha 36
Edirne, *see* Adrianople
Egypt 24, 37, 215, 220–2; *see also*
  Ottoman-Egyptian Wars, First
  (1831–3), Second (1839–40),
  Egyptian-Ethiopian War (1875–7),
  Second World War (1945),
  Arab-Israeli War, First (1948–9),
  Suez War (1965), Six Day War
  (1967), October War (1973), Gulf
  War, Second (1990–1)
Egyptian-Ethiopian War (1875–6)
  159–60
El Aaiún (Aaiún, Aiun, Laayone) 175
El Alamein, Battle of (23 Oct.–4 Nov.
  1942) 57
El Salvador, *see* Second World War
  (1941–5), El Salvador-Honduras
  War (1960)
El Salvador-Honduras War (Football
  War) (1969) 211–12
Elliot, Charles 97–8
Elmina 142, 143
Ems Despatch (13 July 1870) 12
Enmod Convention (1977) 225

Enos 40
Enver Pasha (1881–1922) 38
Eritrea 161–2, 164–5
Erivan (Yerevan) 74
Essamko (Bonsaso) 141
Essau 144–5
Estigarribia, José Félix (1888–1940),
  president of Paraguay 200
Estonia 53, 55, 58
Estoril Peace Accord (31 May 1991)
  180
Ethiopia 174, 215–16, 220–2; *see also*
  Anglo-Ethiopian War (1867–68),
  Egyptian-Ethiopian War (1875–7),
  Italo-Ethiopian Wars: First
  (1887–9), Second (1895–6), Third
  (1935–6), Second World War
  (1942–5); Korean War (1950–3),
  Ethiopia-Somalia Dispute (1964),
  Ogaden War (1977–78)
Ethiopia-Somalia Dispute (1964)
  167–9
Ethiopia-Somalia War, *see* Ogaden
  War
Ethniki Etaria, *see* National Society

Falklands War (1982) 131, 202–4
Fao (F'aw) Peninsula 134
Farrah (Farah) 77
Fashoda 164
Fath Ali (c. 1762–1834), shah of Persia
  72
F'aw Peninsula, *see* Fao Peninsula
Fedayeen 125, 127
Ferdinand I (1751–1825), king of
  Naples 1–3
Ferdinand VII (1784–1833), king of
  Spain 3–4
Ferozeshah, Battle of (21–2 Dec. 1845)
  82
Ferry, Jules (1832–93) 102, 104
Fiji 222–3
Final Act of the Conference on Security
  and Cooperation in Europe *see*
  Helsinki Accords
Finland 45, 215–18, 220–3; *see also*
  Winter War (1939–40), Second
  World War (1941–5)
First Boer War, *see* Transvaal Revolt

First World War 10, 11, 13, 19, 23, 33,
  37, 41, 42–50, 109, 184, 193
Fists of Righteous Harmony, *see* Boxer
  Rebellion
Five Days Revolt (18 March 1848) 14
Flores, Juan José (1800–64), president
  of Ecuador 188, 192
Flores, Venancio (1798–1868),
  president of Uruguay 195
FNLA, *see* National Front for the
  Liberation of Angola
Fomena, Treaty of (13 Feb. 1874) 142,
  143
Foochow (Fuzhou) 98, 104
Foochow, Battle of (23 Aug. 1884) 104
Football War, *see* El
  Salvador-Honduras War (1969)
Formosa (Taiwan) 104–5
Fort Bullen 144
Fort Bullen Convention (5 Jan. 1832)
  145
Fort Lamy, *see* N'djamena
Fort López (Pitiantuta) 199–200
Fournier, Ernest (1842–1934) 103
France 5, 14, 24, 25, 29, 36–8, 49, 51,
  52, 105, 134, 145, 163, 166, 173,
  174–5, 180–2, 213, 215, 217,
  220–3; *see also* Franco-Spanish War
  (1823), Greek War of Independence
  (1821–33), Crimean War (1853–6),
  Opium War, Second (1856–60),
  Franco-Indochina War, First
  (1858–63), Austrian War with
  France and Piedmont (1859),
  Mexican-French War (1861–7),
  Franco-Prussian War (1870–1),
  Franco-Indochina War, Second
  (1882–3), Sino-French War
  (1883–5), Dahomey Wars, First
  (1890), Second (1892–4), Boxer
  Rebellion (1900), First World War
  (1914–18), Second World War
  (1939–45), Franco-Vietminh War
  (1945–54), Korean War (1950–3),
  Suez War (1956), Bizerta Crisis
  (1961), Gulf War, Second (1990–1)
Franco, Francisco (1892–1975) 174
Franco-Dahomey Agreement (3 Oct.
  1890) 146

Franco-Indochinese Wars: First (1858–62) 100–2, Second (1881–3) 102–3

Franco-Prussian War (1870–1) 12–13, 19, 42, 102

Franco-Spanish War (1823) 3–4

Franco-Tunisian Dispute, *see* Bizerta Crisis (1961)

Franco-Vietminh War (1945–54) 69, 109–11

Frankfurt, *see* Seven Weeks' War (1866)

Frankfurt, Treaty of (10 May 1871) 13

Franz Ferdinand (1863–1914), archduke 42

Franz Joseph (1830–1916), emperor of Austria 17–18

Frederick VII (1808–63), king of Denmark 6–8

French Indochina Wars: First (1858–63) 100–2, Second (1882–3) 102–3

Frere, Bartle (1815–84) 151

FROLINAT, *see* National Liberation Front (Chad)

Fuzhou, *see* Foochow

Gaddadi, Mu'ammar, *see* Qadaffi

Gaeta 18

Galicia 45

Gallipoli 46

Galtieri, Leopoldo (b. 1926), president of Argentina 203–4

Gamarra, Agustín (1785–1841), president of Peru 188–90

Gambia, *see* Barra War

Gandamak, Treaty of (26 May 1879) 78, 79

Ganja, Battle of (26 Sept. 1826) 72

García Moreno, Gabriel (1821–75) 191–3

Garibaldi, Guiseppe (1807–82) 16, 18

Gastein Convention (14 Aug. 1865) 9, 10

Gaza 124–5, 129

Gelele, king of Dahomey 145–6

Gemayel, Bashir (1947–82) 131

Geneva, Convention of (1864) 18

Geneva Accords (21 July 1954) 111

Geneva Accords (14 April 1988) 81

Geneva Agreement (5 Aug. 1988) 180

Geneva Convention (1928) 165

Geneva Protocol (1925) 224

George (1869–1957), prince of Greece 35–6

Georgia 23, 72

German Confederation 5, 19; *see also* Schleswig-Holstein Wars: First (1848–9), Second (1863–4)

German Democratic Republic 62, 69, 133, 220, 222

German-Polish Treaty (14 Nov. 1990) 71

German-Soviet Convention (28 Sept. 1939)

Germany 55, 105, 213–18, 220, 222; *see also* Boxer Rebellion (1900), First World War (1914–18), Second World War (1939–45)

Germany, Treaty on the Final Settlement with Respect to (12 Sept. 1990) 70–1, 220

Ghana 221–3; *see also* Ashanti

Ghashmi, al- (c. 1941–78), president of North Yemen 132

Gia Dinh 102

Giap, Vo Nguyen 110

Gladstone, William (1809–98), British prime minister 3, 154

Glegle, *see* Gelele

Goethe, Johann (1749–1832) 20

Gorbachev, Mikhail (b. 1931), president of the Soviet Union 81, 179

Gordon, Charles (1833–85) 163

Gough, Lord (1779–1869) 82, 85, 98

Gouvernement d'union nationale de transition (Chad) (GUNT) 181

Graeco-Ottoman War (1897) 35–6

Graeco-Turkish War (1920–2) 51–3

Grahovo 29

Gran Colombia, *see* Peru-Gran Colombia War (1828–9)

Granadine Confederation, *see* Colombia

Great Britain 3, 5, 8–9, 17, 24, 25, 36–8, 51, 52, 122–4, 134, 165, 169, 187, 213, 215–8, 220–4; *see also*

Greek War of Independence (1821–33), Anglo-Burmese War, First (1823–6), Ashanti War, First (1824–31), Barra War (1831), Anglo-Afghan War, First (1839–42), Opium War, First (1839–42), Sikh Wars: First (1845–6), Second (1848–9), Anglo-Burmese War, Second (1852), Crimean War (1853–6), Anglo-Persian War (1856–7), Opium War, Second (1856–60), Anglo-Ethiopian War (1867–8), Ashanti War, Second (1873), Anglo-Afghan War, Second (1878–80), Zulu War (1879), Transvaal Revolt (1880–1), Anglo-Burmese War, Third (1885), Ashanti War, Third (1895–6), Sudanese War (1896–9), Benin War (1897), Boer War (1899–1902), Ashanti War, Fourth (1900), Boxer Rebellion (1900), Sokoto War (1903), First World War (1914–18), Anglo-Afghan War, Third (1919), Second World War (1939–45), Korean War (1950–3), Suez War (1956), Malaysian-Indonesian Confrontation (1963–6), Falklands War (1982), Gulf War, Second (1990–1)

Greater Colombia, *see* Gran Colombia

Greece 32–3, 37, 213–17, 220, 222–3; *see also* Greek War of Independence (1821–32), Graeco-Ottoman War (1897), Balkan Wars: First (1912–13), Second (1913), First World War (1916–18), Graeco-Turkish War (1920–2), Second World War (1940–5), Korean War (1950–3), Gulf War, Second (1990–1)

Greek Civil War 60

Greek War of Independence (1821–32) 20–2, 23, 24

Guadalupe-Hidalgo, Treaty of (2 Feb. 1848) 207

Guam 209

Guangzhou, *see* Canton

Guatemala 213–15, 217; *see also* First World War (1917–18), Second World War (1941–5)

Guayaquil, Treaty of (22 Sept. 1829) 188

Gucili, *see* Agoli-Agbo

Guelta Zemmour, Battle of (13 Oct. 1981) 175

Guinea 221

Gujrat, Battle of (21 Feb. 1849) 85

Gulf Wars: First (1980–8) 133–5, Second (1990–1) 135–8

Gulistan, Treaty of (12 Oct. 1813) 72

Gundet, Battle of (13 Nov. 1875) 160

GUNT, *see* Government d'union nationale de transition (Chad)

Gura, Battle of (25 March 1876) 160

Guyana 222

Gyulai, Ferencz (1798–1868) 17

Ha Tien 102

Habibullah (1872–1919), amir of Afghanistan 79

Habré, Hissène, president of Chad 181–2

Hafiz Pasha 25

Hafizullah Amin, *see* Amin, Hafizullah

Hailie Selassie (1891–1975), emperor of Ethiopia 166, 170, 174

Haiphong 103, 110

Haiti 213–15, 217, 220; *see also* First World War (1918), Second World War (1941–5)

Halab, *see* Aleppo

Haleb, *see* Aleppo

Halepa, Pact of (Oct. 1878) 35

Hamasan 159

Hang-chou, *see* Hangchow

Hangchow (Hang-chou, Hangzhou, Lin-an) 105

Hangö, *see* Hanko Peninsula

Hangzhou, *see* Hangchow

Hanko Peninsula 58

Hanoi 102, 103, 109–10

Hanover 9; *see also* Seven Weeks' War (1866)

Harar 159

Hardinge, Sir Henry (1785–1856) 82

Hassan II (b. 1929), king of Morocco 173–4

Hayes, Rutherford (1822–93), US president 196
Helsinki Accords (1 Aug. 1975) 70, 220, 225
Heng Samrin (b. 1934) 119
Herat, 76–7, 78; *see also* Persia-Herat War (1836–8)
Herzegovina 30–1; *see also* Bosnia-Herzegovina
Hesse-Cassel, *see* Seven Weeks' War (1866)
Hesse-Darmstadt; *see* Seven Weeks' War (1866), Franco-Prussian War (1870–1)
Hewitt, Admiral 160
Hewitt Treaty, *see* Treaty of Adowa (3 June 1884)
Hindenburg, Paul von (1847–1934) 45
Hiroshima 69
Hitler, Adolf (1889–1945) 47, 53, 59, 60, 166
Ho Chi Minh (1889–1945) 109, 117
Ho Chi Minh City, *see* Saigon
Ho Chi Minh Trail 115
Hoare-Laval Pact (Dec. 1935) 165
Hodgson, Sir Frederick 143–4
Hoko-retto, *see* Pescadores Islands
Holy Alliance 3
Honduran-Nicaraguan War (1907) 210–11
Honduras 213–15, 217, 220; *see also* Honduran-Nicaraguan War (1907), First World War (1918), Second World War (1941–5), El Salvador-Honduras War (1969), Gulf War, Second (1990–1)
Hong Kong 68, 98, 100
Houdong, Treaty of (11 Aug. 1863) 102
Houphouët-Boigny, Félix (b. 1905), president of Ivory Coast 184
Houston, Sam (1793–1863) 102
Hsia-men, *see* Amoy
Hsin-chiang, *see* Sinkiang
Huambo 179
Hue, Treaty of (25 Aug. 1883) 103
Hugo, Victor (1802–85) 20
Humaitá 195
Hungary 16, 215–18, 220, 222–3; *see also* Second World War (1941–5); *see also* Austria
Hung-Hoa 103
Husein Pasha 29
Hussein, Saddam (b. 1937), president of Iraq 134–8

Ibrahim Pasha (d. 1848) 22, 24–5
Iceland 220
Ifrane, Treaty of (15 June 1969) 174
Iglesias, Miguel 197
Imbros (Imroz) 52
Imroz, *see* Imbros
Inchon 112
India 74, 119, 220–3; *see also* Kashmir Dispute (1946–9), Sino-Indian War (1962), Second Indo-Pakistan War (1965), Third Indo-Pakistan War (1971)
Indian Mutiny 77, 99
Indonesia 20–3; *see also* Malaysian-Indonesian Confrontation (1963–6); *see also* Dutch East Indies
Indo-Pakistani Wars, First, *see* Kashmir Dispute, Second (1965) 88–9, Third (Bangaladesh War of Independence) (1971) 89–91
INF Treaty (1987) 225
Ingavi, Battle of (18 Nov. 1841) 190
Inkerman, Battle of (5 Nov. 1854) 28
Ioannina (Janina, Yanina) 40
Iran 215, 217, 220, 222; *see also* Second World War (1943–5), Gulf War, First (1980–8), Persia
Iran-Iraq War, *see* Gulf War, First (1980–8)
Iraq 49, 128, 129, 133, 215, 217, 220–1; *see also* Second World War (1943–5), Arab-Israeli War, First (1948–9), Gulf Wars: First (1980–8), Second (1990–1)
Ireland 44, 220–3
Isandhlwana, Battle of (22 Jan. 1879) 153
Ismail (1830–95), khedive of Egypt 159–60
Israel 137; *see also* Arab-Israeli War, First (1948–9), Suez War (1965), Six Day War (1967), October War

(1973), Lebanon Conflict (1976–)
Istanbul, *see* Constantinople
Istria 49
Italian National Society (Societa
Nazionale Italiana) 17
Italian Somaliland 164–5
Italo-Austrian War (1866) 18–19
Italo-Ethiopian Wars: First (1887–9)
160–2, Second (1895–6) 162–3,
Third (1935–6) 164–66
Italo-Ottoman War (Tripolitanian War)
(1911–12) 36–8
Italy 31, 36, 51, 134, 213–18, 220–3;
see also Italo-Austrian War (1866),
Italo-Ethiopian Wars: First
(1887–9), Second (1895–6), Boxer
Rebellion (1900), Italo-Ottoman
War (1911–12), First World War
(1915–18), Third Italo-Ethiopian
War (1935–6), Second World War
(1940–5), Gulf War, Second
(1990–1)
Ituzzingó, Battle of (20 Feb. 1827) 187
Izmir, *see* Smyrna

Jaén 187
Jakarta, Pact of (11 Aug. 1966) 113
Jalalabad (Jalalkot) 76, 78, 79
Jalalkot, *see* Jalalabad
Jamaica 222
Jamba 179
James Island 144
Jameson Raid (1896) 155
Janina, *see* Ioannina
Japan 213–18, 222; *see also*
Sino-Japanese War (1894–5), Boxer
Rebellion (1900), Russo-Japanese
War (1904–5), First World War
(1914–18), Second World War
(1941–5)
Jehol (Ch'eng-te, Chengde) 64
Jerusalem 24, 27, 46, 124, 127
Jiang Jieshi, *see* Chiang Kai-shek
John IV (1839–89), emperor of
Ethiopia 159–61
Johnson, Lyndon (1908–73), US
president 115
Jordan 129, 133, 223; *see also*
Arab-Israeli War, First (1948–9), Six

Day War (Third Arab-Israeli War)
(1967)
Joubert, Piet (1831–1900) 154
Juárez, Benito (1806–72), president of
Mexico 207–8
Julundar 84
Juncal 187
Jutland, Battle of (31 May 1918) 47

Kabul 74, 75, 78–81
Kachar, *see* Cachar
Kampala 183
Kampuchea, *see* Cambodia
Kamran, amir of Herat 74, 76
Kandahar (Qandahar) 74, 75–6, 98–9
Kandahar, Battle of (1 Sept. 1880) 79
Kangra 84
Kano 149
Karabash 72
Karmal, Babrak (b. 1929), president of
Afghanistan 81
Kars 22, 28, 33
Kashmir 84, 88–90
Kashmir Dispute (First Indo-Pakistani
War) (1947–9) 85–6
Kassem, Abdul Karem (1914–63) 135
Katamanso, *see* Dodowa
Katyn Massacre 55
Kaunda, Kenneth (b. 1924), president
of Zambia 169
Keane, General 75
Kenya 222–3; *see also* Kenya-Somalia
Dispute (1963–7)
Kenya-Somalia Dispute (Shifta War)
(1963–7) 169–70
Keren 161
Kettler, Baron von (d. 1900) 161
Khafji 137
Khan, Yahya (1917–80), president of
Pakistan 89
Khania, *see* Canea
Kharg (Khark) Island 75, 77, 134
Khartoum 163
Khiva 78
Khmer Rouge 118
Khomeni, Ayatollah (1900–89) 133
Khorramshah (Khorramshar,
Mohammerah, Muhammarah) 134
Khrushchev, Nikita (1894–71) 116

Khuzestan 134
Khyber Pass 79
Kiev 51
Kim il Sung (b. 1912) 111
Kim Ok-Kiun (d. 1894) 104
Kimberley 156
Kissinger, Henry (b. 1923) 129
Kitchener, Lord (1850–1916) 163–4
Kiutayeh, Convention of (14 May 1833) 24
Kofi Karikari, Ashanti king 141–2
Königgrätz (Sadowa), Battle of (3 July 1866) 11, 19
Konya, Battle of (21 Dec. 1832) 24
Korea, 62, 65, 104–5, 107; *see also* Korean War
Korean War (1950–3) 69, 111–12
Kosygin, Alexei (1904–80) 117
Kruger, Paul (1825–1904), president of the Transvaal 154–6
Kruger Telegram 155
Kuang–chou, *see* Canton
Kumasi 141–4
Kundt, Hans 199
Kuram valley 79
Kurdistan 133–4 138
Kursk, Battle of (5–13 July 1943) 62
Kutahiya, *see* Kiutayeh
Kuwait, *see* Gulf War, Second (1990–1)
Kuwait Crisis, *see* Gulf War, Second (1990–1)
Kwangchow, *see* Canton
Kwangchow Bay 105
Ky Hoa, *see* Chin Hoa

La Paz 190, 198
Laayone, *see* El Aaiún
Ladakh 87
Ladysmith 156
Lahore 84, 89
Lahore, Treaty of (9 March 1846) 84
Laibach, Congress of (1821) 1
Laing's Neck, Battle of (28 Jan. 1881) 154
Lal Singh 82
Lambert, Commodore 95
Langson (Lang Son) 104, 120
Langson, Battle of (28 Feb. 1885) 104
Lao Kay 120

Laos 103, 109, 116, 220
Larrea-Gual Treaty, *see* Guayacil, Treaty of
Latas, Omar Pasha, *see* Omar Pasha Latas
Lattre Line, de 110
Latvia 53, 55, 58
Lausanne, Treaty (24 July 1923) 52
Lausanne, Treaty of (18 Oct. 1912) 37
Lebanon 25, 49, 133, 215, 217, 220; *see also* Second World War (1945), Arab-Israeli War, First (1948–9), Lebanon Conflict (1976–)
Lebanon Conflict (1976–) 130–2
Lenin, V. I. (1870–1924) 45
Leningrad (Petrograd, St Petersburg) 58, 61, 62
Leningrad, Siege of (Oct. 1941–Jan. 1944) 62
Leopold I (1790–1865), king of the Belgians 5
Leopold of Hohenzollern-Sigmaringen, Prince (1835–1905) 12
Leuven, *see* Louvain
Leyte Gulf, Battle of (23–6 Oct. 1944) 68
Li Hongzhang, *see* Li Hung-chang
Liadong, *see* Liatung peninsula
Liaotung (Liao-tung, Liaodong) peninsula 105
Liberia 213–15, 217, 220–1; *see also* First World War (1917–18), Second World War (1944)
Libya 57, 183; *see also* Chad-Libya War (1978–87)
Liechtenstein 220
Li-Hung-chang (Li Hongzhang) (1823–1901) 103
Lima 197
Lima, Preliminary Peace Convention (19 April 1840) 189
Lima, Treaty of (12 June 1883) 194
Lima, Treaty of (30 Oct. 1980) 212
Lin Tse-hsu (Lin Zexu (1785–1850) 97
Lin Zexu, *see* Lin Tse-hsu
Lin-an, *see* Hangchow
Lissa, Battle of (20 July 1866) 19
Li-Sung-man, *see* Syngman Rhee
Lithuania 53, 55

Locarno Pact (1 Dec. 1925) 50
Lomba River, Battle of (Sept. 1987)
    179
Lombardy-Venetia 14–18
London, Conference of (1830) 5
London, Convention of (Oct. 1861)
    207
London, Convention of (27 Feb. 1884)
    154
London, Treaty of (6 July 1827) 22
London, Treaty of (7 May 1832) 22
London, Treaty of (19 April 1839) 5,
    42
London, Treaty of (30 May 1913) 40
London, Treaty of (26 April 1915) 38
London Naval Treaty (1930) 224
London Naval Treaty (1936) 224
London Protocol (1852) 8
London Protocols (3 Feb. 1830) 22
López, Francisco (1826–70), president
    of Paraguay 194–6
López War, *see* Triple Alliance, War of
    the
Louis XVIII (1755–1824), king of
    France 3
Louvain (Leuven) 5
Ludendorff, Erich (1865–1937) 45
Lugard, Frederick (1858–1945) 149
Lule Burgas, Battle of (28–30 Oct.
    1912) 38
Lushunkow, *see* Port Arthur
Luxembourg 4–5, 213, 215, 217, 220;
    see also First World War (1914–18),
    Second World War (1940–5),
    Korean War (1950–3)
Lytton, Lord (1831–91) 78–9

MacArthur, Douglas (1880–1964) 68,
    112
Macarthy, Sir Charles (d. 1824) 139–41
McKinley, William (1843–1901), US
    president 209
MacMahon, Marshal (1808–93) 17
McMahon, Sir Henry (1862–1949) 87
McMahon Line 87–8
Madeira 199
Madrid 3
Madrid, Treaty of (28 Jasn. 1885) 194
Madrid Agreement (14 Nov. 1975) 175

Mafeking 156
Magdala 158–9
Magenta, Battle of (4 June 1859) 17
Mahdist State 160, 161; *see also*
    Sudanese War (1896–9)
Maiwand, Battle of (27 July 1880) 78
Majnoon Island 134–5
Majuba Hill, Battle of (27 Feb. 1881)
    154
Malaya, *see* Malaysia
Malaysia 221–3; *see also*
    Malaysian-Indonesian Confrontation
    (1963–6)
Malaysian-Indonesian Confrontation
    (1963–6) 112–14
Mali 174, 221; *see also* Christmas War
    (1985)
Mali, Federation of, *see* Mali, Senegal
Malloum, General (b. 1937) 181
Malmö, Convention of (26 Aug. 1848)
    8
Malta 220
Malvinas, *see* Falklands War
Mamoré 199
Manchukuo 64–7, 215, 217; *see also*
    Second World War (1941–5)
Manchuria 62–7, 105, 107–9; *see also*
    Manchukuo
Mandalay 68, 96
Manila Bay, Battle of (1 May 1898)
    209
Manipur 94
Mannerheim, Carl (1867–1951),
    president of Finland 57
Mannerheim Line 58
Mao Tse-tung (Mao Zedong)
    (1893–1976) 65, 110, 116–17
Mao Zedong, *see* Mao Tse-tung
Marchand, Jean-Baptiste (1863–1934)
    163–4
Marco Polo Bridge 64
Mariana Islands 209
Marne, Battle of (5–10 Sept. 1914) 44
Massawa (Mesewa) 159–61
Mauritania, *see* Saharan War (1975–)
Maximilian (1832–1867), emperor of
    Mexico 208
Maynas 187
Mazzini, Giuseppe (1805–72) 16, 36

Media 40

Medun 31

Megiddo, Battle of (19–21 Sept. 1918) 46

Mehemet Ali (1769–1849), khedive of Egypt 22, 24–5, 163

Menelik II (1844–1913), emperor of Ethiopia 161–2

Mengistu, Haile (b. 1937) 170–1

Metaxas, Ioannes (1871–1941) 59

Mettemma 161

Metternich, Prince (1773–1859) 1, 14

Meuse-Argonne Offensive 45

Mexican-American War (1846–8) 205–7

Mexican-French War (1861–7) 207–8

Mexico 215, 217, 220–1; *see also* Mexican-American War (1846–8), Mexican-French War (1861–7), Second World War (1942–5)

Michael, Grand Duke (1832–1909) 32

Midway, Battle of (4–6 June 1942) 68

Milan 14–17

Milan, (1854–1901) prince (later king) of Serbia 31, 34

Milan, Treaty of (6 Aug. 1849) 16

Milner, Alfred (1854–1925) 155–6

Milovgrad 31

Mindon (d. 1878), king of Burma 95

Miraflores, Battle of (15 Jan. 1881) 197

Mirko, Prince (1820–67) 29

Mission of the Representative of the UN Secretary-General in the Dominican Republic (DOMREP) (1965–6) 222

Missolonghi 22

Mitre, Bartolomé (1821–1906), president of Argentina 195

Mitterand, François (b. 1916), president of France 181–2

MNF, *see* Multi-National Force (Lebanon)

Modena 14–16, 18

Mogadishu (Muqdisho) 171

Mohammed Ali, *see* Mehemet Ali

Mohammed Shah 74

Mohammed Yusuf Sadozzi, amir of Herat 76–7

Mohammerah, *see* Khorramshah

Moloney, Captain (d. 1902) 149

Molotov-Ribbentrop Pact (Aug. 1939) 53, 55, 57, 61

Moltke, Helmuth von (1800–91) 11–12, 25

Monaco 220

Monastir, Battle of (5 Nov. 1912) 38

Mongolia 215, 217; *see also* Second World War (1945)

Montenegrin-Ottoman Wars: (1858) 29, (1852–3) 26, (1861–2) 30

Montenegrin-Serbian-Ottoman War (1876) 30–2

Montenegro: *see* Montenegrin-Ottoman War (1852–3), Montenegrin-Ottoman War (1858), Montenegrin-Ottoman War (1861–2), Montenegrin-Serbian-Ottoman War (1876), Russo-Ottoman War (1877–8), Balkan Wars: First (1912–13), Second (1913), First World War (1914–18)

Montreux Convention (20 July 1936) 52

Morocco 36–7, 129, 221; *see also* Sands, War of the (1963), Saharan War (1975–), Gulf War, Second (1990–1)

Moscow, Treaty of (12 March 1940) 58

Mosquera, Tomás Cipriano de (1798–1878) 191–3

Mostar 31

Mosul 135

MPLA, *see* People's Movement for the Liberation of Angola

Mudki, Battle of (18 Dec. 1845) 82

Muhammarah (Khurramshah) 77

Mujaheddin, *see* Soviet–Afghan War (1979–89)

Mukden Incident (19 Sept. 1931) 62–3

Mukti Bahini 90

Multan (Mooltan) 84

Multi-National Force (Lebanon) (MNF) 132

Munich Conference (1938) 56

Munzinger, Werner (1832–75) 159–60

Mussolini, Benito (1883–1945) 57, 59, 164, 166

Myanma, *see* Burma

Nagasaki 69
Najibullah (b. 1947), president of
    Afghanistan 81
Nakhichevan 74
Namasigue, Battle of (18 March 1907)
    210
Namibia (South West Africa) 179
Nan-ching, *see* Nanking
Nanjing, *see* Nanking
Nanking (Nan-ching, Nanjing) 64
Nanking, Treaty of (21 Aug. 1842) 98
Napier, Lord (1810–90) 158–9
Napier, Sir Charles (1782–1853) 85
Naples 3
Naples (Kingdom of the Two Sicilies)
    14–16, 18; *see also* Neapolitan War
    (1821) 1–3
Napoleon III, emperor of the French
    (Louis Napoleon Bonaparte)
    (1808–73) 11–13, 17–19, 27, 101,
    207–8
Napoli, *see* Naples
Nasir ad-Din (1831–96), shah of Persia
    76
Nassau, *see* Seven Weeks' War (1866)
    10–11
Nasser, Gamal Abdel (1918–70),
    president of Egypt 125, 127–8, 174
National Democratic Front (Yemen)
    (NDF) 133
National Front for the Liberation of
    Angola (FNLA) 177–9
National Liberation Front (Chad)
    (FROLINAT) 181
National Society (Ethniki Etaria) 35
National Union for the Total Liberation
    of Angola (UNITA) 177–80
Navarino, Battle of (20 Oct. 1827) 22,
    33
NDF, *see* National Democratic Front
    (Yemen)
N'djamena (Fort Lamy) 181
Neapolitan War (1821) 1–3
Nehru, Jawaharlal (1889–1964), prime
    minister of India 85, 87–8
Nepal 221–2
Netherlands 215, 217, 220–2; *see also*

Belgo-Dutch War (1830–3), Second
    World War (1940–5), Korean War
    (1950–3), Gulf War, Second
    (1990–1)
Neuilly, Treaty of (27 Nov. 1919) 49
New Granada, *see* Colombia
New York Agreements (22 Dec. 1988)
    180
New Zealand 215, 217–18, 220–2; *see
    also* Second World War (1939–45),
    Korean War (1950–3),
    Malaysian-Indonesian Confrontation
    (1963–6), Vietnam War (1964–73),
    Gulf War, Second (1990–1)
Nezib, Battle of (24 June 1839) 25
NFD, *see* Northern Frontier District (of
    Kenya)
Nicaragua 213–15, 218, 220; *see also*
    Honduran-Nicaraguan War (1907),
    First World War (1918), Second
    World War (1941–5)
Nice 17–18
Nicholas, Grand Duke (1831–91) 32
Nicholas, prince of Montenegro
    (1841–1921) 31
Niger, *see* Gulf War, Second (1990–1)
Nigeria 221–2; *see also* Benin War
    (1897), Sokoto War (1903)
Nightingale, Florence (1820–1910) 29
Nikolsburg, Preliminary Peace of
    (5 July 1866) 11
Nikshich (Nikšić) 31, 33
Ningpo (Ning bo) 98
Nish (Nisch, Niš) 33
Nivelle Offensive (16–20 April 1917)
    45
Nixon, Richard (b. 1913), US president
    115, 118
Nizib, *see* Nezib
Non-Proliferation Treaty (1968) 224
North German Confederation, *see*
    Franco-Prussian War (1870–1)
    12–13
North Korea, *see* Korean War (1950–3)
North Vietnam, *see* Vietnam War
    (1964–73)
North Yemen (Yemen Arab Republic),
    see North Yemen-South Yemen
    Dispute (1979)

North Yemen-South Yemen Dispute (1979) 132–3
Northern Frontier District (of Kenya) (NFD) 169
Norway 215, 217–18, 220–3; *see also* Second World War (1940–5), Gulf War, Second (1990–1)
Nouakchott 175
Novarra, Battle of (28 March 1849) 16
Nuclear Risk Reduction Centers, Agreement on (1987) 225
Nugent, General Count 16

OAS, *see* Organization of American States
OAU, *see* Organization of African Unity
Obote, Milton (b. 1924), president of Uganda 182–3
Obregoso, Luis, president of Peru 188–9
October Revolution (1905) 109
October War (Fourth Arab-Israeli War) (1973) 128–30
Oder-Neisse Line 69, 71
Ogaden 167, *see* Ogaden War
Ogaden War (Ethiopia-Somalia War) (1977–8) 170–1
Ologbosheri, Chief 148
Oman, *see* Gulf War, Second (1990–1)
Omar Pasha 30
Omar Pasha Latas 26
Ombdurman, Battle of (2 Sept. 1899) 164
ONUC, *see* United Nations Operation in the Congo
Opium Wars: First (1839–42) 97–9, Second (1856–60) 99–100, 101
Orange Free State, *see* Boer War (1899–1902)
Ospina, Mariano (1805–85) 191–2
Otto (1815–67), king of Greece 22
Ottoman Empire 124, 135, 213–14; *see also* Greek War of Independence (1821–32), Russo-Ottoman War (1828–9), Ottoman-Egyptian Wars: First (1831–3), Second (1839–40), Montenegrin-Ottoman War (1852–3), Montenegrin-Ottoman

War (1858), Montenegrin-Ottoman War (1861–2), Crimean War (1853–6), Montenegrin-Serbian-Ottoman War (1876), Russo-Ottoman War (1877–8), Graeco-Ottoman War (1897), Italo-Ottoman War (Tripolitanian War) (1911–12), Balkan Wars: First (1912–13), Second (1913), First World War (1914–18); *see also* Turkey
Ottoman-Egyptian Wars: First (1831–3) 24; Second (1839–40) 25, 27
Ouchy, Treaty of (15 Oct. 1912) 37
Oueddi, Goukouni (b. 1944) 181
Outer Space Treaty (1967) 224
Outram, James (1803–63) 77
Ovenramwen, *see* Overami
Overami (Ovenramwen), oba of Benin (d. 1914) 148

Peng-hu ch'untao, *see* Pescadores Islands
Pacific, War of the (1879–84) 194, 196–8
Pagan Min, king of Burma 94–5
Pakistan 81, 220–2; *see also* Kashmir Dispute (1946–9), Indo-Pakistani Wars: Second (1965), Third (1971)
Palestine 49
Palestine Liberation Organization (PLO) 130–2
Palmerston, Lord (1784–1865), British prime minister 75, 98, 99
Panama 213, 215, 218, 220, 222; *see also* First World War (1917–18), Second World War (1941–5)
Panmunjon Armistice (27 July 1953) 112
Papal States 14–16, 18
Paraguay 215, 218, 220; *see also* War of the Triple Alliance (1864–70), Chaco War (1932–5), Second World War (1945)
Paris 44, 57
Paris, Siege of (19 Sept. 1870–28 Jan. 1871) 13
Paris, Treaties of (10 Feb. 1947) 69–70, 166, 220

Paris, Treaty of (30 March 1856) 28
Paris, Treaty of (4 March 1857) 77
Paris, Treaty of (14 Aug. 1879) 194
Paris, Treaty of (21 Aug. 1879) 194
Paris, Treaty of (10 Dec. 1898) 209
Paris Peace Accords (27 Jan. 1973) 116
Parma 14–16, 18
Parna, Treaty of (7 March 1856) 187
Passchendaele, Battle of (31 July–10
     Nov. 1917) 45
Paso del Rosario, Battle of (20 Feb.
     1827) 187
Patras (Patrai, Patrae) 20
Paucarpata, Treaty of (17 Nov. 1837)
     189
Peaceful Nuclear Explosions Treaty
     (1976) 225
Pearl Harbor 68
Pechenga, *see* Petsamo
Pegu, 94, 95
Peiwar Kotal, Battle of (2 Dec. 1878)
     78
Peking (Beijing) 64, 100, 105, 106–7
Peking, Conventions of (18–24 October
     1860) 100
Peking Convention (1887, 1895) 120
Penghu Qundao, *see* Pescadores Islands
People's Movement for the Liberation
     of Angola (MPLA) 177–80
Pepe, Guglielmo (1783–1855) 3
Persano, Carlo 19
Persia 23; *see also* Russo-Persian War
     (1826–8), Persia-Herat War
     (1836–8), Anglo-Persian War
     (1856–7), Iran
Persia-Herat War (1837–8) 74–5
Peru 215–18, 220–2; *see also*
     Peru-Gran Colombia War (1828–9),
     Peru-Bolivian War (1841),
     Spanish-Peruvian War (1864–6),
     Pacific, War of the (1879–84),
     Ecuador-Peru War (1941), Second
     World War (1945), Ecuador-Peru
     War (1981)
Peru-Gran Colombia War (1828–9)
     187–8
Peruvian-Bolivian Confederation, *see*
     Peruvian-Bolivian Confederation,
     War of the (1836–9)

Peruvian-Bolivian Confederation, War
     of the (1836–9) 188–90
Peruvian-Bolivian War (1841) 190
Peruvian-Spanish War (1864–6) 193–4
Pescadores Islands (P'eng-hu ch'untao,
     Penghu Qundao, Boko-retto,
     Hoko-retto) 104–5
Peshawar 75, 85
Peshawar, Agreement of (26 Jan. 1857)
     85
Peshawar, Treaty of (30 March 1855)
     77
Petrograd, *see* Leningrad
Petropolis, Treaty of (17 Nov. 1903)
     199
Petsamo (Pechenga) 58, 70
Pézet, Juan Antonio (1810–79),
     president of Peru 193
Philiki Etaira 20
Philippines 68, 209, 220–1; *see also*
     Vietnam War (1964–73)
Phillips, J. R. (d. 1897) 148
Phnom Penh (Pnom Penh) 119
Physical Protection of Nuclear Material,
     Convention on the (1980) 225
Piedmont; *see* Austro-Piedmontese War
     (1848–9), Crimean War, Austrian
     War with France and Piedmont
     (1859); *see also* Italy
Pilsudski, Józef (1867–1935), president
     of Poland 51
Pinzaquí, Treaty of (30 Dec. 1864) 192
Pirot, Battle of (26–7 Nov. 1885) 34
Pishin 79
Pitiantuta, *see* Fort López
Placido de Castro 198
Pleven, *see* Plevna
Plevna, Siege of (19 July–10 Dec.
     1877) 32
Plevna (Pleven)
PLO, *see* Palestine Liberation
     Organization
Plombières Agreement (20 July 1858)
     17
Pnom Penh, *see* Phnom Phenh
Podgoritsa (Podgorica, Titograd) 31, 33
Pol Pot (b. 1928) 118
Poland 45, 215, 217–18, 220, 222; *see
     also* Second World War (1939–45)

POLISARIO (Popular Front for the
Liberation of Saguia el Hamra and
Rio de Oro), *see* Saharan War
Polish-Soviet War (1920) 50–1
Pollock, George (1786–1872) 76
Popular Front for the Liberation of
Saguia el Hamra and Rio de Oro
(POLISARIO), *see* Saharan War
Port Arthur (Lushunkow, Ryoyunuko)
105, 108
Porto Novo 145–7
Portsmouth, Treaty of (5 Sept. 1905)
108
Portugal 156, 177, 180, 213–14,
220–2; *see also* First World War
(1916–18)
Potsdam Conference (17 July–2 Aug.
1945) 69
Pottinger, Eldred (1811–43) 75
Pottinger, Sir Henry 98
Poulo Condore 102
Prado, Mariano Ignacio 193
Prague, Treaty of (23 Aug. 1866) 11
Prempeh, Ashanti king 143
Pretoria, Convention of (3 Aug. 1881)
155
Pretorius, Marthinus (1819–1901),
president of the Transvaal 154
Prevention of Accidental Nuclear War,
Agreements on the 224, 225
Prevention of Dangerous Military
Activities Agreement (1989) 226
Price, Dr 94
Principalities, *see* Romania
Prussia 1, 3, 5, 19, 25, 28; *see also*
Schleswig-Holstein Wars: First
(1848–9), Second (1863–4), Seven
Weeks' War (1866),
Franco-Prussian War (1870–1); *see
also* Germany
Puebla, Battle of (5 May 1862) 208
Puerto Alonso 198
Puerto Rico 209
Punjab 78, 82, 86
Puno, Treaty of (7 June 1842) 190
Pusan (Busan) 112
Pyongyang 105

Qadaffi, Mu'ammar (b. 1942) 180–3

Qandahar, *see* Kandahar
Qingdao, *see* Tsingtao
Quadrilateral 14, 17–18
Quetta 79

Rabat Agreements (15 June 1972) 174
Radetzky, Joseph (1766–1858) 14–16
Ragusa (Dubrovnik) 29
Rahman, Mujibur (1920–75) 89–90
Rangoon 92
Ranjit Singh (1780–1839) 82
Rann of Kutch 88
Rapallo, Treaty (16 April 1922) 49
Raratonga, Treaty of (1985) 225
Ratib Pasha 160
Rawalpindi, Treaty of (8 Aug. 1919) 80
Rhodesia (Zimbabwe) 177
Riacuelo, Battle of (June 1865) 195
Rieti, Battle of (7 March 1821) 1
Riga, Treaty of (18 March 1921) 51
Rio de Janiero, Convention of (27 Aug.
1828) 187
Rio de Janiero, Protocol of (29 Jan.
1942) 201
Rio de Janiero, Treaty of (8 Sept. 1909)
199
Rio Protocol (1941) 201–2
Ripon, Lord (1827–1909) 79
Rivadavia, Bernardino (1780–1845),
president of Argentina 187
Roberts, Lord (1832–1914) 78
Romania 20, 23, 27–8, 213–8, 220; *see
also* Russo-Ottoman War (1877–8),
Balkan War, Second (1913), First
World War (1915–18), Second
World War (1941–5)
Rome 57
Rome-Berlin Axis (Oct. 1935) 166
Roosevelt, Theodore (1858–1919), US
president 108, 209
Rorke's Drift, Battle of (22–3 Jan.
1879) 153
Rubattino Co. 160
Rumaila Oilfield 136
Runjit Singh, *see* Ranjit Singh
Russia 1, 5, 24, 25, 26, 29, 31, 34–5,
36, 100, 105, 213–14; *see also*
Greek War of Independence
(1821–32), Russo-Persian War

(1826–8), Russo-Ottoman War
(1828–9), Crimean War (1853–6),
Russo-Ottoman War (1877–8),
Boxer Rebellion (1900),
Russo-Japanese War (1904–5), First
World War (1914–18); *see also*
Soviet Union
Russo-Finnish War, *see* Winter War
Russo-Japanese War (1904–5) 62,
107–9
Russo-Ottoman War (1828–9) 22–3
Russo-Ottoman War (1877–8) 32–3,
78
Russo-Persian War (1826–8) 72–4
Ryoyunuko, *see* Port Arthur

Sabah 113
Sadat, Anwar el- (1918–81), president
of Egypt 128–30
Sadowa, *see* Königgrätz
SADR, *see* Saharawi Democratic
Republic
Saharan War (1975–) 174–6
Saharawi Democratic Republic (SADR)
175–6
Sa'id Mahommed, amir of Herat 76
Saigon (Ho Chi Minh City) 101, 109
Saigon, Treaty of (5 June 1862) 101–2
Saigon, Treaty of (15 March 1874) 102
St Germain, Treaty of (10 Sept. 1919)
47
St Petersburg, *see* Leningrad
Sakhalin Island 108
Sakhiet 172
Sakkaria River, Battle of the (24
Aug.–16 Sept. 1922) 52
Salam, Saeb (b. 1905) 131
Salaverry, Felipe (1806–36), president
of Peru 189
Salerno, landing (9 Sept. 1943) 57
Salonika (Thessaloniki) 38, 46
SALT Treaties 81, 225
Salvador, Daniel 191
San Francisco, Treaty of (8 Sept. 1951)
70 ,220
San Jacinto, Battle of (21 April 1836)
205
San Juan Hill, Battle of (1 July 1898)
209

San Marino; *see* First World War
(1915–18), Second World War
(1944–5) 213–15, 218
San Stefano, Treaty of (3 March 1878)
33
Sands, War of the (Morocco-Algeria
Dispute) (1963) 173–4
Sankara, Thomas (d. 1987), president of
Burkina Faso 183–4
Santa Anna, Antonio López de
(c. 1795–1876), president of
Mexico, 205–7
Santa Cruz, Andrés (c. 1792–1865),
president of Peru 188–90
Santiago, Treaty of (20 Oct. 1904) 198
Santiago Bay, Battle of (3 July 1898)
209
Santo Domingo, *see* Dominican
Republic
Sarajevo 42–60
Sarawak 113
Sardinia, *see* Piedmont
Saudi Arabia 81, 128, 129, 133, 215,
218, 220; *see also* Second World
War (1945), Gulf War, Second
(1990–1)
Savoy 17–18
Saxony 9; *see also* Seven Weeks' War
(1866) 10–11
Scheldt 5
Schiller, Johann (1759–1805) 20
Schleswig-Holstein Wars: First
(1848–9) 6–8, Second (1863–4)
8–10
Schlieffen Plan 42, 44
Schwarzkopf, Norman (b. 1934) 137
Schzechuan (Sichuan) 103
Scott, Sir Francis 143
Scott, Winfield (1786–1866) 205–7
Scutari, Convention of (31 Aug. 1862)
Seabed Treaty (1971) 224
Sebastopol (Sevastopol) 28
Second World War 13, 37–8, 53–71,
166
Sevastopol *see* Sebastopol
Sedan, Battle of (1 Sept. 1870) 12
Senegal, 221–2; *see also* Gulf War,
Second (1990–1)
Senussi 37

Serbia 23, 35, 213–14; *see also*
  Montenegrin-Serbian-Ottoman War
  (1876), Russo-Ottoman War
  (1877–8), Serbo-Bulgarian War
  (1885), Balkan Wars: First
  (1912–13), Second (1913), First
  World War (1914–18); *see also*
  Yugoslavia
Serbo-Bulgarian War (1885) 34–5
Seven Weeks' War (Austro-Prussian
  War) (1866) 9, 10–11, 19
Sèvres, Treaty of (10 Aug. 1920) 49
Sèvres Protocol (24 Aug. 1956) 126
Shah Shuja (Shah Shoja, Shoja Mirz,
  Shoja-ul-Mulk) (1780–1842), amir
  of Afghanistan 75–6
Shanghai 64, 98
Sharm el-Sheikh 125–7
Shasi (Sha-shih, Shashi) 105
Shastri, Lal (1904–66), prime minister
  of India 89
Shaw, George Bernard (1865–1950) 35
Shelley, Percy (1792–1822) 20
Shenyang, *see* Mukden
Shepstone, Theophilus (1817–1893)
  151, 154
Sher Ali 78
Shifta War, *see* Kenya-Somalia Dispute
Shimonoseki, Treaty of (17 April 1895)
  105
Shirvan 72
Shoja Mirz, *see* Shah Suja
Shoja-ul-Mulk, *see* Shah Suja
Siachin (Siachen) 89
Siam, *see* Thailand
Sichuan, *see* Schzechuan
Sicily, Invasion of (1943) 57
Sidon 131
Sierra Leone 221
Sihanouk, Prince, (b. 1922) 119
Sikh Wars: First (1845) 82–4, Second
  (1848–9) 84–5
Sikhs, *see* Sikh Wars:First (1845),
  Second (1848–9)
Simla Agreement (2 July 1972) 90
Simla Convention (1913–14) 87
Singapore 68, 222
Sinkiang (Hsin-chiang, Xinjiang) 117
Sino-French War (1883–5) 103–4

Sino-Indian War (1962) 86–8, 120
Sino-Japanese War (1894–5) 104–6
Sinope, Battle of (30 Nov. 1853) 27
Sino-Soviet Dispute (1969) 116–18
Sino-Vietnamese Dispute (1979)
  119–21
Six Day War (Third Arab-Israeli War)
  (1967) 127–8
SLA, *see* South Lebanon Army
Slivnitza, Battle of (17–19 Nov. 1885)
  34
Slovakia 215, 218; *see also* Second
  World War (1941–5)
Smyrna (Izmir) 51–2
Sobraon, Battle of (10 Feb. 1846) 82–3
Soccer War, *see* El Salvador-Honduras
  War (1969)
Societa Nazionale Italiana, *see* Italian
  National Society
Society of Eastern Learning, *see*
  Tong-hak
Sofia 41
Sokoto Caliphate, *see* Sokoto War
  (1903)
Sokoto War (1903) 149–50
Solferino, Battle of (24 June 1859)
  17–18
Somalia: *see* Ethiopia-Somalia Dispute
  (1964), Kenya-Somalia Dispute
  (1963–7), Ogaden War (1977–8)
Somme, First Battle of the (24 June–13
  Nov. 1916) 44
Sontay 103
Soochow (Su-chou, Suzhou, Wu-Hsien,
  Wuxian) 105
South Africa 215, 217–18, 220; *see also*
  Second World War (1939–45),
  Korean War (1950–3), South
  Africa-Angola War (1975–88)
South Africa-Angola War (1975–)
  177–80
South Georgia 203
South Korea: *see* Korean War
  (1950–3), Vietnam War (1964–73)
South Lebanon Army (SLA) 131–2
South Sandwich Islands 203
South Vietnam, *see* Vietnam War
  (1964–73)
South West Africa People's

Organization (SWAPO) 179
South Yemen (People's Democratic Republic of Yemen), *see* North Yemen-South Yemen Dispute (1979)
Soviet Union 52, 91, 110, 118–19, 120, 126–7, 129, 133, 137, 167, 170–1, 175, 177–80, 215–18, 220–3; *see also* Polish-Soviet War (1920), Winter War (1939–40), Second World War (1941–5), Sino-Soviet Union (1969), Soviet-Afghan War (1979–89)
Soviet-Afghan War (1979–89) 80–1
Spain 174–5, 222–3; *see also* Franco-Spanish War (1823), Franco-Indochina War, First (1858–63), Spanish-Peruvian War (1864–6), Spanish-American War (1898), Gulf War, Second (1990–1)
Spanish Sahara 174
Spanish-American War (1898) 208–10
Spezia 17
Spizza 29, 31, 33
Spuj 29
Srinagar 86
Stalingrad, Siege of (Aug. 1942–Feb. 1943) 62
START (Strategic Arms Reduction) Treaty 226
Stockholm Document (1986) 225
Straits Convention (13 July 1841) 25
Stresemann, Gustav (1878–1929) 50
Suakkim (Suakin) 159
Su-chou, *see* Soochow
Sucre, Antonio José de (1795–1830), president of Bolivia 188
Sudan 183, 221–2; *see also* Mahdist State
Sudanese War (1896–9) 183, 221–2
Sudetenland 53, 56
Suez Canal 57, 125–9, 159–60
Suez War (Second Arab-Israeli War) (1956) 125–7
Sukarno (1901–70), president of Indonesia 113–14
Suleiman Pasha 31
Suomussalmi, Battle of (11 Dec. 1939–8 Jan. 1940) 58

Suzhou, *see* Soochow
SWAPO, *see* South West Africa People's Organization
Sweden 8, 220–3
Switzerland 220–2
Syngman Rhee (Li Sung-man) (1875–65), president of South Korea 111
Syria 24–5, 49, 133, 215–18, 220; *see also* Second World War (1945), Arab-Israeli Wars: First (1948–9), Six Day War (Third) (1967), October War (Fourth) (1973), Lebanon Conflict (1976–), Gulf War, Second (1990–1)

Tabriz 74
Tacna 197
Taiping Rebellion 99
Taiwan, *see* Formosa
Taku Forts 100, 106
Tangku, Armistice of (31 May 1933) 64
Tannenberg, Battle of (26–31 Aug. 1914) 45
Tanzania, *see* Tanzania-Uganda Dispute (1978–9)
Tanzania-Uganda Dispute (1978–9) 182–3
Taraki, Nur Muhammed (d. 1979), president of Afghanistan 80
Tarapacá 196–7
Tarqui 188
Tashkent, Declaration of (10 Jan. 1966) 89
Tatnall, Commodore 100
Taylor, Zachary (1784–1850) 205–7
Tedale, *see* Dogali
Tegetthoff, Wilhelm (1827–71) 19
Tegucigalpa 210, 211
Teheran 134
Teller Amendment 209
Tembien, Battle of (29 Feb. 1936) 165
Tenasserim 95
Tenedos 52
Terijoki 58
Test Ban Treaty (1963) 224
Tet Offensive (30 Jan.–26 Feb. 1968) 115

Thailand (Siam) 213–18, 221–3; *see also* First World War (1917–18), Second World War (1942–5), Korean War (1950–3)
Tharrawaddy, king of Burma 94
Theodore (1818–68), emperor of Ethiopia 158–9
Thessaloniki, *see* Salonika
Thibaw (Theebaw) (1858–1916), king of Burma 95–6
Threshold Test Ban Treaty (1974) 225
Tianjin, *see* Tientsin
Tibet 86–7
T'ien-ching, *see* Tientsin
Tientsin (T'ien-ching, Tianjin) 64, 100, 106–7
Tientsin, Treaties of (26–9 June 1858) 100
Tientsin, Treaty of (9 June 1885) 104
Tigre 162
Tindouf 173–4
Ting, Admiral (d. 1895) 105
Tito, Josip (1892–1980) 60
Titograd, *see* Podgoritsa
Tlatelolco, Treaty of (1967) 224
Tofa, King of Porto Novo 147
Togo 222
Tojo, Hideki (1884–1948) 68
Tong-hak (Society of Eastern Learning) 105
Tonkin Gulf Incident (2–4 Aug. 1964) 115
Tonkin Gulf Resolution (7 Aug. 1964) 115
Tonking (Tonkin) 101, 102, 104
Tourane, *see* Danang
Transjordan, *see* Jordan
Transvaal 151–2; *see also* Transvaal Revolt (1880–1), Boer War (1899–1902)
Transvaal Revolt (First Boer War) (1880–1) 154–5
Transylvania 70
Traore, Mousa (b. 1936), president of Mali 184
Trentino 49
Trianon, Treaty of (4 June 1920) 49
Trinidad and Tobago 222
Triple Alliance, War of the (López

War) (1864–70) 194–6
Triple Intervention 105–6
Tripoli 132
Troppau, Congress of (1820) 1
Trotsky, Leon (1879–1940) 45
Tshushima, Battle of (27 May 1905) 108
Tsingtao (Ch'ingtao, Qingdao) 105
Tu Duc (1829–83), emperor of Vietnam 101–2
Tulcán, Battle of (31 July 1862) 191
Tunis 36–7
Tunisia 221–2; *see also* Bizerta Crisis (1961)
Turin, Treaty of (10 Dec. 1858) 17–18
Turkey 215, 218, 220, 222–3; *see also* Graeco-Turkish War (1920–2), Second World War (1945), Korean War (1950–3), Gulf War, Second (1990–1); *see also* Ottoman Empire
Turkmanchai, Treaty of (22 Feb. 1822) 74
Tuscany 14, 18
Two Sicilies, *see* Naples
Tyre 131

Uccialli, Treaty of (2 May 1889) 161, 162
Uganda, *see* Tanzania-Uganda Dispute (1978–9)
Uganda National Liberation Front (UNLF) 183
Ukraine 45, 220
Ulundi, Battle of (4 July 1879) 153
UNAVEM, *see* United Nations Angola Verification Mission
UNCI, *see* United Nations Commission for Indonesia
UNDOF, *see* United Nations Disengagement
UNEF, *see* United Nations Emergency Force
UNFICYP, *see* United Nations Peace-Keeping Force in Cyprus
UNGOMAP, *see* United Nations Good Offices Mission in Afghanistan and Pakistan
UNIFIL, *see* United Nations Interim Force in Lebanon

UNIIMOG, *see* United Nations
Iran-Iraq Military Observer Group
UNIKOM, *see* United Nations
Iraq-Kuwait Observation Mission
UNIPOM, *see* United Nations
India-Pakistan Observation Mission
UNITA, *see* National Union for the
Total Liberation of Angola
United Arab Emirates, *see* Gulf War,
Second (1990–1)
United Arab Republic, *see* Egypt
United Nations Angola Verification
Mission (UNAVEM) 180
United Nations Commission for
Indonesia (UNCI) 221
United Nations Disengagement
(UNDOF) 222
United Nations Emergency Force
(UNEF) 126
United Nations Good Offices Mission
in Afghanistan and Pakistan
(UNGOMAP) 222
United Nations India-Pakistan
Observation Mission (UNIPOM) 222
United Nations Interim Force in
Lebanon (UNIFIL) 130–1
United Nations Iran-Iraq Military
Observer Group (UNIIMOG) 135
United Nations Iraq-Kuwait
Observation (UNIKOM) 223
United Nations Military Observation
Group in India and Pakistan
(UNMOGIP) 221
United Nations Observation Group in
Lebanon (UNOGIL) 221
United Nations Observer Group in
Central America (ONUCA) 223
United Nations Operation in the Congo
221
United Nations Peace-Keeping Force in
Cyprus 222
United Nations Security Force in West
New Guinea 222
United Nations Special Commission on
the Balkans (UNSCOP) 221
United Nations Special Committee on
Palestine (UNSCOP) 221
United Nations Transition Assistance
Group (Namibia) (UNTAG) 222

United Nations Truce Supervision
Organisation (Middle East)
(UNTSO) 221
United Nations Yemen Observation
Mission (UNYOM) 22
United States of America 51, 81, 90,
100, 110–11, 119, 126, 129–31,
133–4, 171, 175, 177–80, 181–2,
194, 197, 200, 202, 203, 210–11,
213–18, 220–3; *see also*
Mexican-American War (1846–8),
Spanish-American War (1898),
Boxer Rebellion (1900), First World
War (1917–18), Second World War
(1941–5), Korean War (1950–3),
Vietnam War (1964–73), Gulf War,
Second (1990–1)
Unkiar Skelessi, Treaty of (8 July 1833)
24
UNLF, *see* Uganda National Liberation
Front
UNMOGIP, *see* United Nations
Military Observation Group in India
and Pakistan
UNOGIL, *see* United Nations
Observation Group in Lebanon
UNSCOB, *see* United Nations Special
Commission on the Balkans
UNSCOP, *see* United Nations Special
Committe on Palestine
UNTAG, *see* United Nations Transition
Assistance Group (Namibia)
UNTSO, *see* United Nations Truce
Supervision Organisation (Middle
East)
Upper Volta, *see* Burkina Faso
Uruguay 185–7, 215, 218, 220–3; *see
also* Triple Alliance, War of the
(1864–70), Second World War
(1945)

Valparaíso 193–4
Vanguardia 193–4
Varna, Siege of (1828) 23
Vassos, Col 35
Vatican State 220
Velasco, José Miguel de (1795–1859)
189–90
Venetia 10, 14–19

Venezuela 194, 215, 218, 220, 222–3; *see also* Second World War (1945)
Venizelos, Eleutherios (1864–1936) 51
Veracruz 207
Verdun, Battle of (21 Feb.–18 Dec. 1916) 44, 45
Vereeniging Agreement (31 May 1902) 156
Verona, Congress of (1822) 3
Versailles, Treaty of (28 June 1919) 45–7
Victor Emmanuel II (1820–78), king of Italy 16–17
Victor Emmanuel III (1869–1947), king of Italy 166
Vienna Awards (1938, 1940) 49
Vienna, Congress of (1814–15) 4–5
Vienna, Treaty of (30 Oct. 1864) 9, 10
Vienna, Treaty of (3 Oct. 1866) 19
Vietcong, *see* Vietnam War (1964–73)
Vietminh, *see* Franco-Vietminh War (1946–54)
Vietnam 118, 220; *see also* Franco-Indochina Wars: First (1858–63), Second (1882–3), Franco-Vietminh War (1945–54), Vietnam-Kampuchea War (1978–9), Sino-Vietnamese War (1979); *see also* North Vietnam, South Vietnam
Vietnam War (1964–73) 69, 114–16, 117, 118
Vietnam-Kampuchea War (1978–9) 118–19, 120
Vigevano, Truce of (9 Aug. 1848) 16
Villafranca, Armistice of (11 July 1859) 18
Vilna (Vilnius, Wilna, Wilno) 51
Vilnius, *see* Vilna
Vinh Long 102
Vladivostock 107, 116
Vuchidol 31

Waldersee, Alfred von (1832–1904) 107
Wal-Wal Incident (Dec. 1934) 165
Warba 136
Warsaw 45, 51, 55, 62
Warsaw, Battle of (16–25 Aug. 1920) 51

Washington, Treaty of (26 March 1979) 129
Washington Naval Convention (Five Power Treaty) (1922) 224
Weaponry Convention (1981) 225
Weihaiwei 105
West African Frontier Force 149
Western Somalia Liberation Front (WSLF) 170
Weyler, Valeriano (1838–1930) 208
Whydah, Treaty of (19 April 1876) 145
Wilhelm I (1797–1888), king of Prussia and German emperor 12–13
Wilhelm II (1859–1941), German emperor 155
Wilhelmina (1880–1962), queen of the Netherlands 5
William I (1772–1843), king of the Netherlands 4–5
William III (1817–90), king of the Netherlands 5
Wilna, *see* Vilna
Wilno, *see* Wilna
Wilson, Woodrow (1856–1924), US president 45
Winter War (Russo-Finnish War) (1939–40) 57–7
Wolseley, Garnet (1833–1913) 142
World War I (1914–18), *see* First World War
World War II (1939–40), *see* Second World War
WSLF, *see* Western Somalia Liberation Front
Wu-Hsien, *see* Soochow
Wurttemberg: *see* Seven Weeks' War (1866), Franco-Prussian War (1870–1)
Wuxian, *see* Soochow

Xiamen, *see* Amoy
Xinjiang, *see* Sinkinag
Xizang, *see* Tibet

Yakub Khan, amir of Afghanistan 78–9
Yalu, Battle of the (17 Sept. 1894) 105
Yandabo 94
Yandabo, Treaty of (24 Feb. 1826) 94
Yangtsu, Battle of (5–6 Aug. 1900) 107

Yanina, *see* Ioannina
Yar Mahommed, amir of Herat 76
Yeh Ming-chen (d. 1859) 99–100
Yemen, *see* North Yemen-South
  Yemen Dispute
Yerevan, *see* Erivan
Young, Owen (1874–1962) 50
Young Plan (7 June 1929) 50
Ypacari, Battle of (25 Dec. 1867) 195
Ypsilanti, Alexander (1792–1828) 20
Yugoslavia, 215–18, 220–3; *see also*
  Second World War (1941–5); *see*
  also Serbia
Yunan 103
Yungay, Battle of (20 Jan. 1839) 189

Zahle 131
Zabljak, *see* Zhablyak

Zagreb 60
Zaire 181, 183
Zambia 222
Zarumilla, Battle of (25 July 1941) 201
Zarumilla-Marañón War, *see*
  Ecuador-Peru War
Zelaya, José Santos (1853–1919),
  president of Nicaragua 210
Zeyla 159–60
Zhablyak (Zabljak) 26, 33
Zhenjiang, *see* Chinkiang
Zhenpao, *see* Chenpao
Zhou Enlai, *see* Chou En-lai
Zhoushan, *see* Chusan Island
Zhukov, Georgy (1896–1974) 61, 67
Zimbabwe, *see* Rhodesia
Zulu Kingdom, *see* Zulu War (1879)
Zulu War (1879) 151–3
Zurich, Treaty of (10 Nov. 1859) 18

69; 111–112